WHAT IS COMPERSION?

DIVERSE SEXUALITIES, GENDERS, AND RELATIONSHIPS

Series Editors

Richard Sprott, California State University,
East Bay and President of APA Division 44
Elizabeth Sheff, Sheff Consulting

The Diverse Sexualities, Genders, and Relationships Series highlights evidence-based approaches to understanding and serving diverse individuals and families whose relational or sexual practices or identities have been marginalized and understudied; reports of emerging empirical research on these topics; and analyses of the latest trends in cultural and societal developments on the status and place of diverse sexualities, genders, and relationships. Books in the series emphasize the intersections of race, culture, age, social class, (dis)ability, and other factors that shape the social locations of relational, sexual, and gender minorities as they intersect with institutions in fields such as education, law, medicine, religion, and public policy.

The books in this series serve as sound and critical resources for the training and continuing education of professionals directly serving diverse communities in professions such as counseling, marriage and family therapy, social work, health-care, criminology, human services, and education. They are also useful for educators teaching undergraduate and graduate level university courses in anthropology, cultural studies, gerontology, psychology, sexuality studies, sociology, and women's and gender studies. Finally, these books interest educated laypeople who wish to better understand diversity among relational, sexual and gender minorities.

Titles in Series

WHAT IS COMPERSION?

UNDERSTANDING POSITIVE EMPATHY IN CONSENSUALLY NON-MONOGAMOUS RELATIONSHIPS

MARIE THOUIN

FOREWORD BY JESSICA FERN

ROWMAN & LITTLEFIELD
Lanham • Boulder • New York • London

Published by Rowman & Littlefield
An imprint of The Rowman & Littlefield Publishing Group, Inc.
4501 Forbes Boulevard, Suite 200, Lanham, Maryland 20706
www.rowman.com

86-90 Paul Street, London EC2A 4NE

British Library Cataloguing in Publication Information Available

Library of Congress Cataloging-in-Publication Data
Names: Thouin, Marie, 1984– author.
Title: What is compersion? : understanding positive empathy in consensually
    non-monogamous relationships / Marie Thouin ; foreword by Jessica Fern.
Description: Lanham : Rowman & Littlefield, [2024] | Series: Diverse sexualities,
    genders, and relationships | Includes bibliographical references and index.
Identifiers: LCCN 2024005898 (print) | LCCN 2024005899 (ebook) | ISBN
    9781538183939 (cloth ; alk. paper) | ISBN 9781538183946 (paperback ;
    alk. paper) | ISBN 9781538183953 (epub)
Subjects: LCSH: Non-monogamous relationships. | Empathy.
Classification: LCC HQ980 .T46 2024 (print) | LCC HQ980 (ebook) | DDC
    306.84/23—dc23/eng/20240223
LC record available at https://lccn.loc.gov/2024005898
LC ebook record available at https://lccn.loc.gov/2024005899

"Dr. Marie Thouin's not just a researcher, she's a philosopher. In her remarkable new book, *What Is Compersion?*, Thouin unlocks the transformative potential of the simple act of noticing how the joy you can receive from your partner's delight can empower you in so many ways, serving to disempower jealousy and territoriality. Thouin's research demonstrates how the world could look from the point of view of compersion, and how taking joy in your partner's (or friend's or relations of any kind's) happiness can bring joy to you in all of your relationships. If you are a seeker of sexual freedom and clean love, as I hope you are, for heaven's sake read this book. And then go shine the light of compersion on your lovers, friends, family, and everyone you care about."
—Dossie Easton, licensed marriage and family therapist; co-author with Janet W. Hardy of *The Ethical Slut*

"Drawing from solid research, Thouin breaks down the nuts and bolts of how compersion actually works—the mindset, context, and special sauce that facilitate this often-misunderstood concept. Whether you're non-monogamous yourself, a professional helping clients, or just a curious human, this book is an essential look at the potential of our hearts to share in each other's joy. Thouin's work pushes us to explore uncharted territory in how we experience intimacy and connection."
—Dedeker Winston, author of *Multiamory: Essential Tools for Modern Relationships* and *The Smart Girl's Guide to Polyamory*

"Marie Thouin has been at the vanguard of compersion research for a decade, and her book is destined to become a classic. *What Is Compersion?* boldly and compassionately presents both the first evidence-based model of compersion and a plethora of practical tools to cultivate this jealousy-transforming positive emotion in everyday life. Regardless of whether you lean toward monogamy or polyamory (or somewhere in-between), this groundbreaking book will assist you to achieve freer and more-fulfilling intimate relationships—and to open your heart beyond what both culture and history have considered possible."
—Jorge N. Ferrer, PhD, California Institute of Integral Studies; author of *Love and Freedom: Transcending Monogamy and Polyamory*

"Marie Thouin's *What Is Compersion?* delves into an under-researched topic in the wider area of non-monogamies—the titular 'compersion.' Through a mix of different perspectives, both theoretical and empirical, Thouin resists the urge to talk about emotions as 'new,' 'different,' or merely psychological. Thouin's book has as its greatest strength the capacity to doubt its own topic and to problematize current normative assumptions—not those from mainstream mononormative ideology but those coming from a neoliberal polynormative approach to non-monogamies. Thouin's book shows, time and again, that a DIY approach to relating results in a misunderstanding of how deeply socially embedded emotions are. Through *What Is Compersion?*, readers will be able to engage with the ways in which what they feel—what they are socially allowed to feel, what is easier to feel, and what to do (or what is doable) with those feelings—cannot be considered outside of power, discrimination, access to resources, and many other situated group experiences.

"This book is, fortunately, not for those looking for a facile 'how-to' on compersion. It is, however, very much recommended to those who are looking at the myriad ways power

structures can have an impact on our emotional landscape. Hopefully, this book will serve as a powerful push-back against the oppressive, and weaponized, norms around compersion, jealousy, and (polyamorous) purity politics. At a juncture where some non-monogamies are becoming increasingly visible, this book is a sobering read about the paths—and, more importantly, the constraints—through which we are made to navigate."
—**Daniel Cardoso, PhD, Manchester Metropolitan University; Gender and Sexuality Research Group, RCASS; LUSOFONA University, Lisbon, Portugal**

"Dr. Marie Thouin's book *What Is Compersion?* is a monumental step in helping to rewrite the monogamous script that runs our modern world. Her research and perspectives about compersion challenge this very outdated programming and, I believe, have the potential to shift all relationships in the best possible way. This is how we make real changes within ourselves, which inevitably will extend out into our world, making it a more loving and compassionate place to be."
—**Carrie Jeroslow, best-selling author, relationship diversity advocate, and host of the** *Relationship Diversity Podcast*

"Marie Thouin offers a deep and compelling dive into compersion as it is understood and experienced by people in consensually non-monogamous relationships. The voices of her research participants come through loud and clear, and Thouin handles their experiences with nuance, clarity, and empathy. There is much about all relationships, not just consensually non-monogamous ones, to glean from this important book. Whether you are currently practicing consensual non-monogamy, curious about consensual non-monogamy, or want to bring positive empathy to your monogamous relationship, this book is a must-read."
—**Mimi Schippers, Tulane University; author of** *Polyamory, Monogamy, and American Dreams* **and** *Beyond Monogamy: Polamory and the Future of Polyqueer Sexualities*

"Required reading for anyone working with non-monogamous folks. Thouin's extensive research and compassionate, nuanced approach will give non-monogamous and monogamous people alike a new understanding of themselves and how to feel better in relationships. A landmark work in helping us build a more supportive, connected, and loving world."
—**Irene Morning, somatic pleasure coach, intimacy educator, polyamorous human, and author of** *The Polyamory Paradox: Finding Your Confidence in Consensual Non-Monogamy*

"Dr. Marie Thouin illuminates the transformative and enriching power of compersion. Through relatable stories and deeply researched wisdom, her insightful exploration guides readers toward fostering trust, intimacy, and boundless love in all their relationships!"
—**Joli Hamilton, PhD, MHC, CSE, founder of the Year of Opening; author of** *Project Relationship*

"*What Is Compersion?* speaks to diverse relationships, including and beyond non-monogamy. Dr. Marie Thouin's research edifies as it highlights the better relating made possible when we support our loves in enjoying the touch and care of another. Developing compersion in one's body, heart, and/or mind can help nurture our one-on-one relationships and may help us build stronger webs of sustaining relations across our lives."
—**Kim TallBear, author of** *The Critical Polyamorist* **blog; professor, Native Studies, University of Alberta**

This book is dedicated to all those who dare to transcend conventional rules of love in order to live authentically and relate more deeply.

BRIEF CONTENTS

CONTENTS

CONTENTS

CONTENTS

CONTENTS

CONTENTS

CONTENTS

FOREWORD

When I first came across the concept of compersion at a non-monogamous meetup, I felt a blend of curiosity and skepticism. Being someone who values the intricacies of language, upon hearing compersion defined by another meetup participant, I initially perceived It as a secular equivalent of the age-old Buddhist notion of sympathetic joy—the vicarious joy and pleasure that comes from someone else's well-being. As an advocate for making profound concepts more accessible, I appreciate encountering secular interpretations of spiritual ideas. These interpretations can serve as bridges, allowing individuals who may not align with specific religious or philosophical frameworks to access the wisdom and insights inherent in these concepts through a more psychological lens. Consequently, I found compersion to be an appealing new term for what I had long known as sympathetic joy.

During the meetup, as people shared their positive experiences with compersion, my curiosity remained piqued. As I listened, I still thought everyone was just talking about another version of sympathetic joy, but I could see how feeling joy because your partner is having pleasurable experiences with another lover wasn't something the Buddha covered. My skepticism entered when, amid the discussion, one person became insistent about her past association with the individual who she claimed coined the term "compersion." It seemed very important to her that the group understands how her previous partner was the sole innovator behind this idea, which apparently their relationship was the muse for, suggesting that we owe them (and by extension, her) recognition for their pioneering contribution. While it's possible her previous partner did introduce the term, I couldn't shake off the irony of someone claiming ownership over a word inherently promoting nonpossessive love.

This assertion left a bad taste in my mouth, yet despite my reservations, I recognized the importance of new language and how new words have the potential to shape our perceptions, construct new realities, and how new language is particularly important for those at the forefront of social change. Armed with this newfound term, I returned home to share it with my husband, Dave, who also found it interesting. We both agreed it was perplexing for someone to stake such a strong claim over a term representing nonpossessive love, and we moved on from the topic. Little did I know then, it would soon hold profound significance in our lives.

Thankfully it wasn't too long after the meetup when I experienced compersion firsthand. Watching Dave return home uplifted after a date with another and then hearing him talk about the things they had in common, my first feelings of compersion arose. Previously in our marriage, I frequently experienced a sense of genuine happiness and fulfillment in Dave's successes even when that joy was not contingent upon my direct benefit. However, rarely did his joy actually represent a threat—whether real or perceived—to me or our relationship. However, Dave's return home, eager to share his positive experiences with another woman, could absolutely pose a significant threat, challenging the very core of the monoromantic paradigm that had conditioned me to see other women as dangerous. Within the traditional confines of monogamy, Dave acknowledging his affection for another person is tantamount to one of the gravest breaches conceivable, one that would conventionally justify a vehement emotional response from me. And yet, here I found myself, devoid of those anticipated reactions. Instead, I was genuinely excited to hear about Dave's outing and pleased he had discovered a connection with someone else. As Dave and I transparently talked about what would have previously been forbidden, I could feel my brain and body actively rewiring itself. As I celebrated Dave's emotional connections and positive experiences with others as enriching rather than threatening to our bond, my mental horizon expanded and my heart opened in new ways, where traditional anxieties were supplanted by a deeper sensation of love. This experience transcended mere sympathetic joy; it was a paradigm shift that reshaped my understanding of love, connection, and relationships.

Then came the moment when I found myself on the receiving end of compersion. This took more time to come by. By then, however, Dave's genuine happiness for my budding feelings toward someone else was more than just a heartwarming gesture—it was a testament to our journey. In the face of a lot of challenges with our opening up process through painful bouts of jealousy, primal panic, and insecurity, his eventual compersion became a healing balm, bridging the gap between our past struggles and our evolving relationship. On this one night when I was returning from a date, I sensed a significant shift in his approach when Dave inquired about my evening. His questions stemmed not from a need for self-assurance or a desire to probe, even interrogate, but from genuine curiosity. As I delved into my growing fondness for this new person, Dave's curiosity didn't just persist; it transformed into genuine happiness for my experience. This interaction underscored a deeper level of emotional intelligence and mutual support in our relationship, showcasing a shared joy in each other's happiness that transcends conventional insecurities. I was floored.

As we sat together talking that evening and I was finally at the receiving end of compersion, I felt a deep sense of gratitude for him and us, but I also experienced something beyond us—something transpersonal. As Dave embraced my sexual and emotional exploration with another, I felt a profound resonance with the experiences of countless women across history, whose bodies, hearts, and sexuality were constrained under the guise of monogamy—a standard disproportionately applied, with men often exempt from such rigorous scrutiny. This moment connected me to a long lineage of women who were maligned for their sexual desires, desires that have been celebrated (or at least accepted) in men as intrinsic facets of their humanness. It was a liberating counterpoint to centuries of double standards, serving as a testament to the potential for our collective progress toward recognizing and honoring the equality and autonomy of women's desires and identities. It was as if centuries of societal constraints had been lifted, allowing us to love freely and authentically. In that moment, compersion became not just a feeling, but a political statement—a testament to the transformative power of love unbound by convention.

I was struck by the completion of the cycle of giving and receiving. Practicing compersion seemed to reprogram the monogamous wiring inside me while being on the receiving end of compersion felt like it unlocked and released the concept of monogamy beyond me. This dual experience highlighted a transformative journey, not just in redefining my personal beliefs around relationships but also in expanding my understanding of love's vast potential beyond societal norms.

As a psychotherapist specializing in polyamory, my journey with compersion took a different turn. When polyamorous clients brought up the topic in my office, I anticipated engaging in enriching discussions about cultivating compersion. However, I was met with something else. Instead of seeking ways to deepen their experience of compersion, clients often expressed deep-seated hurt and frustration because there wasn't enough compersion. They shared stories of feeling neglected or rejected by partners who didn't reciprocate their compersion, and to my surprise, some partners felt entitled to the compersion their partner *should* feel for them. What was meant to be a beautiful concept of empathetic joy had morphed into a weapon, used to measure and judge their partners' level of poly *enoughness.*

Witnessing this was disheartening. As one partner struggled to understand why their partner wasn't experiencing compersion for them, they grew resentful. Meanwhile, partners on the other end felt judged and shamed for their inability to fully embrace compersion, further perpetuating a cycle of guilt and frustration between them. In my therapy sessions, I found myself navigating through not only the difficult layers of clients' jealousy and attachment insecurity but now also their misplaced expectations about compersion. It became clear that compersion wasn't just a switch that some people could turn on as they wished. Rather than fostering understanding and compassion, the pursuit of compersion had inadvertently become a source of division and discord.

This realization prompted a shift in my approach. Instead of solely focusing on cultivating compersion, I began to explore the underlying issues that hindered its expression. Often I would tell clients to actually take compersion off the table as a goal, and instead focus on a less reactive baseline of neutrality as a more realistic goal. This was certainly helpful, and ironically, releasing the expectation of compersion often allowed it to naturally emerge in time. But for me, it didn't feel like enough. In my quest to elevate the services I provide to my clients, I delved into the professional landscape seeking guidance on the subject, only to find it surprisingly barren of useful resources. Diving into the mainstream advice on compersion offered some valuable nuggets, yet many of my clients felt the prevailing narrative painted compersion as something innate—you either had it or you didn't, or it was described in such elevated terms that it appeared almost out of reach, creating a sense of exclusivity around the concept that didn't resonate with everyone's experience.

Enter Marie Thouin.

When Marie reached out to me to discuss her original research on compersion within consensually non-monogamous (CNM) relationships, I was thrilled. While the phenomenon of jealousy has been more extensively studied, there is a notable deficit in the scholarly exploration and understanding of compersion. Although investigating jealousy holds its importance, attempting to decode compersion through the prism of jealousy falls short. Just as researchers in the field of psychology acknowledged that focusing their research on mental illness did not pave the way to an enhanced understanding of mental wellness, or how scholars within the domain of conflict resolution recognized that the study of warfare did not contribute to a deeper understanding of peace (the disciplines of Positive Psychology and Peace Studies were inaugurated to bridge these knowledge voids and broaden our understanding), Marie's research endeavors to do precisely this by shedding light on compersion itself—contributing to a richer, more comprehensive understanding of our emotional experiences and relationship dynamics.

As our understanding of human relationships evolves and non-normative relationship structures become increasingly legitimate, the pursuit of understanding our emotional architecture has never been more paramount. This book, a labor of intellect and passion, stands at the frontier of that exploration. Marie's pioneering research into compersion is more than a scholarly endeavor; it is a journey into the heart of empathy, joy, and the human capacity for complex emotional experiences. As a relationship coach herself, Marie's wisdom is practical, compassionate, and field-tested.

By delving into the nuanced experiences of those in CNM relationships, this book illuminates the vast potential of human affectivity and its implications for how we relate to one another. Marie's research sheds light on the complexities of compersion, enriching our understanding by presenting not only nuanced ideas but also practical tools for exploring its various dimensions (which is my favorite part!). She introduces the concept of compersion as a spectrum, and perhaps most crucially, provides a blueprint for CNM people to assess how their personal, relational, and societal contexts might influence the presence or absence of compersion in various scenarios. This blueprint will empower both seasoned polyamorists and those just getting started with non-monogamy to pinpoint the areas where they can focus their efforts to foster compersion most effectively. By going beyond merely sharing her findings, she offers invaluable guidance for CNM individuals, as well as their therapists and coaches.

Additionally, Marie's work addresses the unfortunate weaponization of compersion that can happen through either shaming oneself or one's partner into not being "poly enough." She sheds light on this dynamic by offering a more nuanced understanding of compersion (e.g., the distinction between attitudinal and embodied compersion in Chapter 4) offering readers a more inclusive perspective that resonates with individuals at various stages of their CNM journey. There is something in this book for both folks who've struggled with compersion and those who've ridden the wave of its ecstatic highs. I also believe this work is fostering increased awareness, comprehension, and dialogue about compersion across both academic circles and wider societal discourse, serving as a pivotal step toward cultivating a social framework that appreciates and normalizes intimate relationships outside the traditional monogamous paradigm. For me, this book extends beyond the scope of academic curiosity. It speaks to the very essence of societal transformation. Compersion is not just a feeling or heightened experience—it is also political.

In a world that often heralds monogamy as the sole arbiter of romantic fulfillment, Marie's work invites us to broaden our emotional horizons with compersion, challenging long-held beliefs about love, jealousy, and possession. In these pages, you will discover how compersion can serve as a catalyst for personal growth and relational harmony. Through the voices of diverse individuals, Marie's research underscores the potential for compersion to foster deeper connections and challenge the stigmas surrounding non-monogamy.

Welcome to a groundbreaking exploration of compersion. May this book not only inform but also inspire you to approach relationships with a renewed sense of possibility, understanding, and, most importantly, a heart open to the myriad ways we can love and support each other's happiness.

—*Jessica Fern*

ACKNOWLEDGMENTS

Academic research is a lot like compersion. Both require a team effort and flourish best among ecosystems of individuals who sincerely desire and work hard for the highest interests of the collective. This book is a testament to the true and actual labors of love of many exceptional individuals; it could not have been brought to life without them.

First, this work is rooted in the wisdom of my research participants, who generously donated their time, insight, and personal expertise on compersion through our in-depth interviews. Their contribution to this book is integral and immense; it cannot be overstated. I am also deeply grateful to my dating and relationship coaching clients, who broaden my perspectives on love on the regular—and thus, continually inform my thinking and writing.

On my path as a scholar, I have been blessed with several colleagues, mentors, and thought partners who, through their dedication and support, catalyzed the evolution of my work. Jorge Ferrer—thank you for fueling my inquiry into compersion through your own writing and for closely supporting my research throughout my PhD studies and beyond. Glenn Hartelius—you have demonstrated how a combination of radical curiosity and rigorous scholarship can change the world, and you made this inspiration tangible in my life through your steadfast mentorship. Elisabeth Sheff—your devotion to building a strong and diverse body of CNM literature has sparked the inspiration for this book, and your close editorial support and guidance has shepherded it into existence. Jessica Fern—thank you for inspiring me with your splendid work on non-monogamy, for believing in my project, and agreeing to write the foreword to this book—this is one of the great honors of my life!

I am endlessly grateful to the many colleagues who supported this project with their valuable insights, feedback, and soulful enthusiasm. While I cannot mention every person who has positively impacted this work, I would like to specifically thank those who most directly influenced the contents of this book, including: Joli Hamilton, Kathy Labriola, Sharon Flicker, Craig Chalquist, Nicolle Zapien, Kassia Wosick, Eden Nasher, Derrell Cox,

ACKNOWLEDGMENTS

Evita "Lavitaloca" Sawyers, William Winters, Kevin Patterson, Sarah Stroh, and Millie Boella.

I am deeply thankful to the editorial team at Rowman & Littlefield, who have caringly ushered this book into being through its many iterations and growing pains: Mark Kerr, Lilith Dorko, Sarah Rinehart, Jonathan Joyce, and series editors Elisabeth Sheff and Richard Sprott. I also owe special gratitude to my friend and editor, Tracy Friesen, who not only helped improve the presentation of my ideas but also greatly strengthened my writing through a number of important suggestions. Likewise, a huge thank you to my friend Philip Simmons for his incalculable assistance with the cover graphic design.

To my life partner Derek Chan: your steadfast integrity, kindness, courage, patience, and love are a daily wake-up call to my heart! Thank you for choosing to navigate this life with me, teaching me about love in ways I never imagined possible, and making me laugh throughout my many existential rabbit holes.

Last but not least—to my wonderful friends, family members, and conversation partners who supported me and my research over the years: There are simply too many of you to mention individually here, which is a testament to my good fortune! To each one of you, thank you from the bottom of my heart. I love you so much! Your happiness is my happiness.

INTRODUCTION

Just having a concept which acknowledges that you have the potential of feeling joy and expansion rather than fear and contraction in response to a loved one's sharing their love with others can go a long way toward transforming jealousy.

—Deborah Anapol[1]

The language we have at our disposal to describe human experiences has a critical effect in shaping our emotional landscapes. Thus, expanding our awareness and understanding of *compersion* and developing an informed and candid conversation around it, in both academia and the broader culture, is a powerful step in engendering a social paradigm that values and normalizes intimate connections beyond mononormative scripts and assumptions.

In a majority of positive social interactions, the value of positive empathy is not put into question. When someone we care about receives a promotion, falls in love, or achieves a personal goal, most people consider it emotionally appropriate to rejoice with them. However, if this person is our romantic partner, and they experience joy from an intimate relationship *with somebody else*—the socioemotional convention then quickly shifts from expecting positive empathy to anticipating painful feelings of jealousy, rage, betrayal, sadness, loss, or possessiveness.

This socioemotional convention is a central feature of mononormativity[2]—the cultural norm that designates monogamy (including serial monogamy) as the healthiest, most natural, and morally superior way to form and maintain intimate bonds. Mononormativity greatly relies on the assumption that jealousy is the only valid reaction to a romantic partner developing an intimate relationship with someone outside the couple.

As it turns out, this assumption is simply inaccurate. Many people regularly experience positive thoughts, attitudes, emotions, and behaviors regarding their partner's other intimate connections. Without denying the common coexistence of other emotions such as jealousy in those contexts (see Chapter 6, "Coexistence of Jealousy and Compersion"), this reality, referred to as *compersion*, compels a revisioning of deeply rooted social scripts and

1

conventions about love, attachment, and intimate bonds. In other words, *the existence of compersion in consensually non-monogamous (CNM) relationships throws a wrench in the wheels of mononormativity.* Uprooting the false constructs that hold mononormativity in place in our culture is the first of three reasons why I decided to document compersion and write this book.

The second reason that compelled me to study compersion is that it positively correlates with relationship satisfaction in CNM relationships.[3] Understanding compersion—what it is, what promotes it, and what hinders it—is intrinsically helpful in uncovering the factors that create harmonious and fulfilling CNM relational ecosystems. Until now, there is far too little research and study about the impact of compersion within relationships and society as a whole, both in academia and in CNM communities.

Third, I believe our understanding of compersion can unlock untapped relational potentials for every type of relationship. Jealousy, competitiveness, and envy are not unique to non-monogamy but impact every kind of connection—including monogamous partnerships, relationships with friends, siblings, parents, children, work colleagues, and even virtual or social media connections.

It is exceedingly common for people to feel powerless to handle, navigate, or heal painful emotional dynamics based on jealousy and competition. Alternatively, they may suppress feelings of jealousy, or inhibit their love as a result. Without the ability to imagine a different reality, a potent opportunity to grow and heal is lost. Thus, gaining awareness of the potential for compersion—the capacity to genuinely want the best for others and rejoice in their success—may illuminate new personal and relational possibilities for all of us.

WHAT IS COMPERSION?

At the time of this writing, the word compersion has not yet been included in the main English dictionaries and therefore lacks a consensus definition. However, I recently coauthored a seminal entry on compersion in the *Springer Nature Encyclopedia of Sexual Psychology and Behavior,*[4] with Dr. Sharon Flicker, which is a meaningful step toward legitimizing and disseminating the word. The entry includes three definitions:

1. Compersion refers to a broad range of positive emotions experienced in relation to one's intimate partner's extra-dyadic intimate relations.
2. Compersion refers to the broad range of positive attitudes, thoughts, and/or actions manifested in relation to one's intimate partner's extra-dyadic intimate relations.
3. Compersion refers to the broad range of positive emotions, attitudes, thoughts, and/or actions manifested in relation to another person's gratifying experience in any context.

The first two definitions apply to CNM contexts where a person is experiencing positive thoughts, attitudes, actions, and/or emotions regarding their partner's intimate joy with someone else. Together, these two definitions encapsulate the original meaning of the term compersion as it was coined and defined by the Kerista community, a San Francisco–based polyamorous group that disbanded in the early 1990s.[5] As with many communities outside the cultural mainstream, CNM people have had to "invent their own language" to reflect their unique experiences—experiences that are not yet portrayed in conventional language and dictionaries.[6]

Dr. Flicker and I added the third definition because many people have begun to adopt the word compersion to describe their nonromantic experiences of positive empathy. Since there are no other words in the English language to describe this experience, compersion is a helpful term to describe what is roughly the equivalent of the German term *freudenfreude*—joy for someone else's joy (which is the opposite of its better-known antonym, *schadenfreude*—pleasure derived from someone's misfortune). While this book focuses on the first two definitions of compersion in its original CNM context, a short detour through the land of Buddhism is necessary to understand the spiritual import of compersion in broader relational contexts.

COMPERSION AND BUDDHISM

Although non-monogamists were the first to add the term compersion to the English language in the 1970s, the concept of sharing someone's joy even in the absence of a direct personal benefit is ancient. As psychologist and scholar Jorge Ferrer has discussed at length,[7] there is a clear connection between compersion and the Buddhist concept of *muditā*—the Sanskrit word for sympathetic joy. Buddhist scriptures describe mudita as one of the "four immeasurable states" (*brahmaviharas*) or qualities of the enlightened person—the other three being loving-kindness (*metta*), compassion (*karuna*), and equanimity (*upeksha*). In its original context, Buddhists first practiced sympathetic joy toward friends or loved ones, then directed it to people toward whom they felt neutral, and finally in relation to difficult or hostile people, until the practice would encompass all beings. Considered the most difficult brahmavihara to achieve, mudita is said to remedy the illusory separateness between self and others and can therefore be a powerful vehicle on the path to liberation.[8]

Many other spiritual traditions suggest that transforming self-centeredness and egotism into altruism and generosity is a critical part of spiritual progress. For example, in Christianity, the practice of *agape* (or selfless love) includes desiring the well-being and happiness of all human beings. Similarly, Sufism suggests that opening the "eye of the heart" can allow a person to attune themselves to the omnipresence of divinity, and thus rejoice in the presence of anyone's happiness.[9] Why are sexual and romantic realms completely omitted from those teachings? According to Ferrer, it is probably because "genetic selfishness is so archaic, pandemic, and deeply seated in human nature that it invariably goes unnoticed in contemporary culture and spiritual circles."[10]

However, as societies around the globe are evolving toward increased secularity and gender equality, many people look for meaning, self-expression, and even spirituality in their intimate relationships.[11] This departure from patriarchal, transactional, and highly scripted versions of marriage as the norm toward wider acceptance of nontraditional relationships and family structures[12] invites not only an interest in the morality of monogamy and non-monogamy,[13] but also an increased adoption of, and interest in, diverse forms of CNM.

PREVALENCE OF CONSENSUAL NON-MONOGAMY

CNM relationships are intimate relationships in which all partners explicitly agree that each partner may have romantic or sexual connections with others.[14] CNM encompasses several types of relationships—the main ones being open relationships, swinging, relationship anarchy, and polyamory.

Open relationships are relationships in which partners agree that they can have extradyadic sex; *swinging* refers to when a couple practices extradyadic sex with members of another couple; *relationship anarchy* is an anticategorical and antihierarchical stance that blurs the distinctions between friends and intimate partners, and in which individuals are free to be what they want with whoever they choose; and *polyamory* is the form of CNM that is typically characterized by long-term and loving intimate bonds with more than one partner at a time.[15]

According to a 2017 study that surveyed two national samples of Americans (nearly 9,000 people), approximately one out of five Americans have engaged in CNM at some point during their lifetime.[16] Moreover, it is estimated that approximately 4–5% of Americans are currently involved in CNM relationships.[17] Additionally, interest in seeking more information about CNM has been increasing: an analysis of Google searches between 2006 and 2015 revealed that the frequency of CNM-related searches had markedly risen during that decade.[18] More recently, a 2020 poll by YouGov found that about one-third (32%) of Americans described their ideal relationship type as non-monogamous (43% for millennials), while 56% responded it would be completely monogamous.[19] Only four years earlier, 61% had then said their ideal relationship would be completely monogamous—showing a clear trend toward greater interest in CNM between 2016 and 2020.[20]

Why are we seeing this increase? It appears that in realizing how infidelity and jealousy are the main causes of conflict and separation in romantic partnerships,[21] academics and laypeople alike are increasingly questioning whether humans are suited for lifelong monogamy.[22] A growing number of people are warming up to the idea that consensually non-monogamous relationship styles may ethically help solve the conflict between the desire for long-term partnership and the need for romantic and sexual freedom.

Yet, health professionals and scholars still commonly pathologize CNM behaviors;[23] many insist, among other arguments, that jealousy is the only normal or healthy response to extradyadic intimacy.[24] They generally interpret the absence of jealousy as "pathological tolerance,"[25] where a partner pathologically denies a real threat to the relationship. There is no room or understanding for the possibility of compersion in this interpretation. This belief in the inalterability of jealousy is a cornerstone of mononormativity,[26] which is the assumption that romantic and sexual relationships can only occur, or are only normal, between two monogamous partners.

MONONORMATIVITY AND COMPERSION

Mononormativity relies in great part on a language that reflects monogamy as the only legitimate, healthy, and acceptable way to conduct romantic and sexual relationships. In that vein, Ritchie and Barker argued that the conventional mononormative language that saturates modern Western culture and mainstream media is, to a certain extent, constraining the potentials of polyamory.[27] From a social constructionist perspective, people build their identities from the vocabulary they are given to make sense of their emotions and experiences. Thus, the lack of adequate and popular words to express the concepts and experiences particular to CNM lifestyles perpetuates mononormativity, as well as a cycle of ostracization and marginalization for those who practice non-monogamy. As Ritchie and Barker pointed out,

> We come to understand ourselves in terms of the concepts that are available to us in the time and place we live in. The language around us shapes our self-identities (Burr, 1995) and our understanding of sexual identity depends on the language of sexuality available to us. The language and everyday experience of sexuality are thus intrinsically linked (Weeks, 2003). . . . People are further constructed through the language of emotions that we have available to make sense of our experiences.[28]

As such, the invisibility of the word compersion in popular vocabulary makes it seem as though it would be impossible for someone to experience it. However, it is a slow process for a word to become mainstream. At the time of this writing, I have emailed the Merriam-Webster editorial department three times—once in February 2017, again in August 2019, and finally in May 2023 following the publication of the encyclopedia entry in Springer Nature's *Encyclopedia of Sexual Psychology and Behavior*[29]—to advocate for the inclusion of the words compersion and mononormativity into their online dictionary. On the first occasion, one editor responded that "at this point in time, 'compersion' and 'mononormativity' don't have enough widespread general use to merit entry into our online dictionary."[30] My 2019 and 2023 attempts were left unanswered.

Why am I so keen on pursuing dictionary editors to disseminate the word compersion? I believe that a dictionary inclusion could be key to transforming personal and collective narratives around the inevitability of sexual jealousy and possessiveness, in a similar way that the "emergence of the label 'gay' in the early 1970s was important in terms of the public expression of homosexuality as a legitimate sexual identity."[31] In the same vein, Deri made the argument that "having a word can force a reinterpretation of an experience within that context or even create its potential. . . . Learning the word compersion could increase the likelihood that it will occur."[32]

The lack of foundational literature on the phenomenon of compersion has created the inspiration and opportunity for this work. A main goal of this book is to contribute to the collective understanding, visibility, and inclusion of compersion in both common language and academic literature.

HOW IS COMPERSION RELEVANT TO MONOGAMOUS PEOPLE?

In my coaching practice, I have often witnessed monogamous couples struggling with envy, jealousy, or competitiveness—even in the absence of threats to sexual or romantic exclusivity. For example, some folks might feel that their partner spends excessive energy at work or with their friends, and insufficient time cultivating their intimate relationship. At times, they might also feel uncomfortable around the depth of connection their partner is having with a friend or colleague, even when that connection is platonic. Or, they may grow envious of their partner's success in areas where they feel insecure or disadvantaged.

It may be extremely difficult to share one's partner's happiness in such instances, especially when one feels neglected, left out, or under-resourced. While these scenarios can cause painful rifts, examining them through the lens of compersion may help monogamous folks build more mutually supportive relationships. As I elaborate on in this book, the solution is not to shun jealousy or envy, or to pressure oneself or others to *feel* compersion—but rather to use these difficult emotions to illuminate the places where one's needs, especially those related to inner and relational security, aren't met. With this information, one can become aware of what it would take to meet these needs, both individually and as a team with one's partner(s).

Indeed, the process of developing a compersive *attitude* (see Chapter 4 for more detail about this distinction) in one's relationships applies well beyond CNM. It is partly about identifying opportunities to fill one's individual and relational plates more abundantly so that being supportive and generous becomes easier. It also includes developing an orientation to love that honors every person's sacred autonomy as well as embraces collaboration and deep interconnectedness within partnerships. In other words, seeking compersion is about cultivating greater alignment with one's loved ones and *being on the same team*—which is a way of relating that transcends the distinction between monogamy and non-monogamy.

THE RESEARCH BEHIND THIS BOOK

The concepts presented in this book are sourced from my original research in the context of my PhD dissertation on the topic of compersion in CNM relationships.[33] My initial study included seventeen participants. For this book, I conducted five additional journalistic interviews to bring in more racially and ethnically diverse perspectives, as well as seven interviews with CNM experts and community leaders for further perspectives on the yet uncharted field of social positionality and compersion (see Chapter 11).

Thus, my final sample included 22 CNM individuals with whom I conducted in-depth qualitative interviews. Wonderfully, nine participants from the original group (initially interviewed in 2018) agreed to follow-up interviews in 2022 and 2023—yielding a small set of longitudinal data points. The study sought to address two research questions:

1. What is the experience of compersion?
2. What factors impact compersion?

Thus, the main objectives of this study were (a) to describe the experience of compersion, and (b) to describe the factors that promote or hinder the occurrence of compersion. To this end, I used a classic grounded theory research design[34] to identify patterns among participants' descriptions of their experiences of compersion.

Overview of Research Participants

My final sample (at the time of the second interviews) comprised eleven women, eight men, one trans man, and two nonbinary-identified persons. Two of the men and two of the women specified some flexibility in their gender identity through the following descriptors: "Male-ish," "Male—though not too heavily," "Female genderqueer," and "Female (very loose attachment to my gender identity)." One participant, Jo, was in the process of transitioning from female to male between their initial (2018) and second (2022) interview, and now used "he/they" pronouns; I changed their pseudonym from Alice (in my 2021 dissertation[35]) to Jo in this book to accommodate their different gender identities across the two interviews, and to reflect the fact that they changed their name in real life. I also used the "they" pronoun to refer to them in this book for the sake of consistency (rather than "she" for the quotes taken from the first interview and "he/they" for quotes from the second interview). Additionally, Bethanne, who identified as cis-woman in 2018, identified as gender nonbinary at the time of the second interview (2023), and used "she/them" pronouns. I did not change her pseudonym (as she did not change her name in real life) and elected to use the pronoun "she" to refer to her in this book, for consistency between quotes from each interview.

Participant ages (at the time of their first interviews) ranged from 26 to 83 years, closely distributed among participants in their 20s (n = 4), 30s (n = 4), 40s (n = 6), and 50s (n = 4). There were two participants in their 70s (n = 2), and one participant each in their 60s (n = 1) and 80s (n = 1).

The majority of the participants were in a committed relationship at the time of the first interviews. Marriage was the most common status (n = 12). A majority of participants were childless (n = 14), four participants had children but no grandchildren, and four had children and grandchildren. One person, in his 80s, also had several great-grandchildren.

Only five participants identified as completely heterosexual. The vast majority (n = 17) of the sample identified as somewhere on the LGBTQ+ spectrum: eight participants identified as queer or pansexual, six as bisexual, and three as heteroflexible. One of the bisexual-identified individuals also added "poly" as part of their sexual orientation—which reflected the perception of polyamory being a categorical orientation, rather than a fluid choice, for this person.

Racially, the sample was split as such: White (n = 13), Black (n = 3), half-Black/half-White (n = 1), Ashkenazi Jew (n = 1), half White/half Ashkenazi Jew (n = 1), Asian (n = 1), half White/half Asian (n = 1), and Indigenous/Dakota (n = 1).

The demographics questionnaire asked participants to identify their spiritual or religious affiliations. The most common spiritual or religious affiliation was none and/or atheist and/or agnostic (n = 10), then Pagan and/or Unitarian Universalist (n = 5), followed by Buddhism or loose Buddhism (n = 3), Hinduism (n = 1), Dakota (n = 1), Catholic (n = 1), and Personal

Meditation & Ashtanga Yoga (n = 1). This distribution concurs with Kolesar and Pardo's study on the spiritual identities of CNM people as heavily slanted toward nonreligious but spiritual identities, with an emphasis on Paganism.[36]

This sample was highly educated, with seven participants holding doctorate degrees, six with master's degrees, another seven with BA or BS degrees, one with an associate's degree, and one with a high school diploma. Income levels were varied and generally correlated with the participants' geographical locations and their cost of living. Eight participants earned over $100,000/year, three earned between $60,000–$80,000/year, six between $40,000–$60,000/year, another three between $20,000–$40,000, and two earned less than $20,000/year.

Geographically, the largest group of participants lived in the western states of the United States (n = 16) followed by the eastern states (n = 3), the Midwest (n = 1), the southern states (n = 1), and Canada (n = 1). California was the most popular state (n = 10), followed by the state of Washington (n = 4). This distribution is reflective of the well-known high concentration of CNM folks on the West Coast of the United States and largely Democratic areas.[37] However, the paucity of responses from East Coasters and non-US countries where polyamory is also known to be prevalent (such as England) appears to be in part a function of the recruiting.

CONTRIBUTIONS AND RELEVANCE OF THIS BOOK

Understanding the phenomenon of compersion has the potential to deepen our knowledge of human relationships with significant repercussions in several fields, in particular: (a) psychology, neuroscience, and social sciences; (b) sexuality and CNM studies; (c) philosophy and ethics; and (d) law. Next, I describe how I expect that this book, and compersion research more generally, may contribute to these fields.

Psychology, Neuroscience, and Social Sciences

Compersion provides a direct window into the study of empathic joy. In psychology, neuroscience, and social sciences, empathy has mainly been examined in the context of reacting to others' distress; almost no research has addressed the mechanisms by which humans share others' positive emotions. To this point, Pittinsky and Montoya have noted that empathic responses are typically measured by assessing the degree to which one feels "sympathetic, compassionate, softhearted, warm, tender and moved" (Batson, 1991) or by assessing the "tendency to experience feelings of sympathy and compassion for unfortunate others." . . . Researchers tend to explicitly ignore the possibility of empathic joy.[38]

Additionally, the scant body of research on empathic joy focuses on platonic contexts, ignoring sexual or romantic ones.[39] The phenomenon of compersion opens the door to studying positive empathy under this powerful lens. At the interpersonal level, research on positive emotions indicates that positive empathy is a significant mechanism for interpersonal bonding,[40] and is linked to more positive attitudinal responses toward others.[41] All these findings are highly relevant to the study of compersion[42]—and conversely, the study of compersion has the potential to make a significant contribution to these fields of study. I describe this in more detail in Chapter 2, "Positive Empathy."

Sexuality and CNM Studies

The burgeoning subfield of CNM studies has produced a vast increase in literature in recent decades. However, very few research studies have focused on compersion specifically. Yet, compersion is a concept and an experience that is highly meaningful in the lives of CNM individuals and has been shown to positively correlate with CNM relationship satisfaction.[43]

This book offers a theoretical groundwork to understand compersion, as well as the contextual factors that promote and inhibit it. This knowledge should support CNM individuals as well as their therapists and counselors on the path of creating a hospitable environment for compersion—individually, relationally, and socially—which in turn may enhance relational satisfaction. Additionally, my hope is for other researchers to build upon the avenues of inquiry brought forth in this book and continue developing this area of study.

Philosophy and Ethics

Mononormative societies consider monogamy to be the moral ideal in intimate relationships and cast non-monogamy as synonymous with betrayal, deviance, or moral deficiency. However, in conjunction with the increased legitimacy of CNM relationships, partly derived from an influx of research documenting that these relationships are as committed and successful in the long run as their monogamous counterparts,[44] several philosophers have been examining the ethical underpinnings of intimate relationship choices and sexual dynamics.[45]

One of the main ethical objections to CNM is the supposed inevitability and inflexibility of jealousy in intimate extradyadic dynamics. The possibility of compersion as a legitimate response to non-monogamy weakens moral objections to CNM, and therefore may impact the philosophical discourse on intimacy.

Law

Mononormativity has deep legal and institutional implications. The legal system in the United States and most countries rewards monogamous unions and punishes non-monogamy. Folks in CNM partnerships and families, as well as uncoupled adults, do not benefit from equal privileges to monogamous couples when it comes to parental rights, marriage rights, tax advantages, immigration privileges, and other institutional privileges.[46] This functions in much the same way as cisheteronormativity, which has historically discriminated against people on the LGBTQ+ spectrum.[47]

Discrimination based on non-monogamous behavior—for example, in housing, workplace, or child custody cases—does not yet have legal recourse under the US Constitution because discrimination protections are legally defined for certain categories or protected classes. These include race, religion, and gender, but not relationship status.[48] Because the documented reality of compersion weakens the philosophical foundation of mononormativity, research on compersion and the findings in this book have the potential to play an indirect but significant role in fostering legal protection and equality for CNM individuals.

SHOULD COMPERSION ALWAYS BE THE GOAL?

Unfortunately, I have often seen compersion being weaponized or misused in CNM contexts. For example, as a dating and relationship coach who supports CNM people, I have witnessed circumstances where folks approached me impatiently wanting to supplant painful emotions—their partner's or their own—with compersive feelings. Understandably, feeling compersion represents an ultimate desired state for many people practicing CNM. However, there can be a naive idealism associated with this goal when the "ideal of compersion" gets misused or weaponized as a form of *toxic positivity*.[49]

This can show up as putting pressure on oneself or others to "just feel happy" in moments where emotional pain needs to be directly dealt with. This pressure can add shame and disconnection to a situation where addressing fears, resentments, or conflicts is needed. In other words, telling oneself or one's partner to "just have compersion!" when relational or personal issues are still unresolved is counterproductive to fostering relationship closeness and harmony.

Furthermore, compersion is not the goal for every person involved in CNM—and nor should it be. People who struggle with intense fear or jealousy due to their personal history around trauma, abandonment, and/or monogamous enculturation may be better served in aiming for "benevolent neutrality" (see Chapter 5, "Spectrum of Compersion") than for compersive feelings, as neutrality may be a more realistic and achievable goal. Further, in cases where disrespectful or harmful dynamics are at play, attempting to invoke feelings of compersion could be akin to gaslighting or spiritual bypassing.[50] If one's partner repeatedly disregards established agreements or boundaries, or acts in abusive or nonconsensual ways, looking for ways to transform problematic dynamics when possible or exiting a relationship altogether, if all else fails, might be a more promising route than attempting to pave over one's issues with the "ideal of compersive bliss."

Similarly, if a person is poly under duress (PUD) and has not wholeheartedly consented to embark into CNM from a place of personal agency, compersion might remain out of reach until they reclaim their personal power and autonomy within their relationship(s). Illuminating such information can be an opportunity to create relational ecosystems that best serve the needs of those involved, instead of a reason to shame someone for not being sufficiently compersive.

It is also worth noting the common pitfall of confusing painful emotions that arise within truly healthy and consensual, yet emotionally difficult situations, with those that arise due to abusive situations. Both instances may invoke an inner narrative of being a victim of one's circumstances. In truly consensual situations, however, a person's task is to connect to their personal agency, find supportive resources, and frame challenging situations in empowered terms. In contrast, under abusive circumstances, framing those painful emotions as normal CNM-related challenges would be counterproductive and even delusional. CNM people and their counselors need to discern the difference, as these situations require very different approaches and interventions. Relationship coach Sarah Stroh explained this phenomenon eloquently, so I cite her at length:

> Some people may have a particularly difficult time distinguishing between pain that is productive and that which is damaging. One reason can be that they've been abused, emotionally or physically, by a loved one in the past—maybe their parents. So that dynamic: pain, love, then pain then love, started to feel normal, comfortable even. And so some people may unconsciously seek this unhealthy relationship dynamic as adults. In this case, encouraging people to embrace some discomfort and pain in non-monogamy might be triggering, and I can empathize with that. What makes it even more confusing, is that sometimes this abuse occurs within the context of "polyamory." There are people who emotionally manipulate their partners into being non-monogamous even though it's not really what they want. That said, the pain I'm talking about is fundamentally different than this type of abusive pain. The pain I feel sometimes because of jealousy is one I have actively chosen. I've decided I want to be non-monogamous with the adult understanding that this type of pain will probably emerge. And I've chosen this not because that pain is a necessary part of being loved—I know very well that I can be loved without this type of pain—but because ultimately, this pain comes from my partner enjoying his life. And being able to endure that pain feels meaningful to me. Here the pain is in support of beautiful things, like love, lust, and connection. Whereas in the case of abuse, enduring that pain is in support of something that's unhealthy from all sides. Furthermore, I see it as a personal challenge to find peace within myself while my partner is on a date. I see it as a call to minimize the importance of needing to be number one out of a sense of competitiveness. I see it as an invitation to see the world as abundant and full of love, as opposed to scarce. And here, I'm courageously acting out of curiosity, love, and opportunity, not out of fear. That's the big difference.[51]

In this quote, Stroh voiced the crucial importance of distinguishing between two forms of pain that may occur in the context of non-monogamy: pain that derives from abusing dynamics and is entered subconsciously because of one's trauma history, leading a person to associate abuse with love; or, a more agentic, consciously chosen form of pain that may be a vector for personal and relational growth.

The line is sometimes a fuzzy one—but in my experience, and as Stroh explained, the difference lies in whether a person is navigating their relationship(s) out of personal autonomy and conscious choice, and is sufficiently resourced to maintain a sense of balance as well as grow their comfort zone over time. Along that fuzzy line, some circumstances may not lend themselves to compersive feelings, but there may be a healthy opportunity for cultivating a compersive attitude. I refer readers to Chapter 4's section, "Is Compersion Necessary?" for a discussion of the importance of attitudinal versus embodied compersion in CNM relationships.

OVERVIEW OF THE BOOK

Because the inevitability of jealousy is typically the first objection people bring up when encountering the idea of compersion, it is vital to understand how compersive individuals deal with jealousy. Thus, this book opens with a chapter titled, "Developing a Non-Mononormative Relationship to Jealousy as a Foundation for Compersion." In this chapter, I show how a proactive, agentic, and non-mononormative relationship with jealousy creates the foundation upon which compersion may arise.

Then, Part I, "Components of Compersion," addresses the first research question, "What is compersion?" with two chapters, each describing a main component of compersion: "Positive Empathy" (Chapter 2) and "Gratitude" (Chapter 3). Each chapter describes various avenues through which my study participants found these components to constitute compersion in their CNM relationships.

Next, Part II, "Dimensions of Compersion," dives into the many ways, flavors, and characteristics with which CNM folks may experience compersion. It includes three chapters: Chapter 4, "Two Kinds of Compersion: Attitudinal and Embodied," spells out the distinction between these two kinds of compersion and shows why the existence of compersion beyond its emotional quality is of utmost relevance to CNM individuals. Chapter 5, "Spectrum of Compersion," proposes that a spectrum of compersion encompasses jealousy, benevolent neutrality, attitudinal compersion, and embodied compersion. While this spectrum is not linear, it is a helpful visual representation of the fluidity with which CNM folks experience their emotions. Chapter 6, "Coexistence of Jealousy and Compersion," discusses the nuance and dynamism with which jealousy and compersion interact in CNM relationships.

Part III, "A Compersion Roadmap," addresses the second research question that guided this study: "What promotes and hinders compersion?" In this section, I provide a blueprint for CNM individuals to evaluate how their individual, relational, and social contexts may contribute to the presence or lack of compersion in different situations. Chapter 7, "What Promotes Compersion?" describes elements that foster compersion, while Chapter 8, "What Hinders Compersion?" describes those that block it. This is perhaps the most practical section of this book, as it can support CNM folks and their therapists, coaches, or counselors in assessing where, in their relational ecosystems, they can direct their attention to invite compersion most effectively.

Part IV, "A Comprehensive Model of Compersion," combines the findings of Parts I, II, and III, culminating in "A Proposed Theory of Compersion" (Chapter 9). I frame this model as a *dual control model*, inspired by the Kinsey Institute's *Dual Control Model of Sexual Response*.[52] Using the analogy of break and acceleration pedals in a car, the model shows that some contexts "accelerate" compersion, while other factors act as a "break" to its occurrence. This model may support both CNM and monogamous individuals to identify and understand how their unique contexts promote or hinder different aspects of compersion. I offer a visual schema for readers to grasp visually how the different factors relate to one another.

Part V, "Social Lenses on Compersion," applies social perspectives on the phenomenon of compersion. In Chapter 10, "The Role of Coming Out and Pride in Compersion," I explain how CNM identity development impacts the experience of compersion through the process of coming out to oneself and others—a phenomenon greatly mitigated by belonging to supportive communities. I also suggest a parallel between compersion in CNM relationships with pride in LGBTQ+ communities. Then, in Chapter 11, "Social Positionality and Compersion," I investigate how systems of social privilege and power can impact personal experiences of compersion. I explore the surprising impact of compounded discrimination on compersion, compersion as a strategy of resistance, and dissect how the variables of age, disability, race, socioeconomic status, gender, and sexual orientation may intersect with one another and with non-monogamy—affecting different people's propensity to experience compersion.

Finally, I bring the book to a close with Part VI, "Concluding Thoughts." Chapter 12, "Can Compersion Be Learned?" addresses this important question—distilling the most concrete wisdom in this book. Finally, I conclude the book with Chapter 13, "Parting Words: Compersion, Personal Transformation, and Social Change," leaving readers with broader philosophical considerations on the personal and collective impacts of compersion.

I omitted a formal section on future research directions from this book for the sake of conciseness; however, I have pointed out several ideas for research throughout the book. Readers may also refer to my PhD dissertation (which is freely available online) for elaboration on possible studies that would enhance the understanding of compersion in CNM relationships and beyond.[53]

I hope you enjoy this book and that the pages ahead inspire you to create a more love-filled, reflective, fulfilling, and emancipated relationship life—however this looks on your unique journey.

NOTES

1. Anapol, 1997, p. 64.
2. Pieper & Bauer, 2006. The term *mononormativity* was coined by Marianne Pieper and Robin Bauer, organizers of the first International Conference on Polyamory and Mono-Normativity in 2005, and has been developed by several scholars since. See, for example, Ansara, 2023; Emens, 2004; Ferrer, 2018, 2021; Kean, 2015; Klesse, 2016; Rothschild, 2018; Sandbakken et al., 2022.
3. Aumer et al., 2014.
4. Thouin-Savard & Flicker, 2023.
5. Ferrer, 2007.
6. Ritchie & Barker, 2006.
7. Ferrer, 2007, 2019, 2021.
8. Coren, 2023; Ferrer, 2019.
9. Ferrer, 2019.
10. Ferrer, 2019, p. 187.
11. Perel, 2006.
12. Haag, 2011.
13. Clardy, 2019; Chalmers, 2019, 2022; York, 2020.
14. Conley, Moors, et al., 2013.
15. Anapol, 2010; Barker & Langdridge, 2010.
16. Haupert et al., 2017.
17. Conley, Moors, et al., 2013, p. 3.
18. Moors, 2017.
19. Ballard, 2020.

20. Moore, 2016.
21. Betzig, 1989.
22. For example, Ferrer, 2021; Haag, 2011; Perel, 2006.
23. Moors & Schechinger, 2014.
24. Ferrer, 2018.
25. Pines, 1998, p. 13.
26. For example, Ferrer, 2018; Schippers, 2016.
27. Ritchie & Barker, 2006.
28. Ritchie & Barker, 2006, p. 585.
29. Thouin-Savard & Flicker, 2023.
30. Lee Goodrich, personal communication, February 3, 2017.
31. Ritchie & Barker, 2006, p. 585.
32. Deri, 2015, p. 41.
33. Thouin-Savard, 2021.
34. Glaser & Strauss, 1999; Holton & Walsh, 2017; see Thouin-Savard, 2021, for a more detailed description of the research process.
35. Thouin-Savard, 2021.
36. Kolesar & Pardo, 2019.
37. Sheff & Hammers, 2011.
38. Pittinsky & Montoya, 2016, pp. 513–514.
39. Batson et al., 1991; Perry et al., 2012; Pittinsky & Montoya, 2016.
40. Gable et al., 2006; Gable et al., 2012; Gable et al., 2004; Morelli et al., 2015; Pittinsky & Montoya, 2016.
41. Pittinsky et al., 2011b; Tam et al., 2008.
42. See also Flicker et al., 2022.
43. Aumer et al., 2014.
44. Sheff, 2014.
45. For example, Chalmers, 2019, 2022; Clardy, 2019; Cruz, 2016; Jenkins, 2015; York, 2020.
46. See Conley et al., 2013; Emens, 2004; Klesse, 2016; Rambukkana, 2015; Rothschild, 2018; Stein, 2020.
47. Rhoten et al., 2021.
48. Dryden, 2015.
49. Goodman, 2022.
50. For example, Fox et al., 2020.
51. Sarah Stroh, personal communication, August 9, 2023.
52. Bancroft, 1999.
53. Thouin-Savard, 2021.

CHAPTER 1

DEVELOPING A NON-MONONORMATIVE RELATIONSHIP TO JEALOUSY AS A FOUNDATION FOR COMPERSION

> From ancient Greek mythology to modern reality television, triangles of jealousy spark the imagination and remind us that any time we have a valuable relationship, there is the potential for that relationship to be interrupted by another person.
>
> —Joli Hamilton and colleagues[1]

> The key is to approach managing jealousy as a shared project both can cooperate on instead of pitting one person against another or allowing one partner to use his or her jealousy to manipulate the other or make the other wrong.
>
> —Deborah Anapol[2]

Jealousy is a universal human experience. In its simplest interpretation, it is a survival mechanism—just like anger, fear, or hunger—that serves to guard and protect one's access to valued relationships from perceived intruders. As such, jealousy shows up in babies as young as six months old when a primary caregiver's attention gets interrupted by a third party.[3] The jealous impulse, which is registered as a negative experience, provides an indicator that basic needs are going unfilled, or are under threat. This is valuable information toward the goal of self-preservation. However, just like thirst or hunger can become excruciating—and even lead to interpersonal violence when one's needs for water and food are not satisfied—the pain of jealousy can become gut-wrenching when compounded with a sense of powerlessness to meet one's emotional needs. It can lead to a wide array of challenging dynamics, from internalized shame and self-harm to interpersonal conflict and aggression.

On the one hand, the emergence of interpersonal jealousy is usually steeped in personal shame and inadequacy and is "socially scorned as a character flaw largely attributable to low self-esteem or lack of relational skills,"[4] as jealousy researcher Joli Hamilton and her colleagues explained. On the other hand, the consequences of jealousy can be fatal when a mononormative culture excuses its violent outcomes. Psychologist Jorge Ferrer noted, "Perhaps due to its prevalence, jealousy is widely accepted as 'normal' in most cultures, and many of its violent consequences have often been regarded as understandable, morally justified, and even legally permissible."[5] To illustrate, Hamilton continued: "No other emotion is considered as a possible excuse or reasonable motive for murder, from the ancient mythological texts right through the modern justice system."[6] Indeed, as late as in the 1970s the law of states such as Texas, Utah, and New Mexico considered "reasonable" the homicide of one's adulterous partner if it happened at the scene of discovery.[7] It therefore is not surprising that the overwhelming majority of cases of domestic violence and spousal murders worldwide are caused by jealous rage.[8]

While the jealous impulse itself is morally neutral (like hunger or fear), the way people treat themselves and one another based on that impulse is where complexities emerge, and questions around ethics, values, personal agency, and power dynamics come in. In the context of an imperfect world where people do not get everything they want or need, humanity's reckoning with jealousy cuts to the core of what it means to be a social—and socialized—animal.

THE ENTANGLEMENT OF JEALOUSY AND MONONORMATIVITY

Understanding jealousy and mononormativity—and how they operate together in particular social contexts—is essential to contextualizing and understanding the emergence of compersion. While jealousy is an innate, and therefore morally neutral, response to a need—again, like hunger—the ways one interprets its meaning are socialized and can vary from culture to culture (see the next section for examples of divergent views on jealousy and monogamy). In the United States, for example, social institutions like immigration, taxation, and healthcare provide legal and socioeconomic incentives to monogamous couples; meanwhile, the enculturated belief that jealousy is inflexible and absolutely inevitable outside of monogamy creates a moral justification for its institutional enforcement.[9]

Indeed, the fact that most people view jealousy as the only proper—or even imaginable—reaction to an intimate partner enjoying sexual and/or romantic intimacy with others morally justifies the pedestalization of monogamy as the only legitimate relationship structure. In other words, *the assumption that jealousy is the single valid response to extradyadic intimacy is a moral cornerstone of mononormativity.* If compersion became a more commonly known and available response to non-monogamy, compulsory monogamy and the moral arguments that maintain it[10] would have little left to stand on.

In this chapter, I survey literature that demonstrates, through the interplay of biology and social construction, that jealousy is *not inflexible*, and can be experienced in different ways depending on the meanings attributed to it. I then investigate how CNM people typically engage with jealousy in intentional ways that make compersion possible. Their distinctive views and modes of participation with jealousy is a phenomenon I coin "non-mononormative jealousy." Thus, I hypothesize that disentangling jealousy from mononormativity is the foundation upon which compersion is most likely to emerge, and that this particular way of relating with jealousy can also benefit people of all relationship styles—including those who choose monogamy—who wish to create a more intentional, proactive, and transformative relationship with their partner(s)—and with the green-eyed monster.

DIFFERENT TYPES OF JEALOUSY

Jealousy is a complex emotion that can be viewed through many lenses—including biological, archetypal, interpersonal, and sociocultural. In romantic contexts, Guerrero and colleagues defined jealousy as a "multi-faceted set of affective, behavioral, and cognitive responses that occur when the existence or quality of a person's primary relationship is threatened by a third party."[11] As such, jealousy is distinct from envy—which is desiring something another person has. Jealousy can be visually represented with a triangular shape where the jealous person, the prized person or object, and the perceived interrupter make up the three points of the triangle—while envy is dyadic and can be depicted as a line between the envious party and the object of their envy.[12] Envy is often an aspect of jealous dynamics, however, and can play a particularly intense role in CNM situations where a person envies their partner's relationship with a metamour, or their metamour's qualities.

There are qualitative distinctions that can be made between different types of jealousy—many of which can apply to both monogamous and CNM dynamics. One is the difference between *suspicious* and *fait accompli* jealousy.[13] Suspicious jealousy is the feeling of distrust toward a partner's fidelity, and fait accompli jealousy occurs when the threat is real, such as when a lover has left one person for another. Clinical sexologist Ronald Mazur[14] separated jealousy into five different categories: *possessive jealousy*, which arises when one assumes exclusive possession of a love object, and this possession is threatened; *fear jealousy*, which happens when one fears being rejected by one's partner and replaced by someone else; *competition jealousy*, a form of jealousy rooted in comparison and feelings of inadequacy; *ego jealousy*, the fear of being judged by others and of having one's pride hurt; and *exclusion jealousy*, which happens when someone feels left out or deprived of equitable time or attention. Jessica Fern and David Cooley coined the term *justice jealousy* in their latest book, *Polywise*,[15] to refer to situations where a partner gives something to a metamour—for example, particular romantic behaviors such as gift giving or planning elaborate dates—that the initial partner had been wanting and asking for to no avail; the pain of comparison and the perceived unfairness in these situations can bring feelings of competition jealousy, ego jealousy, and exclusion jealousy all at once.

From a mental health perspective, there are three categories of jealousy: symptomatic, pathological, and normal.[16] *Symptomatic* jealousy derives from mental illness such as paranoia, schizophrenia, substance abuse, or other disorders. Jealousy is considered *pathological* when it becomes a personality trait rather than a solely episodic emotion. Finally, *normal* jealousy is the relatively common sensitivity to relationship threats in the absence of psychological or personality disorders. Scholars and mental health professionals widely accept the latter form of jealousy as a normal, even healthy, human emotion[17] that can bring a positive component in romantic relationships. As Maya Angelou put it, "Jealousy in romance is like salt in food. A little can enhance the savor, but too much can spoil the pleasure and under certain circumstances, can be life-threatening."[18] Indeed, there seems to be a "sweet spot" when it comes to jealousy. Hamilton contended with Angelou: "If my lover is not jealous, I might wonder if they genuinely long for me. If my lover is overly jealous, I might wonder if they truly value my autonomy and otherness."[19]

Where the "sweet spot" of jealousy lies can vary from person to person. Moreover, it is not simply the quality or intensity of the emotion, but how one's jealousy gets expressed or worked out that can distinguish whether members of a relationship consider their jealousy "healthy." As I stated earlier in this chapter, jealousy is fundamentally amoral; however, the behavioral responses that people enact from jealous feelings are often fraught. For a deeper philosophical inquiry into the morality of monogamy and non-monogamy, including the role of jealousy in investigating this question, I recommend Justin Clardy's *Why It's Okay to Not Be Monogamous*,[20] Jorge Ferrer's *Love and Freedom: Transcending Monogamy and Polyamory*,[21] as well as articles by Jason Cruz,[22] Harry Chalmers,[23] and Kyle York.[24] In the following section, I explore evolutionary and socially constructed perspectives on jealousy that further contextualize how people may experience and relate to jealousy outside of mononormativity.

ESSENTIALIST, CROSS-CULTURAL, AND SOCIALLY CONSTRUCTED PERSPECTIVES ON JEALOUSY

What is the purpose of jealousy in sexual or romantic contexts? It depends on who you ask. According to evolutionary psychologist David Buss,[25] intimate jealousy likely emerged around 3.5 million years ago as an adaptive survival response for both genders. For men, jealousy served to ensure that they would not invest resources into offspring who were not biologically theirs—and thus used mate-guarding behaviors to ensure *paternity certainty*. For women, jealousy served to prevent men from abandoning them and investing their resources into a rival woman, a scenario that could leave them and their children vulnerable to starvation. As Ferrer synthesized, "from an evolutionary standpoint the main purpose of both monogamy and jealousy is to secure the dissemination of one's DNA."[26] Following this logic, men would be likely to feel greater sexual jealousy (where their partner's sexual infidelity could cause them to nurture a child that was not their own), whereas women would be more likely to feel greater emotional jealousy (where their partner's emotional attachment to another mate could lead to a loss of resources). Researchers have observed this phenomenon in several cultures, including the United States, in modern times.[27]

That said, there are reasons to question claims of biological determinism when it comes to jealousy. For one, the gender differences stated earlier appear to vanish in countries where gender equality is more advanced[28]—which questions whether sexual jealousy still serves human evolution in sociocultural contexts where women no longer depend on men's resources to survive. To this point, Buss has called intimate jealousy a "living fossil"[29] of human evolution: a behavior that may be deeply imprinted in humans, but no longer necessary and thus destined to lose its grip over time. While this assessment does not necessarily make the lived experience of jealousy less painful or challenging, it provides perspective on why its compelling intensity may warrant more creative and compassionate behavioral responses, rather than the "assumption of entitlement"[30] to controlling a partner's sexuality.

Furthermore, jealousy is undeniably linked to variable social conditions. There are many cultures where monogamy is not the norm, and where instances of sexual jealousy are looked down upon rather than normalized. The Mosuo, a matrilineal ethnic minority in southwest China, might be the best-known example. They do not practice marriage, and women take as many lovers as they please. Their brothers contribute to the raising of their children, rather than their lovers. Jealousy among lovers is considered shameful and is typically met with ridicule by members of the community.[31]

Along the same lines, Sylvia, a 59-year-old Dakota participant, noted that the verbal expression of jealousy is considered "undignified" in her culture. Even though her parents practiced monogamy, she grew up "knowing that [her] ancestors were non-monogamous"—and that compulsory monogamy had been enforced by European colonizers by way of coerced conversion to Christianity, imposed patriarchal rules, and economic incentives to marry monogamously. She explained that

> marriage was tied up with the dissolution of the tribal land based into private property. So when they took the land, and they had settlers, they gave it away to homesteaders, and they divided it up into 160-acre parcels, you got more if you were married, and more if you had children, and women couldn't have access to land unless they were married. So marriage and monogamy really became central to anybody having any property.

While Sylvia lamented how modern Dakota communities often fail to challenge those inherited monogamous templates, she did recount that her relationship to jealousy had always been a non-mononormative one from the perspective of her meaning-making process: "It's not that I don't feel an embryo of jealousy, it's that I kill it immediately. Because I view it as undignified, I just won't go there."

Many other traditional societies around the globe have practiced forms of non-monogamy, a fact that challenges claims of biological determinism when it comes to pair bonding and the "naturalness" of monogamy.[32] Polygyny (one husband, many wives) has been widespread throughout history, and instances of polyandry (one wife, many husbands) are not as rare as previously believed and are found in many parts of the world.[33] Polyandrous societies typically have little interest in paternity certainty.[34] Furthermore, in a substantial number of Lowland South American societies, when a woman has several sexual partners before and during pregnancy, each of them is considered the biological father of the child and deemed to have contributed his strengths to her offspring; thus, all of them share the responsibilities of fatherhood.[35] When biological paternity is either shared or ambiguous, sexual jealousy takes on a different meaning.

Therefore, cross-cultural analysis supports the idea that sexual jealousy is more influenced by cultural conditioning than by biological programming.[36] When one sees jealousy through the lens of social construction rather than biological determinism, it becomes apparent that jealousy is mutable. As de Sousa stated,

> Jealousy fits no one simple template. In truth, it is driven less by a deep lionesque desire to ensure paternity of the offspring one helps to nurture, than by a variety of socially variable conditions. The diversity found in experiences of jealousy, as well as in attitudes toward it, is a clue to its nature as a product of culturally variable ideology rather than biological necessity. That may give us reason to think it might be tamed.[37]

In alignment with a social constructionist view of emotions, many authors also argued that romantic jealousy is intrinsically linked to compulsory monogamy, patriarchy, private property, and colonialism. While jealousy manifests itself in the body, it is also undeniably culturally fostered. Jillian Deri,[38] Mimi Schippers,[39] and Angela Willey[40] have each highlighted the interplay of biology and culture in the normalization of jealous feelings, employing interdisciplinary and queer feminist critical approaches to elucidate the significance of jealousy in the context of mononormativity. Building upon Harding and Pribram's contention that emotions, while generally understood as individual phenomena, are also "formed and function as part of the historical, cultural, and political contexts in which they are practiced to reproduce, and potentially resist, hegemonic relations,"[41] Deri, Schippers, and Willey suggested that emancipation from the ideological adherence to patriarchy could result in a different embodied experience of jealousy and compersion.

For example, Deri investigated how polyamorists' cultural and collective beliefs "translate into embodied feeling, at times both enabling *and* preventing the experience of jealousy and compersion"[42]—an assertion de Sousa later used to suggest the possibility of transmuting jealousy into compersion.[43] Deri also coined the term *intersectional emotion* to "illustrate the complexity of factors which contribute to our experiences of emotion, including biology, psychology, neurological composition, gender, age, culture, class, context and other relevant factors."[44] This constructivist understanding of emotions as dynamically intersecting with systems of power set the stage for an analysis of how both jealousy and compersion are impacted by power dynamics.

JEALOUSY AND POWER DYNAMICS IN CNM RELATIONSHIPS

In *Love's Refraction: Jealousy and Compersion in Queer Women's Polyamorous Relationships*, Deri emphasizes the role of power relations in the embodied experience of jealousy: *interpersonal dynamics* (class, gender, age, beauty, race, ethnicity, quantity of partners, etc.), *institutional power* (mononormativity, heterosexism, sexism), and *perceived power* within specific relationships all contribute to one's feelings of security or insecurity, which in turn shift the dial on one's propensity to experience jealousy or compersion at any given time:

> Many people describe jealousy as a result of insecurity coming from an imbalance of power, real or perceived. Jealousy can be experienced as vulnerability linked to the fear of losing a relationship or of a decline in its quality, which again is inseparable from how one understands power within a relationship. For example, a person may not be threatened in their relationship, but their perception of an imbalance of power could trigger a jealous response.[45]

Under that lens, jealousy might carry valuable information about both a person's ingrained insecurities and perceptions, and the actual health of a relationship and its power dynamics. Clanton's relationship assessment model[46] helps understand how jealousy is connected to perceptions of interpersonal power dynamics, naming circumstances such as "who loves whom more, who is thought to be more likely to find another partner sooner upon break-up, who has access to more financial resources, etc."[47] While my study participants did not typically use the term "power" to describe the reasons why they may feel more jealousy than compersion in some circumstances, reading between the lines of interview data reveals themes that point to power dynamics. For example, perceiving that a metamour might embody certain desirable characteristics that feel "threatening" to an established balance of power in a relationship such as youth, beauty, success, or other personally compelling or socially privileged qualities—often resulted in jealous responses for my participants. In Chapter 11, "Social Positionality and Compersion," I explore in more depth the intersection between compersion and social identities. What I found is a paradoxical reality: while lacking social power in certain areas may indeed aggravate jealousy, I also found that people from marginalized communities often view and practice compersion as a form of solidarity, pride, and even resistance to interconnected systems of power and oppression. Both trends are true—mirroring the fact that compersion and jealousy are not mutually exclusive (see Chapter 6, "Coexistence of Jealousy and Compersion") and that the interconnectedness between jealousy, compersion, and the myriad contextual elements impacting those experiences in each person's life is a complex and irreducible tapestry.

Nevertheless, while jealousy functions as an attempt to regain power when faced with a perceived threat to a valued relationship, the expression of jealousy can ironically, in itself, have disempowering effects—at least in some relationships. As Deri explained,

> Jealousy is culturally associated with shame, low self-esteem, insecurity, and immature emotional development—all things that evoke a sense of vulnerability. Thus, exposing one's jealousy may exacerbate power differences, which in turn may increase one's jealousy.[48]

The disempowering effects of jealousy can be particularly present in CNM subcultures where normative expectations are that partners *should* feel compersion rather than jealousy, and the latter gets labeled as a problem stemming from one's lack of confidence or security. Unless partners explicitly agree to become safe havens for the expression of jealousy as a normal, healthy, and acceptable part of their emotional landscape, this expression can unwittingly become an emotional territory fraught with shame and fear—which compounds jealous feelings into further disempowerment. Deri continued,

> To expose oneself as feeling jealous may seem like a declaration of the other person's power, potentially exacerbating the (sensation of) vulnerability. One partner's expression of jealousy can be interpreted as the other person having power, or it can shift perceived power. In mainstream culture, jealousy on the part of a partner can be interpreted as a sign of care or love, but for polyamorous people, a partner's jealousy is more often seen as a barrier to intimacy, in that it gets in the way of closeness and makes polyamorous practice more challenging.[49]

On the bright side, a majority of my interviewees emphasized the importance and the benefits of normalizing jealousy and its expression within CNM relationships, to avoid compounding shame or secrecy around already challenging feelings. Many people reported making explicit agreements with their partners that they could safely ask for reassurance when experiencing jealous feelings—and agreed to do their best to meet each other's vulnerability with compassion, patience, and kindness. This was an intrinsic part of building the safety and trust necessary for compersion to emerge. I explore this theme further in Chapter 7.

In the next section, I turn to the central question of how CNM people view and relate to jealousy differently than their monogamous counterparts. This particular aspect of people's worldview and emotional landscape lays the ground for compersion to emerge.

HOW CNM PEOPLE RELATE TO JEALOUSY DIFFERENTLY: THE ADVENT OF NON-MONONORMATIVE JEALOUSY

The fact that compersion—a concept that is antithetical to mononormativity—takes place in CNM relationships reflects the agency that non-monogamous individuals embody in the process of making meaning of their emotional and relational experiences. Each interviewee in my study challenged the standard mononormative narrative by looking at jealousy from the lens of the values and beliefs they held around honoring their partner's sexual and romantic autonomy. This process subverts the mononormative "assumption of entitlement"[50] to controlling one's partner's sexual behavior on the basis of one's jealousy.

That is not to say that CNM folks experience less jealousy than monogamous people. Practicing non-mononogamy "virtually guarantees [jealousy] must be dealt with openly and directly."[51] Indeed, most of my participants reported extensive experience with jealousy, as well as the tense coexistence of jealousy and compersion—a phenomenon that Joli Hamilton and I coined "comperstruggle" (see Chapter 6 for more detail). However, CNM interviewees took an unconventional stance, in that they generally strived to utilize occurrences of jealousy to increase the depth of intimacy with themselves and their partners, rather than seeing jealousy as an emotion to be avoided at all costs. They also believed that jealousy was not inevitable, nor inflexible. A few participants stated that they had never very much struggled with jealousy, while the majority said that they had learned to shift, transform, and progressively heal their relationship with jealousy over time.

All participants expressed a sense of personal responsibility and agency vis-à-vis jealousy. For most participants, this meant doing the work of identifying and understanding the source of their jealousy, as well as learning to self-soothe, self-regulate, and replace shame with compassion. At the relational level, it also meant strategizing with their partners to create more attachment security and reassurance, minimize specific triggers, get more of their needs met, and maintain relationship boundaries and agreements that would keep jealousy more manageable. In all cases, participants had developed a sense of proactive engagement, rather than avoidance, in relation to jealousy and its associated feelings.

For example, Simon, an 83-year-old retired professor, reported establishing a clear behavioral boundary toward jealousy over 35 years prior—as well as a commitment to healing what lay underneath the emotion. After displaying aggressive and entitled jealous behaviors with his girlfriend in the context of a personal development workshop, he gained a new awareness of "how [jealousy] really fucked up [his] life":

> I felt like a terrible, terrible person. I was *really* embarrassed. I can't imagine why I did what I did, except that it was driven by this sense of abandonment of not being loved. I . . . you know, it's a whole bunch of feelings. . . . I realized that could not happen again. *I just had to not let that happen again.*

Simon's epiphany and depth of embarrassment had served to shift his perspective on jealousy from something that he felt entitled to use as a tool for controlling his lovers, to an emotion that was rooted in a lack of self-love, and one that could be healed. He went on to participate in many Human Awareness Institute (HAI) workshops for many years, and at the time of the first interview, had recently celebrated 25 years of non-monogamous marriage with his wife.

What exactly allows CNM people to build successful non-monogamous partnerships despite unavoidable encounters with jealousy? Hamilton and colleagues studied how CNM individuals relate to jealousy differently than monogamous people. In a *Comparison of Monogamous and Consensually Non-Monogamous Women's Experience*, they described how both monogamous and CNM women viewed jealousy as a normal part of relationships, as well as containing valuable information. However, how CNM women differed from monogamous ones was in how they interpreted and then responded to jealous feelings. To illustrate, one CNM interviewee said that while she valued the information that jealousy was giving her about how much she cared about her partner, she felt "it was her responsibility to 'parse out' and to navigate her next steps so she didn't act on that jealousy information with a sense of entitlement to someone's attention, body, or time."[52]

This view represented a rejection of mononormativity that is distinctive of CNM individuals. It led this participant to reframe jealousy from a reason to feel betrayed by one's partner to a source of inquiry and intentional meaning-making based on CNM beliefs and values. Conversely, a belief specific of *monogamous* participants was that "there is a qualitative type of attention that is reserved for, expected from, and only experienced within the monogamous dyad container."[53] A breach of this expected attention-exclusivity was understood to be a violation of the core value and purpose of monogamous relationships, but not CNM ones. This points to the different paradigms—mononormative or non-mononormative—that jealousy can be viewed from, and how engaging with jealousy from a non-mononormative standpoint leads to different behavioral outcomes and relationship structures. Again, doing so does not mean that jealous feelings simply evaporate—but it creates a certain disidentification and distance from them, which in turn creates more room for compersion to grow.

The journey from proactively engaging with jealousy to nurturing compersion is certainly not a linear one (see Chapter 5, "Spectrum of Compersion"); yet, it is a helpful one to schematize. Hamilton and her colleagues created such a framework from their analysis of how CNM participants successfully dealt with jealousy. They suggested that clinicians might consider employing this framework to support clients in managing jealousy. The framework or "roadmap" through jealousy included five steps:

1. *Notice.* CNM participants reported that noticing jealousy early made it easier to manage. This took the form of attending to uncomfortable thoughts, bodily sensations, and feelings of insecurity or threat.
2. *Name.* Naming jealousy was key for participants who described jealousy as a manageable emotion—unless they experienced internalized shame and/or judgment from their partners. Destigmatizing jealousy allowed them to manage the emotional content as well as address unmet relational needs.
3. *Narrate.* Comfort with jealousy came through the process of reimagining jealousy as a source of information without automatically presuming a relationship was in imminent danger. This went hand-in-hand with questioning common cultural narratives of jealousy portrayed in literature, films, television, and social media content.
4. *Navigate needs.* CNM participants used explicit communication, boundary-setting, agreement-making, emotional attunement, and rupture and repair skills to respond to feelings of jealousy—which highlighted the importance of being able to identify one's needs.
5. *Nurture compersion.* Most CNM participants reported consciously nurturing compersion to counterbalance feelings of jealousy.[54]

These five steps are congruent with my participants' accounts of how they manage jealousy and cultivate compersion. For example, Bethanne, a 29-year-old nonprofit activist, explained how she was able to move from jealousy toward compersion in the following steps:

I would say, first: validate, validate, validate, validate those feelings, those are real. Second is the enormous category of doing the work. Like, understand where that comes from. Understand your background, do a shit ton of therapy, identify your trigger points, know what's causing that jealousy. And then, be super clear about where you want to get to, what does compersion mean to you, when do you feel that . . . and cultivate those moments of joy.

Tyrone, a 38-year-old facilitator, had similar recommendations for handling jealousy:

One, feel it, don't push it away. Listen to it. Be clear on what it is trying to say. I feel like our emotions are always telling us something, and listening to our jealousy is like, what is it that you're jealous of? Do you want the thing that this other person is getting? . . . What is the actual truth, and what is the story there? I think it's always important to be clear on the truth and the story. . . . I like to be very clear with and frank with myself and speaking like, "This is a story. This isn't reality. This is illogical, I'm being real irrational right now." And, all of those things are okay because I feel those things. Those are my truth. In this moment, I feel really irrational. And I need the moment to be in that, to narrow down to my truth. I just need to be clear on that. So just allowing space and not taking action when it comes to jealousy, until I'm clear on what it is; not be proactive when I feel jealous. You're going to act out certain ways that could cause a rift if you're not present to the story that's there. So it's just allowing yourself to be in it. Feel it. Figure it out; and then speak to where the truth is. What is it trying to tell you? What is the truth there?

Both Bethanne and Tyronne's responses were compatible with Hamilton et al.'s five-step framework. While CNM folks view jealousy in different terms than their monogamous counterparts, such a process of dissecting challenging emotions can be extremely helpful for people in all relationship types.

THE MALLEABILITY OF JEALOUSY

If jealousy is at least in part socially constructed, individuals have a certain amount of power and agency to intentionally alter their subjective experiences of it. Several of my participants exemplified this by speaking of their relationship to jealousy and compersion as a fluid dance that could change over time and depending on contexts (I further describe the coexistence of jealousy and compersion in Chapter 6).

To illustrate how intentional meaning-making could impact one's emotional outcomes, Alexis, a 26-year-old professional cuddlist and event program director, explained how "raw emotional arousal" from their partner's intimate engagement with others could lead to either compersion or jealousy, and that they could exercise freedom and agency in determining the emotional and psychological impacts of these contexts:

There will be the seed of envy or jealousy, however it got there—whether it's socialized in or whether I would have it regardless—there's a little bit of a seed. And there . . . there's a gateway. And when I'm tired, sometimes, I'll just go into the envy or jealousy, or if I don't feel like using resources. With that seed, I can choose pleasure, I can choose to tap into the pleasure my partner's feeling, I can choose to tap into the love that I feel for them, and for their other partner, because I like to have some sort of relationship or connection with the other partner. And so, it just feels good. Because I'm choosing pleasure, I'm choosing love. . . . The way I view jealousy . . . is a mix of emotions and stories that tells us about our childhood, and about our fears about ourselves, and our partners. And they're really good teachers for personal growth. . . . So teaching agency about what stories we have, and how to work with them, and also agency about what to do with jealousy and envy. They're both stories. What story are you going to choose?

Some participants also got playful, even kinky, with jealousy. They interacted with jealousy's intensity in positive, enlivening, and even arousing ways. This was another way participants expressed agency in their relationship to jealousy and experienced their ability to "dance" with jealousy, rather than simply feeling that they were victims of it. For example, Bethanne recounted how she had learned to accept and invite jealousy more fully into her life, after many years of practicing polyamory. Counterintuitively, in her 2023 interview, she recounted how she had been feeling more jealousy in recent months compared to the time of her first interview in 2018. She attributed this change to her increased ability to hold many emotions, an ability that had increased from her ongoing meditation practice. Instead of "forcing" herself to just feel compersion, because that is what was expected of her in CNM contexts, she had learned to embrace more of her emotional depth—which in turn led to "more authentic compersion." When asked about her recent experiences of compersion compared to five years prior, she responded:

It feels like [compersion] has gotten in some ways harder, but it feels connected to me being more open to the complexity and diversity of my human experience and feelings, rather than it being less accessible. . . . I think one thing that I really appreciate about this [current] relationship is that we just practice being really honest about shadow. So recently, I had my first full intimate experience with someone else . . . and it was so beautiful for us to connect about that and then him to just be like, "Okay, I'm feeling my full caveman that wants to rip this other person apart." And then he just channeled that, and I could receive it, and we played with it, and I did this whole thing where I told him all the ways that this other experience was way better. And then I did the flip and I told him I have all the ways that this other experience was way worse, and like, reaffirm. Anyway, it was just super fun to play with. And I'm finding a lot of life in doing the inverse of compersion. I find my inner caveperson that wants to rip this other person apart, and channel that with my intimate person. And like, let that free the shadow parts and that actually enables a more authentic compersion to emerge.

In this description, Bethanne credited her increased capacity to hold a variety of emotions as well as intentional shadow work for her deepening relationship with *both* jealousy and compersion. She then suggested that this evolution had to do with age, to some extent.

As I get older, I have more capacity to feel more things . . . I can move through emotions more easily. I can not take them as personally or as seriously, and also take them more seriously . . . there's just a lot more capacity. There's less, like, "oh, I *should* feel compersion so I'm going to feel compersion right now." There's more permission to feel whatever.

I explore deeper in Chapter 2 how jealousy was used by some of my participants to enhance sexual arousal, into what I coined as "erotic compersion." This is one more way in which CNM folks often relate to jealousy in unconventional, non-mononormative, and highly agentic ways.

In conclusion, my research with CNM individuals has demonstrated that the subjective experience of jealousy, rather than being inflexible, can evolve and change through intentional meaning-making and mindful practice. The multifaceted process of recognizing, naming, destigmatizing, understanding, and working constructively with jealousy creates a foundation for compersion. Again, engaging with jealousy from a non-mononormative standpoint does not mean that feelings of jealousy just disappear—but it allows enough space and disidentification from jealous feelings to invite compersion to take place. Jealous feelings often coexist with compersion, particularly in its attitudinal and behavioral forms. Indeed, the fact that jealousy and compersion can arise simultaneously (see Chapter 6) means that jealousy does not have to vanish for compersion to arise.

NOTES

1. Hamilton et al., 2024. Reprinted with permission.
2. Anapol, 2010.
3. Hart & Carrington, 2002.
4. Hamilton et al., 2024.
5. Ferrer, 2019, p. 186.
6. Hamilton, 2020, p. 8.
7. Buss, 2000.
8. Daly et al., 1982; Goetz et al., 2008; Wilson & Daly, 1996.
9. For example, Emens, 2004; Heckert, 2010; Kean, 2015; Klesse, 2016; Rothschild, 2018; Willey, 2015.
10. For example, York, 2020.
11. Guerrero et al., 2005, p. 233.
12. Hamilton, 2020.
13. Parrot, 1991.
14. Mazur, 1973.
15. Fern & Cooley, 2023.
16. White, 1991.
17. Pines, 1998.
18. Angelou, 1994, p. 129.
19. Hamilton, 2020, p. 8.
20. Clardy, 2023.
21. Ferrer, 2021.
22. Cruz, 2016.
23. Chalmers, 2019, 2022.
24. York, 2020.
25. Buss, 2000.
26. Ferrer, 2007, p. 39.
27. Buunk & Dijkstra, 2004.
28. de Sousa, 2017; Harris, 2003; Hupka & Bank, 1996.
29. Buss, 1994, p. 222.
30. de Sousa, 2017.
31. Namu & Mathieu, 2007; Ryan & Jethá, 2010.
32. For example, Fisher, 2016.
33. Starkweather & Hames, 2012.
34. Bhugra, 1993.
35. Knight, 2004; Ryan & Jethá, 2010.
36. For example, Bhugra, 1993.
37. de Sousa, 2017, p. 4.
38. Deri, 2015.
39. Schippers, 2016.

40. Willey, 2016.
41. Harding & Pribram, 2004, p. 865.
42. Deri, 2015, p. 19.
43. de Sousa, 2017.
44. Deri, 2015, p. 20.
45. Deri, 2015, p. 99.
46. Clanton, 1996.
47. As cited in Deri, 2015, p. 99.
48. Deri, 2015, p. 99.
49. Deri, 2015, pp. 117, 118.
50. de Sousa, 2017, p. 5.
51. Hamilton, 2020, p. iii.
52. Hamilton et al., 2024.
53. Hamilton et al., 2024.
54. Hamilton et al., 2024.

PART I

COMPONENTS OF COMPERSION

A primary goal of my research has been to elucidate the question that titles this book. *What is compersion?* To this aim, I inquired about what compersion is, exactly, in the experience of my study participants. I explored questions such as: *What are its primary constituents? What does it take for an experience to qualify as compersion? To what extent is it self-focused, versus other-focused?* Because of the foundational nature of these topics, I investigated them using grounded theory—a qualitative research method that does not begin with a hypothesis, but allows themes to emerge from the "ground" of raw interview data (please refer to the introduction for more details on my research process).

The initial section of this book describes what *constitutes* compersion. This is distinct from the *dimensions* of compersion described in Part II, as these refer to the various nuances and ways that people may experience it, rather than its fundamental constituents. To use a culinary analogy—if compersion were a cake, the components described in Part I would be the basic ingredients, and the dimensions described in Part II would represent the different baking methods and flavors.

I found two overarching components that together constitute compersion: positive empathy and gratitude. These components were present across the board in all of my interviewees' accounts. The following two chapters describe each of these themes, respectively, and depict the many ways in which they manifest in CNM people's lives.

POSITIVE EMPATHY

I'm going to give you the thing that I know you enjoy. Because that's how I show my love, by intentionally giving you what you actually want, what gives you joy, the things that you desire in your life. I want to give that to you because I'm your partner.

—Tyrone, 38, facilitator

I learned to love and let go, not be attached to what I wanted, but to be attached to what WE, my partner and I, wanted.

—Simon, 83, retired professor

The first component of compersion is *positive empathy*. This includes a wide range of empathic emotions, sensations, thoughts, and feelings that individuals may experience in reaction to their partners' enjoyment of other intimate relationships. While a majority of participants emphasized the *emotional* component of positive empathy (i.e., empathic joy), many folks depicted their experiences of compersion as *cognitive, attitudinal, or behavioral*. Additionally, many participants reported experiencing many different "flavors" of compersion, depending on the context. I describe these distinctions more fully in Chapter 4, "Two Kinds of Compersion: Attitudinal and Embodied," and Chapter 5, "Spectrum of Compersion." To this point, I have renamed the present section from "empathic joy" in my original dissertation work[1] to "positive empathy" in this book to more accurately reflect the nuances of participants' accounts.

Before diving into the varieties of ways positive empathy manifests in CNM dynamics, it is helpful to understand how academic literature has conceptualized empathy. This next section reviews different definitions of empathy, and explores how a budding body of research on positive social emotions can support the understanding of compersion.

CHAPTER 2

WHAT IS EMPATHY?

The term *empathy* was derived from the German term *einfühlung*, which literally translates as "feeling into." Titchener later named this concept "empathy."[2] At the core of it is the idea of "going into a strong feeling-connection with another."[3] Researchers have assigned a variety of clinical and theoretical meanings to the term empathy in recent decades,[4] to the extent that some scholars characterized the field as being in "conceptual disarray."[5] One of these many perspectives is that empathy refers strictly to emotional state-matching (i.e., "I *feel* what you feel")—a phenomenon coined as "contagion."[6] An opposing perspective is that empathy refers instead to a cognitive perspective-taking process (i.e., "I can *imagine* what you feel").[7] Other scholars view empathy as "an experience that is both emotional and cognitive, either because these two elements are intertwined or because the emotion results immediately from the cognitive state of perspective-taking."[8]

For the present study, I deemed the third perspective—a combined experience of perspective-taking and the resulting emotional state—best suited for the task of describing the experience of compersion, as participants' accounts included interconnected emotional/embodied and cognitive/attitudinal components (see Chapter 4, "Two Kinds of Compersion: Attitudinal and Embodied"). Further, I selected the term *positive empathy* as a label for the first component of compersion (rather than simply *empathy*) to convey the specific meaning of compersion as a shared positive experience, and to distinguish it from the more widely studied form of empathy toward negative emotions and sensations. Pittinsky and Montoya, who investigated empathic joy in the context of intergroup relations, noted that "research on empathy focuses almost exclusively on its negative variety, empathic sorrow, either by defining empathy as a state involving negative emotions or by confining its empirical study to the negative."[9] In other words, scholars typically see and study empathy as the ability to understand the sorrow and suffering of other people. This bias might be due to the fact that the human brain reacts far more intensely to the distress and sadness of others than to their joy, even though the two phenomena employ the same brain circuitry.[10] This is potentially connected to negativity bias—the psychological phenomenon by which humans pay more attention to, and give more weight to, negative rather than positive information.[11]

However, a growing body of research on positive social emotions indicates that positive empathy is a significant mechanism for interpersonal bonding,[12] and is linked to more positive attitudinal responses toward others.[13] For example, *broaden-and-build theory* has shown that positive empathic emotions are particularly important for building connections among groups—which can map well onto groups of partners and metamours, or polycules, who share intimate space in CNM.[14] The theory indicates that arousing empathic joy generates positive emotions, positive thoughts, more flexible thinking, and the psychological states that prepare a person to build friendships and social networks. The theory also shows that positive emotions broaden people's sense of self, resulting in feelings of *self–other overlap*[15]—a phenomenon repeatedly described by my study participants when discussing compersion.

In turn, self–other overlap is thought to result in a more complex understanding of others,[16] which may lead to more fully understanding one's partner's perspective. This process may help explain how someone may experience compersion from a relationship that does not include them. *Self-expansion theory* also shows a connection between positive emotions and self–other overlap, suggesting that as people get closer emotionally, they begin to perceive the other as part of the self.[17] This is also consistent with *crossover theory*, which focuses on the emotional influence that close dyadic partners have on each other.[18]

All these findings are highly relevant to the study of compersion[19]—and conversely, the study of compersion has the potential to make a significant contribution to the nascent psychological field of positive empathy research. Next, I illustrate how positive empathy showed up in my research.

PARTICIPANTS' ACCOUNTS OF POSITIVE EMPATHY

Positive empathy was a central tenet in all my participants' accounts of compersion. They described compersion as sharing their partners' positive experiences of new crushes, new relationship energy (NRE), emotional fulfillment, erotic pleasure, and other positive experiences associated with other relationship(s). Five themes were particularly evocative: (1) "their joy is my joy": expansion of personal boundaries; (2) compersion as an expression of romance; (3) from "what serves *me*" to "what serves *us*": being on the same team; (4) positive relational feedback loop; and (5) erotic compersion.

"Their Joy Is My Joy": Expansion of Personal Boundaries

At the heart of the experience of compersion is the inclusion of one's partner(s) and/or metamour(s) into one's circle of care and empathic concern. The term *personal boundaries* refers to how one's sense of self, identity, desires, and emotions is experienced as separate from that of others. With impervious personal boundaries, a person's joy would not impact another; but the expansion of personal boundaries means that the line between self and other becomes blurred or porous.

As such, the majority of interviewees associated compersion with a felt sense of enhanced closeness to their partners, and described their motivations as interconnected with their well-being. This expansion of personal boundaries made the experience of shared joy possible—epitomizing a sense of togetherness, deep connection, and emotional intimacy. This is consistent with the description of mudita, one of the four Buddhist "immeasurable states" (see introduction), as having the power to dissolve the illusion of separation of the self.[20]

To illustrate, Teresa, a 54-year-old nanny, coined her experience of compersion as "Big Love" to illustrate that compersion is based on an expanded sense of self. She used the analogy of witnessing a child opening a present:

> I feel "Big Love" when my kid opens a present. I see the look on their face, and I get so excited watching them open that present. . . . It's not me wishing that my kid's present was mine. I'm excited for them. And their joy is my joy. In the same way, when Richard was with another woman, where he had really beautiful experiences, even watching him sexually be with her. . . . It's not so much that I was turned on by it . . . his joy, his absolute bliss made me feel like he was opening a gift in front of me. [*laughs*]

Similarly, Bethanne, a 29-year-old nonprofit activist, described compersion as the simple experience of sharing her lover's joy:

> I think it's as simple as, "I love this person, and seeing them be happy is happy making." That is the most basic part of being in love—delighting in the person, wanting the person to be happy. So, seeing them be happy in a relationship with someone else is happy making.

Overall, my participants described compersion as a linchpin of a paradigm of shared joy and shared love, where the experience of "more for you means more for me" replaced the zero-sum game of "more for you means less for me" in the intimate realm.

Compersion as an Expression of Romance

While the traditional romantic paradigm centers jealousy and possession as a main feature of passionate love, folks in my study found that giving their partner what they *really* want—including the encouragement to fulfill one's intimate desires with others—was a romantic stance of the highest order. They saw taking pleasure in their partner's pleasure as a gift of devotion and deep love. Tyrone, a 38-year-old facilitator, described compersion as a "romance-joy," or "romantic joy":

> I love that compersion is romantic. I feel this level of romance-joy. That's like romantic joy! I would do anything for you, and I get to see that you're getting this thing that I know you want, and I love to see you in bliss and pleasure. . . . I love to see that, and I love to witness that . . . it's a level of intimacy and connection and partnership. It's just like if my partner says, "I like flowers," and I bring them flowers once in a while. If their desire is to be tied up and have a guy or girl present and play with them—to me, it's the same thing. It's like, *I'm going to give you the thing that I know you enjoy.* Because that's how I show my love, by intentionally giving you what you actually want, what gives you joy, the things that you desire in your life. I want to give that to you because I'm your partner.

Sabrina, a 41-year-old dance artist, illustrated a similar experience by describing how her long-term partner sees her as a queen when looking at her through a compersive lens:

> He's treating me the way he wants to treat me, which is like a queen who has sovereignty over herself. That's how he envisions me and wants me to be and treats me. And then likewise, I come back feeling like that. So we feel great! [*laughs*]

While these perspectives may, at first sight, seem far removed from a mononormative vision of romantic love, they share many values and attributes with what monogamous people would consider romantic: the willingness to sacrifice one's immediate comfort for the sake of a beloved's pleasure, selfless devotion, joyful generosity, an expanded sense of self to include one's partner's well-being, and a desire to treat our partner(s) regally. In that light, intimate compersion may simply be a natural extension of what most people understand as deep, devotional love—but without the expectation of sexual and romantic exclusivity.

From "What Serves *Me*" to "What Serves *Us*": Being on the Same Team

Nearly all my study participants explained that compersion went hand-in-hand with their sense of being on the same team with their partner(s), and in many cases, with their extended polycule (i.e., one's CNM network of partners/lovers, metamours, and metamours' other partners/lovers). The widening sense of self I described in the earlier sections promotes intimacy by shifting one's attention from a focus on what serves the individual to what serves the whole. This requires a democratization of power that is foundational to successful CNM,[21] where the well-being of the group is prioritized through careful negotiations and communication, aimed at ensuring that every person feels heard, seen, and cared for and that their needs are adequately met. This process is based on a perception of interconnectedness between oneself and others.

Simon, an 83-year-old retired professor with five great-grandchildren, explained his journey to compersion by saying, "I learned to love and let go, not be attached to what *I* wanted, but to be attached to what *we*, my partner and I, wanted." Jamila, a 36-year-old nonprofit program associate, described it as "being a *cheerleader*. I want to make sure that they're happy and that they feel supported and cheered on."

This sense of caring for the team also extended to metamours and their metamours' partners. In a personal interview, Kevin Patterson, author of *Love Is Not Color Blind*,[22] described the sentiment of being part of a team with his wife's other partners:

> I try to see myself as on the team of my partner. So, you know, I'm on *wife team*, and everyone else she's dating is on *wife team*. We need to help each other out because *this is the team*.

Compersion also extends to caring about the well-being of members of one's extended polycule. Several participants expressed the perspective, as did Michael, a 67-year-old musician, that "if everyone is not having a good time, then it's not working." Accordingly, a few folks expressed strong opposition to having any nonconsensual affairs, or even "don't ask, don't tell" dynamics as part of their intimate networks, as these would present obstacles to maintaining the sense of pride, openness, enthusiastic consent, and transparency necessary for compersion to bloom.

This stance demonstrated how my participants felt accountable to other members of their intimate networks, and that if one person in the polycule was disgruntled by, or not supportive of, their partners' other relationships, this would impact everyone's ability to enjoy those connections. Partly, the presence of a resentful partner might indicate the presence of interactions that were not fullheartedly consensual; and compersion is dependent on the full consent of all involved in a network. Conversely, when all parties involved expressed sincere support toward their metamour relationships, a positive relational feedback loop was likely to occur.

Positive Relational Feedback Loop

When a polycule operated with little or no negative tension between its members, the creation of a "positive relational feedback loop" (an expression coined by Martin) would occur. Participants described this phenomenon as a multiplication of love within a network of people sharing a similar desire and commitment toward the CNM values of sharing, respect, communication, autonomy, and authentic expression. Partners and metamours expressing goodwill to one another would create a feedback loop that promoted compersion. Thus, all members of a polyamorous network had to share this desire for mutually beneficial outcomes.

Martin, a 33-year-old software engineer, described compersion as a departure from individual self-centeredness and a dyadic mentality, toward a mindset where all members of a polycule would receive and reciprocate care and joy from everyone else. This created a positive chain reaction:

> There's a feedback loop there . . . if one of my partners is happy about something, and I'm happy about it, then I'm going to be happy about this third person who is providing the initial happiness. It's this transmitted effect.

This "transmitted effect" reflects the awareness of interconnectedness within a group of people—and the contagious character of emotions. This is reminiscent of transpersonal and intersubjective views of human interactions, where personal boundaries may expand to include others.[23] Such an effect can also be interpreted as a departure from a Cartesian worldview that establishes the individual self as a fully separate and self-defining entity,[24] and instead requires a deep experience of interconnectedness that allows for mutually beneficial, rather than zero-sum, outcomes. This is also akin to mudita, or sympathetic joy, in Buddhism.[25]

Additionally, the phenomenon of positive relational feedback loops aligns well with the broaden-and-build theory,[26] the concept of self–other overlap,[27] self-expansion theory,[28] and crossover theory[29]—all of which I described early in this chapter. These established theories, although not developed in the context of CNM, contribute to understanding compersion as an empathic phenomenon that enhances a sense of common good, and is intrinsically connected to the cultivation of close friendships and social support networks.

Erotic Compersion

Many participants identified erotic turn-on as an important factor in their experiences of positive empathy. They described deriving sexual arousal from the knowledge, thought, or experience of their partner being intimately engaged with another person. For some, this type of vicarious eroticism—or *erotic empathy*—had been an initial point of entry into CNM. Whether or not this flavor of turn-on—what I coin here *erotic compersion*—should really "count" as compersion is up for debate, as this particular experience may appear more self-focused than other-focused in some cases. I discuss this in more depth toward the end of this section.

Nevertheless, several participants in my study described a heightened sense of eroticism as a notable and thrilling aspect of their compersion experiences. I categorized their accounts into three themes: (1) resexualization of partner(s) through third-person gaze; (2) taboo quality; and (3) alchemizing of jealousy into desire.

Resexualization of Partner(s) through Third-Person Gaze

The practice of CNM allowed participants to resexualize their partner through a third-person gaze through imagining or witnessing their partner being sexually desired by, or sexually involved with, other people. This experience was especially potent for participants who were in long-term relationships.

As Esther Perel explained in *Mating in Captivity*, cultivating erotic tension within long-term coupledom requires maintaining a sense of separateness and autonomy.[30] Conversely, when partners become deeply entangled with one another, through sharing everyday tasks, parenting, finances, chores, and so on, they often begin to presume they know everything about one another; the mysterious *erotic gap* between them, which once brought sexual aliveness to their connection, fades. However, committed couples—monogamous or not—may notice a renewed spark of desire when they witness their partner through another's eyes—for example, seeing them engage in lively conversation with an attractive stranger at a party, giving a conference presentation, or sharing a dance with someone else. In these scenarios, looking at one's partner from a third-person gaze can re-enliven sexual arousal by reintroducing an erotic gap.

Likewise, CNM contexts introduce a sense of separateness through erotic autonomy. Non-monogamy creates scenarios where partners get to imagine each other, and sometimes witness one another, from a third-person perspective—for example, when they are out on dates, sharing about their crushes, spending time with metamours, or participating in group sex. Many participants recounted how practicing CNM enlivened sexual desire and intimacy with their long-term partner(s) in everyday life. For example, Sabrina explained that CNM brought a sense of sustainable aliveness in her sexual relationship with her boyfriend:

> I don't feel that our sexual relationship is going to peter out over time. I'm in it for the long haul with this man. I just knew right from the beginning that we were going to grow sexually together, and that was going to be a very vivifying and alive part of our dynamic.

Diane expressed a similar experience. Having recently shifted her previously monogamous relationship with her husband of 30 years into a polyamorous one, she noticed that sex with her husband had been re-enlivened as a result of bringing new people into their intimate space:

> Being together for 30 years, boredom sets in the sex life. But being with these people [lovers and metamours], and then you come back, your sex life is even better with your mate. James saw that I'd come back and I'd be like, "Hey, baby, let's get it on!" He liked that! [*laughs*]

Taboo Quality

Erotic compersion also derived from a sense of conspiring, sharing a secret, or engaging with taboo activities. Eroticism is associated with a sense of diving into the unknown or a sense of mystery,[31] and there is ample evidence that many common sexual fantasies revolve around taboos.[32] CNM, while gaining ground in terms of prevalence and normalization, is still highly stigmatized and controversial in mainstream culture. Thus, it makes sense that CNM partners share a special bond based on doing something that is, to a large extent, prohibited—and having to hide their "naughtiness." Some participants reported heightened erotic excitement from this sense of living on the edge. Sabrina pointed out the turn-on associated with the taboo quality of CNM:

> There's a sense of sharing a secret, there's something very titillating about that. There's a taboo quality also. I love to tease my partner, I ask him: "So, at your workplace, did someone catch your eye or attention?" and he shares with me these dynamics. I think it's great! I feel alive. I feel bubbly. I feel more intimate with him.

Similarly, Tyrone pointed out that his propensity toward actualizing fantasies was key in his experience of compersion:

> I live a life of ethical hedonism. I have a lot of group sex. I'm very open about my desires and my fantasies. . . . I like living in my fantasy brain. With my partners, I'm like, "Let's talk about all your deep desires, the shadowy work, the things that you think you can't have"—and I give that to them.

Playing with taboo was often connected with the eroticization of jealousy as a turn-on. For many participants, the veil between "hot jealousy" and destructive jealousy was a thin and malleable one—often used as an entry point to compersive feelings.

Alchemizing Jealousy into Desire

With intentional framing, participants often used jealousy as a sexual catalyst with their partners by introducing elements of unpredictability, tension, threat, and even an edgy, yet tolerable, amount of emotional pain. This theme echoed research findings where jealousy was shown to add "spice" to a relationship by leading to more sexual activity with a partner[33]—a phenomenon I described in more detail in Chapter 1.

Indeed, a "goldilock" amount of jealousy could function as a kink. Agreeing to invite jealousy into one's intimate bond has striking parallels to bondage, discipline, sadism, and masochism (BDSM) practices, as it forces partners to be present and hyperattentive to their own feelings and sensations—thus boosting their sensitivity.[34] For example, Alexis recounted how jealous feelings had enhanced their sexual relationship with a partner:

> I found jealousy and compersion to be kind of interesting and fun additions to my relationships. . . . When I see Jules with another partner, for example, I have envy or scarcity come up and, and that's kind of fun, because then, when we have alone time, I'm like, "Wharf! Mine!"

Tyrone took this a step further by intentionally using jealousy as a kink:

> When I give my partner head as they talk about the things they would rather be doing outside of me, I'm really turned on and I feel really connected. . . . Sometimes I want to feel jealousy and shame. I like to play around with that. Like, I want you to go out and play around with other people that you find attractive in front of me. Or, I want you to tempt me that you can't take me home but you're taking someone else home. There's ways that you can play around with any emotion that can turn it from a negative into a playful positive. You can play around with jealousy just like you can play around with sensuality . . . and not make it this heavy thing—make it this light, playful, sexy, sensual, or connective, intimate thing.

Another interesting facet of erotic compersion is its relevance to the study of *cuckolding* or *troilism*.[35] While no participants in my study mentioned cuckolding or troilism as a fantasy or as an aspect of their compersive turn-on, the earlier themes and quotes point to potential commonalities in their psychology. In my coaching practice, I have received several inquiries from people who have an interest in cuckolding as they see themselves represented in my work on compersion—which led me to investigate the matter more closely. Research by Justin Lehmiller, David Ley, and Dan Savage on gay men's cuckolding fantasy yielded qualitative data that was surprisingly reminiscent of my own participants' narratives around compersion. For example, one gay male in their study reported a clear emphasis on his partner's pleasure within a cuckolding framing:

> I enjoy imagining, hearing about, and witnessing my partner having sex with other men. I am turned on by my partner receiving physical and emotional pleasure with other men because each human being has different qualities

and each can form unique and interesting relationships; I feel that a life fully lived incorporates diverse relationships with others, be they passing, distant, intimate, emotional, or physical. I want my partner to experience pleasure and happiness in whatever way he deems fit for living the fullest life he can.[36]

What exactly is cuckolding? According to Lehmiller and colleagues, a general definition of cuckolding is "a sexual interest in which one obtains sexual arousal from the experience of a romantic partner engaging in sexual activity with someone else."[37] More specifically, "cuckolding" is the colloquial term for a contemporary form of troilism "in which a man obtains sexual arousal from the sight or experience of his wife or girlfriend engaging in sexual activity with another man," where "much importance is typically ascribed to the wife's sexual pleasure."[38] The practice and fantasy of cuckolding is considered to be a form of consensual non-monogamy, although it is distinct from most other forms of CNM due to the cuckold "taking on a submissive, disempowered, and largely voyeuristic role in both the experience and fantasy"—while other forms of CNM "tend to involve more egalitarian sexual interactions or mutual physical participation by all parties."[39]

While the word "cuckold" is most typically used to refer to a heterosexual man,[40] research shows that gay male's interest in cuckold fantasies is on the rise—which makes sense through the lens of *sperm competition theory*:

> The idea is that men evolved to experience biological and behavioral changes that give them a competitive reproductive edge whenever multiple men compete over the same mate, such as by releasing more motile sperm and engaging in more vigorous thrusting during intercourse to displace rival males' semen. Though sperm competition principles have not been tested among sexual minority men, this theory provides a plausible mechanism that could explain why men, regardless of sexual orientation, might find cuckolding scenarios arousing.[41]

There is an intuitive connection between the idea of sperm competition and sexual jealousy, although a deeper dive into this topic is beyond the scope of this book. Also, more research on the erotic aspect of compersion is needed to investigate how cuckolding may fit (or not) under its umbrella—and whether using jealousy and competition as a kink also has a place in lesbian relationships, where sperm competition theory would not apply.

In any case, the similarity between some of Lehmiller and colleagues' data and my own participants' quotes about compersion suggests that the line between compersion and cuckolding may be a fluid one, at least in some cases. The distinction may depend on several factors such as the power and consent dynamics at play, the role of empathy, and to what extent one's erotic focus is on the self or on one's partner's pleasure. While this may be a controversial take from the lens of most CNM research, it certainly deserves more exploration.

Does Erotic Compersion "Count" as Compersion?

On the one hand, it might seem that a self-rewarding fantasy involving one's partner intimately engaging with another is fundamentally different from compersion, which is a form of positive empathy that is other-oriented. On the other hand, there is not always a crisp distinction between self-serving and altruistic behaviors—as I will show in the next chapter. When enough empathy is at play, the line between self-orientation and other-orientation often gets blurred in the dynamics of sex and love. Indeed, evolutionary scientists de Waal[42] and Hoffman[43] argued that the question of whether "true" altruism is devoid of selfish reward may be a false dichotomy, as "empathy may be uniquely well suited for bridging the gap between egoism and altruism."[44] This applies particularly well to erotic compersion.

Other researchers have also started to document erotic compersion. Flicker and colleagues[45] found *sexual arousal* to be one of three core elements in their three-factor scale of compersion, COMPERSe. The three factors were: (1) happiness about partner/metamour relationship; (2) excitement for new connections; and (3) sexual arousal. In their elaboration of the scale, the theme of sexual arousal was validated by research participants' affirmation of the following statements: (a) I experience sexual arousal thinking about my partner and metamour together; (b) I feel sexual excitement when I think about my partner and metamour together; and (c) My partner and metamour's relationship turns me on sexually. Congruent with my research, Flicker and colleagues did not find sexual arousal to be a fundamental part of compersion, but rather that it may be an important part of the experience *for some people*. This is also consistent with Deri's description of compersion as having the potential to "take many forms . . . includ[ing] both non-sexual joy and sexual arousal."[46]

The erotic aspect of compersion also aligns with Justin Lehmiller's research on common sexual fantasies.[47] In his survey of 4,175 Americans, seven major themes emerged. Taboo sex acts (i.e., doing something that is socially or culturally forbidden) and being in a non-monogamous relationship (e.g., swinging, polyamory, cuckolding, or having an open relationship) were both included on this list, which reflects the taboo quality aspect of erotic compersion. Later on, Lehmiller conducted further research exploring fantasies about CNM relationships in a study of people currently involved in monogamous relationships. Nearly one-third (32.6%) of his online sample (N = 822) reported that "their favorite sexual fantasy of all time included being in some type of sexually open relationship—of whom most (80.0%) said that they want to act on this fantasy in the future."[48] It is thus unsurprising that people practicing CNM would often experience sexual turn-on around witnessing, or imagining, their partner(s) connecting intimately with others.

In sum, positive empathy was a core component of the experience of compersion for my study participants—and this often applied to the erotic domain as well as to the emotional, cognitive, and attitudinal domains. Notably, a majority of my interviewees spoke of erotic compersion as a complementary aspect to other manifestations of positive empathy, rather than as a standalone experience. It would be interesting to see further studies investigating the erotic aspects of compersion more fully and compare different styles of CNM (polyamory, swinging, open relationships, cuckoldry) in regard to this theme.

NOTES

1. Thouin-Savard, 2021.
2. Titchener, 1924.
3. Barrett-Lennard, 1981, p. 91.
4. Batson, 2009; Pittinsky & Montoya, 2016.
5. Meneses & Larkin, 2012, p. 153.
6. For example, Singer, 2006.
7. For example, Shamay-Tsoory et al., 2009.
8. Pittinsky & Montoya, 2016, p. 4.
9. Pittinsky & Montoya, 2016, p. 2.
10. Perry et al., 2012.
11. Taylor, 1991.
12. Gable et al., 2006; Gable et al., 2012; Gable et al., 2004; Morelli et al., 2015; Pittinsky & Montoya, 2016.
13. Pittinsky et al., 2011b; Tam et al., 2008.

14. Fredrickson, 2001; see also Fredrickson & Branigan, 2001.
15. Waugh & Fredrickson, 2006.
16. Waugh & Fredrickson, 2006.
17. Aron & Aron, 1986.
18. Westman, 2001; Westman et al., 2009.
19. See also Flicker et al., 2022, for a more in-depth description of the connection between the aforementioned theories and compersion.
20. Coren, 2023; Eisenberg, 2002; Ferrer, 2007, 2019.
21. For example, Deri, 2015.
22. Patterson, 2018.
23. For example, Friedman, 2013; Garcia-Romeu et al., 2015.
24. For example, Bordo, 1987; Tarnas, 1991.
25. Coren, 2023.
26. Fredrickson, 2001; Fredrickson & Branigan, 2001; Waugh & Fredrickson, 2006.
27. Waugh & Fredrickson, 2006.
28. Aron & Aron, 1986.
29. Westman, 2001; see also Westman et al., 2009.
30. Perel, 2006.
31. For example, Sovatsky, 1985.
32. Lehmiller, 2018; Morin, 1995.
33. Bryson, 1991.
34. For example, Greenberg, 2019; Kleinplatz, 2006.
35. See Smith, 1976.
36. Lehmiller et al., 2018, p. 1005.
37. Lehmiller et al., 2018, p. 999.
38. Lehmiller et al., 2018, p. 1000.
39. Lehmiller et al., 2018, p. 999.
40. Block, 2015.
41. Lehmiller & al., 2018, p. 1000.
42. de Waal, 2008.
43. Hoffman, 1981.
44. Hoffman, 1981, p. 133.
45. Flicker et al., 2021.
46. Deri, 2015, p. 33.
47. Lehmiller, 2018.
48. Lehmiller, 2020, p. 2799.

CHAPTER 3

GRATITUDE

Oh, gosh, I am living the happiest life I can imagine. And I have for 26 or 27 years now. My wife and I, when we met, agreed that we did not know how to do monogamy and we would never require it of each other. We got married. Our goal was to have this be the longest marriage. And we have succeeded by having our 25th wedding anniversary last summer.

—Simon, 83

Gratitude is the second core constituent of compersion, along with positive empathy. The perception of deriving benefits from a partner's other relationship(s)—toward oneself, one's partner, or one's relational ecosystem—is in and of itself a source of joy and satisfaction. It also facilitates the emergence of positive empathy, which is then compounded with gratitude to result in compersion.

As a psychological state, gratitude is a felt sense of wonder, thankfulness, and appreciation for life; it is also linked with contentment, happiness, pride, and hope.[1] It is usually experienced in relation to receiving a benefit from another person's intentional action—a perspective that is coherent with my interviewees' experience of compersion. Compersive individuals tend to experience gratitude for an enhanced life as a result of CNM and of their partner(s)' other relationship(s). They then direct gratitude toward their metamours as well as their partner(s) for being the source of more love, freedom, and other avenues of abundance in their lives. Gratitude is also foundational to the positive relational feedback loops often experienced between partners and metamours (as depicted in Chapter 2).

In the following pages, I describe the main ways in which my study participants experienced gratitude in their CNM relationships, and the role of these experiences in invoking compersion. Finally, I explore the thorny question of whether compersion is fundamentally a selfish (i.e., utilitarian) or selfless phenomenon.

CHAPTER 3

PARTICIPANTS' ACCOUNTS OF GRATITUDE

My participants offered many examples of situations that stoked their gratitude toward their partners and metamours and elicited compersion. Some sources of gratitude were expressed with notable regularity: (a) richer emotional and sexual life; (b) richer social life; (c) authentic emotional expression; (d) freedom from fear, emotional congruence, and pride; (e) relief from guilt; (f) personal growth; and (g) enhanced relationship satisfaction.

Richer Emotional and Sexual Life

Compersive individuals were typically very grateful for their ability to engage in concurrent romantic or sexual relationships with multiple people with the knowledge and consent of everyone involved. This fueled compersion toward their partner(s)' other relationships and crushes. A desire for a richer emotional and sexual life was often the primary reason why participants had selected CNM as a relationship style to begin with—and the ability to do so ethically and openly within a vastly mononormative society was a strong source of gratitude. Many had struggled for years to develop an identity that suited both their desires for romantic and sexual variety and for relational depth and commitment. When they found partners who were supportive of these desires, they typically experienced heartfelt thankfulness, which translated into compersion.

For example, Jo, a 29-year-old software engineer, had come to realize that their sexual needs and preferences were better served by several partners than just one. Getting some of their desires and needs met by other people stoked compersion between them and their spouse:

> It's hard to match up everything in your life to one person, including sexuality. And so, one thing that's really beneficial is, if you have different things that you like sexually, you can find different people to do those things with. So, my husband and I do not match up . . . we have good sex, but we don't match up in terms of what our kinks are . . . he just doesn't have a lot of kinks, and I do. If he was going to be anything, he'd be slightly dominant, but I'm very dominant. So, when I find someone that I can do that with, he's like, you know, "yay, good for you!" You know, "and don't ask me to do it!" [laughs]

From the perspective of a non-nesting partner to a married polyamorous man, Teresa, a 54-year-old nanny, experienced great compersion toward her boyfriend and his wife's relationship: she perceived that the quality of their marital relationship enabled her to enjoy the connection with her boyfriend freely. Thus, she was very supportive of their relationship, as she felt she derived a direct benefit from it:

> I certainly don't feel jealous around him and his wife. I actually am a cheerleader for them spending more time. I'll volunteer to babysit. I'm like, "go out, go have fun," you know. Because the happier they are as a couple, I benefit from their happiness. Their healthy relationship makes it possible for me to be with him. So, you know, I want to feed that.

While gratitude for a richer emotional and sexual life was present for all participants, it was especially notable in cases where there was a "more poly" partner—typically the partner who initiated the idea of becoming consensually non-monogamous if the couple was previously monogamous. In those cases, the "less poly" partner developing new relationships would most often be met by compersion by the "more poly" partner, as this would signify that successful CNM would be sustainable, and that they would also be allowed to enjoy their own relationships with others with less, if any, guilt.

For example, Diane, a 54-year-old academic administrator, recalls how she initially, in the first few months of opening her marriage, demonstrated more compersion for her husband James (a 54-year-old scientist engineer) than he did for her because she was the one who had initiated opening their relationship after she had an extramarital affair. She felt that she "owed" him to express compersion for his new relationships, and she was patient about his taking longer to express compersion toward her:

> It's only been really recently that James has given me his full kind of, "I'm happy for you." I think it's only in the last maybe six to eight months, that I've really felt that from him. And when that happens, you feel like, okay, we're all on board here, and we're having a good time. I don't have to come home and apologize. And he's never had to do that with me. Because I've always been very much like, "No, go, I want you to do this." Because I was the one that kind of forced us into this, I felt like I had to be the bigger one.

While Diane and James offered an extreme example of a "more poly/less poly" partnership, their experience illustrates something crucial and common to all participants: the importance of each partner getting enough of their needs met for a CNM relationship to be sustainable. The gratitude that one feels toward a partner's other relationship(s) for enhancing one's romantic and sexual life, while it may, at first sight, seem self-serving, is ultimately rooted in the importance of mutuality, fairness, and reciprocity between all parties. If one partner was enjoying other relationships, then it meant that the other(s) could do the same with less guilt or fear that the relationship would fail due to a lack of balance.

Richer Social Life

Benefits from one's partner's other relationship(s) often included having a rich social life and deep friendships that did not confine people to the rigid normative boxes of either "a platonic friend" or "The One." For example, Jo mentioned that CNM was very compatible with being an extrovert and that they enjoyed making friends with their husband's partners and metamours:

> It gets me a lot more friends because I get to be friends with my partner's partners. And that's really fun. [*laughs*] Yeah, our potlucks every week, people like to joke that they've become a poly potluck. Because a lot of them are made up of people that we've dated, and then people that they're dating, so it brings a lot more people into your life. And I'm a very social person. So that's cool.

Fred, a 75-year-old retired molecular geneticist, expressed that he felt his friendships with lovers and ex-lovers often ran deeper than his purely platonic friendships—and that the result of him and his wife having had so many lovers over the past 40-plus years resulted in a circle of "family-like" friends, where cooperation was common:

> Some of the people that we're lovers with, that raises the value of those relationships in a way. As a scientist I don't want to claim something magical about it, but I think the people we've been lovers with, our friends that we have a level of friendship that we just don't achieve any other way, and the level of trust, the level of feeling connected. . . . So, those are the people I expect will care about me if I become really ill, people we would do something for, you know, help them financially or otherwise if they absolutely needed it. And there have been times. . . . Sort of almost the same levels we would take care of children, for example, if they needed help. . . . I'd say that, it brings those friendships into the feeling of family.

Besides the emotional depth of these friendships being emotionally fulfilling, Fred also recounted how lovers and ex-lovers would support each other in very practical ways, which stoked gratitude and compersion:

> When there are more people cooperating, you can get more different things done. I guess my favorite example is when my daughter turned 16, and she got me to teach her how to drive, we had another husband, a guy named Rod. And my first foray into the parking lot with Sarah in the car was like, she kept popping the clutch, and I just freaked out. Like, that's $600 to replace a clutch! [*laughs*] . . . I just couldn't do it. Rod said, you know, I'll teach her how to drive. Rod is a professional driver, he drives 18-wheelers and city buses, and logging trucks. He was very calm, and I mean, she wasn't his daughter. . . . We cared for each other, and we still see his daughter.

Of course, such situations would stoke gratitude, and in turn, compersion toward metamours. Both Fred (75) and Michael (67) explained that these kinds of social connections were especially valuable in their later stages of life, where health or libido changes resulted in sex not being as important or frequent in their relationships. Still, they appreciated their relationships not being confined to the "hard categories" of either platonic friendships or marriage. Being able to approach every relationship with fluidity and a sense of possibility, instead of being restricted to conventional categories and labels, was an advantage of CNM that many participants brought up. This benefit was also a factor in promoting compersion, according to Jo:

> Whenever I meet someone new, I don't like there to be a boundary on what that relationship can look like, because you never know who's going to come into your life. I like that every relationship can just land where it's supposed to. I don't date everyone I meet, sometimes I want it to be platonic. And there are some people that you want a sexual relationship with, but you don't want to be in a serious romantic relationship with. In monogamy, you kind of have to make a choice, are you in or are you out, you know? Because you're disqualifying other people if you're being sexual with this person. Unless you're doing the whole dating around thing, but then if you meet someone serious, you have to give that person up.

This fluidity in approaching relationships outside traditional categories contributed to a richer social life in participants' eyes, not only in terms of the quantity of people one would meet, but in terms of depth and authenticity, as CNM created more space for different variations of intimacy.

Authentic Emotional Expression

Along these lines, participants specifically expressed gratitude for being able to express themselves authentically with their partners and other people as well. With their partners, authentic emotional expression would enhance intimacy and a sense of both freedom and safety. For example, not having to censor themselves when they had a new crush invited connection into a space where communication is traditionally forbidden or taboo—which could enhance closeness. With other people, authentic emotional expression would manifest in their ability to approach each person with an open sense of possibility, rather than having to make every relationship besides one's nesting partnership a platonic one.

Tyrone, a 38-year-old facilitator, described his gratitude for the ability to experience authentic expression with his partner in a way that bridged safety, emotional intimacy, and sexual turn-on:

> I get to love you through whatever you want, and invite you to share all your desires with me, even if they're not involving me, because that turns me on and it makes me feel close to you, and makes me feel heard and safe that I know you can be as honest as possible, and I can be transparent with you.

For Tyrone and a majority of participants, a standard of transparency with their partners came as a relief from the mononormative norm, where they felt they had to hide intimate desires toward others to protect a committed partner from experiencing jealousy or hurt feelings. In a CNM context, caring about their partner's feelings came with a prerequisite of honesty and openness—and that transparency would be framed in loving and inclusive terms, rather than threatening or confrontational ones.

Freedom from Fear, Emotional Congruence, and Pride

Enhanced emotional authenticity in one's relationships would often bring about a sense of congruence between one's CNM ideology and lived experience. Several participants expressed a sense of relief and gratitude that the way they wanted to structure their relationships was not only possible but could translate into positive emotional experiences despite the stigma associated with CNM. Participants who had been nervous about trying non-monogamy but had encountered a reality that was more pleasurable than expected reported experiencing a sense of newfound freedom, relief, and thankfulness.

This was especially true of folks who encountered compersion somewhat as a surprise. Often, they expected that jealousy would be their main response when getting involved with extradyadic intimacy; but when it turned out to not be as bad as they feared, they felt reassured and comforted. Fred, for example, described this sense of relief when his wife first made love with another man about 20 years prior:

> One time I was interviewed by someone who was writing about polyamory for the *LA Times*, and she asked me how I felt about that experience. I said I felt relieved. The article said, "I'll bet you felt relieved, you know, then you got to fuck other people, right?", but I didn't mean it like that. . . . The reporter thought I felt relieved because it meant that I got permission, but I felt relieved because Sue was happy, Jorge was happy, and it wasn't gonna blow us apart! . . . In terms of jealousy, I didn't feel I had lost anything. I felt that we'd sort of done the initial experiment and it had been a success. I felt a warmth and a happiness. I didn't feel any fear or anger.

While the journalist assumed that Fred's sense of relief was purely utilitarian, he explained that something else was at play. That "something" was not transactional, but rather an experience of joy connected to his emancipation from fear. Fred's experience did not *negate* the additional benefits that both partners derived from the situation, such as having access to richer emotional and sexual lives; however, the gratitude he described was mainly derived from the relief that he had been able to "play with fire" without getting burned, so to speak, and that the success of this initial experiment meant a more exalted and authentic life would be possible going forward.

Colette, a 41-year-old sex and relationship coach, experienced similar emotions when she and her husband did a "full sexual swap" with another couple for the first time. They each experienced unexpected compersion, and she was pleasantly surprised by their lack of jealousy or discomfort. She described how she and her husband shared about their experience afterward:

> As we were sharing this experience, we kept checking with each other, like, "Are you okay? How are you doing?" And we were both like, "Yes, I'm fine. That's weird!" At the end, we were like, what the heck, and we were both, like, high five! We high-fived! We were joking. We called ourselves sticking pasta. So that was definitely like a very, very, very strong compersion moment, for sure.

Colette and her husband's compersive reaction had come as a surprise, as they experienced the weight of fear being lifted. Pride, ecstasy, and gratitude were byproducts of feeling relieved and liberated from fear—and they experienced these feelings as compersion.

In these examples, finding congruence between a CNM ideology and a positive emotional reality gave birth to a sense of pride for my participants. Pride is often a byproduct of overcoming fear, especially when this fear is rooted in a social expectation. Similar to LGBTQ+ pride, CNM and polyamorous individuals tend to feel pride when they overcome the widespread mononormative expectation that extradyadic relationships should only lead to jealousy and conflict, as well as the shame and stigma surrounding those relationships. These emotional experiences can then become a source of gratitude for the opportunity to "be oneself" openly, and live in emotional congruence with one's values and ideologies. This shows how compersion often emerges from the process of "coming out" as CNM. I unpack this connection more fully in Chapter 10, "The Role of Coming Out and Pride in Compersion."

Relief from Guilt

Another benefit most participants named as a source of compersion was a relief from guilt—both around the desire to engage intimately with others, and also around the pressure to fulfill all of one's partner's needs. Tyrone described this sense of relief and gratitude for witnessing his partners' fulfillment with other people, and explained how it helped him reframe jealousy:

> I want to give everything to my partner but I cannot. So I have to reframe being jealous to be like, ah, at least you're getting the thing you want and I don't have to worry about you missing out on this thing, or feeling resentful that you've never got this thing.

Similarly, Michael explained how he and his nesting partner Gisele being in a "fourple" with Rain and Cedric allowed them to partake in activities where their inclinations and abilities differed. Seeing Gisele and Cedric enjoying things that she liked (but that he, Michael, did not enjoy or could not physically do) was a source of joy, relief, and compersion:

> I have a bad knee so I can't hike anymore, and Gisele and Cedric can go and spend five days hiking up to Mount Olympus. That's a joy to know that I'm

not holding Gisele back from doing one of the things that she really loves. . . . The fact that they could go do that makes me really happy. . . . Cedric likes to dance a lot, more than I like to dance, so they can go dancing. I don't have to feel guilty . . . they can go dancing, and Rain and I can do something at home.

As this example illustrates, compersion often arises when the needs and desires fulfilled by a metamour are needs and desires that a person cannot, or is not particularly interested in, fulfilling for their partner. In such instances, one is not "competing for the same spot" with their metamours—and thus they may view their partner's other relationships as a value-added rather than as a threat.

In this way, James felt gratitude toward his wife Diane's other lover because he fulfilled some of Diane's sexual desires that he, James, was not interested in: "Some of the elements that he provided to her was something that she liked. . . . But it didn't really get into a space that I was interested in being in." Thus, James was relieved from feeling that his lack of interest in meeting some of Diane's needs was holding her back in any way, and this translated into compersion for her other relationship. Letting go of being everything to one's partner could, in some cases, trigger one's internalized mononormativity and bring up insecurities. However, when enough safety was present, these situations could invoke more gratitude than threat, resulting in compersion.

Personal Growth

Experiencing growth from connections with different partners was another element frequently identified by my participants as a source of gratitude. Based on the idea that one partner can hardly suffice in witnessing, relating to, and stimulating all different parts of oneself, several interviewees stated that connecting intimately with more than one individual would support their partner's personal development and growth, as well as their own—something they viewed as an all-around benefit that would invoke gratitude and compersion.

Lisa, a 41-year-old faculty counselor, expressed that she loved to witness her partners blossom and self-actualize through their other relationships—and hypothesized that elements of her joy might go "beyond compersion":

I think the highlight of any relationship is when you get to be part of witnessing people growing and blossoming into their fully actualized selves. And if somebody is new to some part of their self-expression, it's so rewarding to support them and celebrate them in doing that. I understand that I feel compersion, but I feel like there's elements of it that go beyond compersion. It's just this joy and celebration of someone's new newfound self and self-definition that I really love.

Perhaps the joy that Lisa experienced witnessing her partners bloom into their actualized selves seemed like it went beyond the romantic meaning of compersion, encompassing a more spiritual sense of positive empathy akin to Buddhist mudita, or sympathetic joy[2] (see the introduction). Such nuances in people's experiences show how compersion is a dynamic concept, rather than a one-size-fits-all.

Enhanced Relationship Satisfaction

Each of the benefits I described earlier could generate enhanced relationship satisfaction, which was in itself a source of gratitude, and thus compersion for my participants. For example, authentic emotional expression often leads to improved intimacy, both emotional and sexual, between partners. Having multiple partners often made it easier for each person to get their needs met, which relieved disappointment from not having all of one's needs filled by one partner. Less guilt, in turn, translated into more satisfying relationships. Experiencing growth from one relationship would then serve the other(s) by helping individuals show up as better, more wholesome versions of themselves in all their relationships. Partners often expressed gratitude to one another for being willing to brave the social stigma of mononormativity together, be "partners in crime," and "do the work" to show up fully in CNM relationships. This gratitude for empowering one another to live an authentic yet countercultural life fueled relationship satisfaction.

When circumstances lent themselves to each person in a relational ecosystem feeling seen, loved, and fulfilled, this chain of events could generate a positive relational feedback loop as described in Chapter 2. When partners felt grateful to one another and to their metamours, they were more likely to feel compersion, which turned into increased relationship satisfaction.[3]

In Part III of this book, I show how the perception of benefits from a partner's other relationship is one of the main factors that promote compersion, as the gratitude derived from these benefits is core to what constitutes compersion. Next, I integrate Part I by addressing how the two components of compersion—positive empathy and gratitude—interact. The coexistence of empathy and gratitude within the experience of compersion begs the question: is compersion selfish or selfless?

IS COMPERSION SELFISH OR SELFLESS?

Is compersion truly an empathic, selfless love phenomenon akin to Buddhist muditā, or is it simply an activation of one's reward system when one derives personal, utilitarian benefits from non-monogamy? The theme of gratitude, taken in isolation, could lead readers to believe it's the latter. However, in the last chapter, I focused on positive empathy as a core component of compersion—which emphasized people's ability to blur the boundaries between self and others and to interpret another person's joy as their own.

So, is compersion selfish or selfless? The perspective most congruent with my research is that both are true—and that in fact, self-focused and other-focused elements seem to be synergistic as it pertains to compersion. This is reflected in two complementary evolutionary theories: *kin altruism*[4]—which portrays a flavor of altruism based on empathic concern rather than an egoistical reciprocity, and *reciprocal altruism*[5]—a form of altruism that revolves around self-centered reward, and is the biological equivalent of the "tit for tat" strategy used in game theory.[6]

From my findings, I would hypothesize that compersion may have roots in both reciprocal altruism and kin altruism. Indeed, I observed that there is not a crisp distinction between self-serving and selfless behaviors when it comes to compersion—but that gratitude and positive empathy seem to feed off each other. As I spelled out in Chapter 2 in the *erotic empathy* section, evolutionary scientists de Waal[7] and Hoffman[8] argued that the question as to whether "true" altruism is devoid of selfish reward may be a false dichotomy, because kin and reciprocal altruism can be reconciled through empathy:

> If altruism is produced by mechanisms, such as empathy and bonding, that produce emotional identification with the other, one may well ask if helping another does not boil down to helping oneself. It does, but . . . this is no reason to call empathy-based altruism selfish. A truly selfish individual would have no trouble walking away from another in need, whereas empathic engagement hooks one into the other's situation. Since the

mechanism delivers intrinsic rewards exclusively via the other, it is genuinely other-oriented. At the same time, it is futile to try to extract the self from the process. There simply is no satisfactory answer to the question of how altruistic is altruism. This is, in fact, the beauty of the empathy-altruism connection: The mechanism works so well because it gives individuals an emotional stake in the welfare of others.[9]

The quote from de Waal echoes the spirit of compersion my participants' interview data described. While a certain level of benefit to oneself, or something to be grateful for, was necessary for compersion to emerge, compersive experiences went well beyond individual self-reward. As I described in Chapter 2, and emphasized under the theme of positive relational feedback loop, participants described compersion as a departure from individual self-centeredness and accessing a state of self–other overlap, where they perceived a benefit to a partner or metamour as a benefit to oneself, thus inducing a mutual desire to be generous and a feedback loop of positive affect. Several psychological theories help explain the functioning and impacts of those feedback loops, and positive empathy more generally: broaden-and-build theory,[10] self-expansion theory,[11] and crossover theory[12]—which are described more in detail in the last chapter.

Thus, gratitude seems to be both a component of compersion in and of itself—as an aspect of the positive emotions, thoughts, and attitudes one may experience in relation to their partner's other relationship(s)—but also, a catalyst for more positive empathy to emerge. It is a rather intuitive phenomenon when imagining, for example, receiving a huge unexpected gift from someone that would change one's life for the better; one would typically take a greater interest in the gift giver's well-being from that point on, as gratitude would have carved a path for a more conscious, heartfelt, and active participation in their joy. Compersion, similarly, is fueled by gratitude.

While research on positive empathy and compersion is still nascent, I hope this book inspires other researchers to further investigate their underpinnings and potentials. In a world plagued by separateness, conflict, and competition, it seems more crucial than ever to understand how engrained impulses toward self-preservation, altruism, and empathy can work synergistically in the realm of all human relationships.

NOTES

1. Emmons & Shelton, 2002.
2. Coren, 2023.
3. Aumer et al., 2014.
4. For example, Ashton et al., 1998; Osiński, 2009.
5. For example, Ashton et al., 1998; Trivers, 1971, 2006.
6. Heap & Varoufakis, 2004.
7. de Waal, 2008.
8. Hoffman, 1981.
9. de Waal, 2008, p. 292.
10. Fredrickson, 2001; Fredrickson & Branigan, 2001.
11. Aron & Aron, 1986.
12. Westman, 2001; Westman et al., 2009.

PART II

DIMENSIONS OF COMPERSION

My research indicated that there is no single way to define compersion. This is akin to other complex experiences, such as happiness, sadness, or jealousy, which do not have a one-size-fits-all definition or model.

This next section delineates the main dimensional characteristics of compersion. These are the particular flavors and variations with which my study participants described compersion. The fluidity and dynamism CNM people use the term with has revealed that compersion can come in different types, intensities, and characteristics. Understanding these distinctions is essential to approaching the topic of compersion with adequate nuance and accuracy.

The next three chapters describe the dimensional aspects of compersion I observed from my qualitative data. These include Chapter 4, "Two Kinds of Compersion: Attitudinal and Embodied," Chapter 5, "Spectrum of Compersion," and Chapter 6, "Coexistence of Jealousy and Compersion."

TWO KINDS OF COMPERSION

Attitudinal and Embodied

I hold an ethic of compersion even when I don't always experience the
FEELING of compersion.

—Evita "Lavitaloca" Sawyers[1]

A notable finding of this study was the distinction, in my participants'
accounts of compersive experiences, between two categories of compersion:
attitudinal and embodied. When interviewed about the nature of their compersion experiences, some participants described their experience as a primarily *cognitive* realization leading to positive attitudes and behaviors toward
their metamour relationships—a phenomenon I coin here as "attitudinal
compersion"; others described it as a more *embodied* experience—an emotional felt sense of joy, gratitude, turn-on, and/or exhilaration.

This distinction between different kinds of compersion was the basis for
choosing to "split" the definition I coauthored, with Dr. Sharon Flicker, in
the *Springer Nature Encyclopedia of Sexual Psychology and Behavior*.[2] The first
two definitions reflect this nuance within CNM contexts, while the third
definition extends the usage of the word compersion to any context:

1. Compersion refers to a broad range of positive emotions experienced
   in relation to one's intimate partner's extra-dyadic intimate relations.
2. Compersion refers to the broad range of positive attitudes, thoughts,
   and/or actions manifested in relation to one's intimate partner's extradyadic intimate relations.
3. Compersion refers to the broad range of positive emotions, attitudes,
   thoughts, and/or actions manifested in relation to another person's
   gratifying experience in any context.

Having distinct definitions highlights the fact that one can experience compersion in many ways, and that contrary to popular belief, compersion is not *only* an emotion. This is good news for those seeking to cultivate more compersion in their relationships, because while it is quite difficult to invoke an emotion, it is easier to agentically choose one's thoughts, attitudes, and behaviors. Therefore, this nuanced understanding renders compersion accessible as a *voluntary* orientation to relationships—rather than being confined to an emotional state that may only arise when the contextual winds are favorable.

Further, attitudinal and embodied compersion are not mutually exclusive. They can be experienced concurrently or in close proximity. Further, attitudinal compersion is often a precursor to embodied compersion for people transitioning from monogamy to CNM—although the relationship between the two is not always linear (I explore this more deeply in Chapter 5, "Spectrum of Compersion"). In the following pages, I describe the two kinds of compersion in depth using participant data.

ATTITUDINAL COMPERSION

I refer to attitudinal compersion as the overall interpretation of one's partner's happiness with another person as a positive event, and one they show support toward. Compersive thoughts and behaviors are included under this category. To illustrate, when I asked Martin, a 33-year-old software engineer, to describe how he experienced compersion, a follow-up question arose as to whether compersion was more of a cognitive or embodied experience for him. He responded with the former:

> Sometimes it's more, like, I'm having a conversation with my partner, and it's not an embodied experience as much as a noticing that something good happened to them. I sort of intellectually think, "Oh, it's a good thing that this happened to Laura-Lee, to Karen, or whatever." And so, when I think of compersion, I think more of the former [cognitive], and a lot less of the latter [embodied].

Similarly, Martin's partner Laura-Lee, a 32-year-old anthropologist, described compersion as an awareness of the value her metamours bring to her and her partners' lives:

> I experience compersion as an awareness that my partners make my life better and make Martin's life better. Martin's partners make his life better and my life better. So, if you're doing it right, everybody's life is better. . . . We're all bringing value into our lives, we're enriching each other's lives. And isn't that wonderful, and magical?

For Laura-Lee, this simple awareness brought about a sense of ease and positivity. For both her and Martin, attitudinal compersion came effortlessly. Other participants, on the other hand, saw attitudinal compersion as a duty that required a more concerted effort.

A Sense of Duty

For some participants, compersion was a chosen behavior rooted in a sense of duty to empower one's partner's pleasure. George, a 53-year-old professor, recounted how he used to drive his ex-wife, who was bisexual, to meet her female lovers—not because it was particularly joyful for him, but because he believed that supporting his spouse in getting her needs and desires met was the right thing to do as a husband. He recounted,

> Knowing of her orientation, I was trying to be the "good husband." You know, it kind of hurt. Not that she was bi, but just seeing her with someone else, no matter their background. But, I would take her around to her female partners' houses and I'd wait in the car, do my thing, until she got finished and then I'd take her home. . . . I'm thinking about compersion being more of a voluntary piece. For me, it was a sense of duty.

George's account very much reflects Evita Sawyer's concept of a "compersion ethic" introduced in the opening quote to this chapter: "I hold an ethic of compersion even when I don't always experience the FEELING of compersion."[3] These quotes show clearly how compersion can be a behavior, not just an emotion. This is reminiscent of the idea, for example, that one can choose compassionate behaviors even when they may not feel compassion emotionally—or that one can uphold a great work ethic even on days when they feel tired and unmotivated. In the context of CNM, this phenomenon also speaks of the potential for jealousy and/or other challenging emotions to coexist with compersion, a theme I explore in Chapter 6, "Coexistence of Jealousy and Compersion."

A Respectful Distance

An adjacent flavor of attitudinal compersion was that of a "respectful distance." Sylvia, a 49-year-old professor, had a unique background and perspective on compersion. As a Dakota woman, she had grown up with core values around honoring each person's sacred autonomy and "minding her own business," especially in the realm of sexuality. This general orientation toward relationships translated into a deliberate distance vis-à-vis other people's choices. Talking about her lovers' other relationships, she described:

> I have compersion for people, but I just don't consider it my business. . . . I'm happy that you're happy, but it's in a more kind of distanced way. I don't need to know everything they're doing. I don't need to know their other partners. I don't need to be a part of it. I'm not into threesomes. I'm not into triads. It's their business. And I have a deep respect for people's autonomy.

While Sylvia's perspective on compersion was a more emotionally detached one than almost all other participants, I believe this is a very important voice to highlight, as it may be reflective of a more common experience for many CNM people who did not self-select for this study because they may not have identified their experience as compersion. On the "spectrum of compersion" (see Chapter 5), Sylvia's experience would squarely reside in the attitudinal category—while the more popularized meaning of compersion is typically the embodied kind, per the next section.

EMBODIED COMPERSION

Embodied compersion was the kind of compersion most popularly known and described in CNM literature. Many participants offered descriptors of their compersion experiences based on physical sensations and strong emotions. They used colorful and textured language, often evocative of a sense of exhilaration. Examples of such language included: a "sense of magic, like winning the lottery" (Fred); "Frubbly," "bubbly," "warm," "fuzzy" (Jo); "delight," "sparkly," "tickly" (Lisa); "buzz," "high" (Colette); "bliss" (Jamila); "romance-joy" (Tyrone); and "titillating" (Sabrina). As an illustration, Lisa, a 41-year-old faculty counselor, compared her experience of compersion to drinking champagne:

I tend to describe it as feeling sparkly, kind of what a sip of champagne feels like . . . it feels kind of tickly and sparkly, in your chest and up into your face. And I might feel a little flushed if I'm particularly excited with them. So I find it to be really, almost intoxicating.

Very similarly, Teresa employed vivid language such as "bubbling up" to describe her compersive feelings. Additionally, employing the term "endorphin rush" pointed to the physiological nature of her experience. In her description of an experience of erotic compersion, she reported feeling excitement within her entire body, "from [her] pelvic floor up":

Joy bubbling up, like just excitement, joy . . . sometimes, I got the endorphin rush. . . . Watching, it was like, they're in front of me, I'm feeling in the mood. We're all feeling something, he's not even with me. He's over there. And I'm like, aww, you know, feeling it all the way in my body, in a sexual way . . . I can't have an orgasm over it. But I could definitely feel the sexual energy running through me. . . . I'm feeling it in my body, from my pelvic floor up . . . it's like watching a cool movie and coming to the good part.

Likewise, Colette described her first experience of compersion as a "total high":

We didn't know if we were going to share everything, but we shared the full details of the entire experience. And it was a total high, the first time you do any of that stuff you're just buzzing. It's like a complete high without the drugs.

What I gathered through these participants' accounts is that embodied experiences of compersion are linked to more intense emotions, and at times, sexual turn-on. Interviewees generally described these experiences of compersion as being felt at a "higher pitch" compared to attitudinal descriptors.

Most interviewees described aspects of both kinds of compersion, attitudinal and embodied. The intensity and attributes of each compersive experience seemed to depend on contextual elements. For example, James noticed that the character of his compersion would vary according to proximity and setting:

If I'm experiencing [compersion] remotely, it's often cognitive. . . . If I'm right there, seeing what's happening, then it's a much more embodied sort of experience. In essence, it can be almost a turn-on to see and appreciate it in the right setting.

The distinction between attitudinal and embodied compersion is thus a fluid line that people may navigate depending on circumstances.

The notable variety in participants' accounts provides a glimpse into the multidimensionality of compersion. Bringing this nuance into the understanding of compersion may help CNM folks avoid the common pitfall of pressuring themselves and/or their partners to *feel* compersion at an emotional or embodied level.

IS COMPERSION NECESSARY?

My findings about different types of compersion can help bring clarity to the controversial question, "Is compersion necessary for successful CNM?"[4] Based on my research and experience as a relationship coach, it seems that embodied compersion is an enjoyable and fortunate experience when it arises, but not a prerequisite to harmonious CNM partnerships. However, partners adopting a *compersive attitude* is more fundamental. In other words, embracing an "ethic" of compersion, behaviorally and attitudinally, brings congruency and integrity to non-monogamy, without being dependent on the ups and downs of one's emotions, moods, and changing relational dynamics. This was beautifully articulated by Evita "Lavitaloca" Sawyers:

> I am practiced in choosing to align my thoughts and behavior, even when my emotions may not be on board, with my polyamorous integrity which is to be a supportive and encouraging partner to my partners as they pursue relationships and connections that bring them fulfillment.[5]

In this quote, Sawyers encapsulated how, while one's feelings might change according to many situational factors, adopting a compersive attitude and behavior is always an option. This may be a helpful perspective for CNM folks who seek to develop compersion in their relationships without disavowing or repressing challenging emotions.

Additionally, it is easier to intentionally invoke an attitude than an embodied affect—and therefore, cultivating attitudinal compersion can be a more reasonable aspiration for those who are experiencing discomfort or anxiety in their CNM relationships. Under this lens, embodied compersion can be seen as a fortunate outcome that may arise when personal, relational, and social contexts are favorable to it, rather than the be-all and end-all of non-monogamy. There is so much to be celebrated through the practice of enacting a compersive orientation to one's relationships through one's compersive attitudes and behaviors—and this need not be diminished by a lack of embodied compersion. I hope this perspective can bring more freedom, acceptance, and fluidity in how CNM people relate to compersion.

CONGRUENCE WITH PREVIOUS RESEARCH

The attitudinal and embodied accounts of compersion I described here are reminiscent of researcher Ulrike Duma's analysis of *trait compersion* versus *state compersion*[6]—albeit with notable differences. In her study, trait compersion refers to the general attitudes, thoughts, emotions, and reactions of a compersive person. In contrast, state compersion relates to positive situational reactions when one is exposed to specific extradyadic contexts, such as a partner's flirting or engaging in sexual activity with someone else.

Trait compersion has parallels with the attitudinal compersion described by my participants, as it is a more consistent, predictable, and lower-pitched experience than embodied compersion. However, I found that attitudinal compersion could also be activated in response to specific and situational extradyadic contexts—and could include behaviors (such as George driving his spouse to meet her lovers) as well as attitudes.

State compersion, which refers to a temporary state of being in Duma's study, echoes the embodied experience of compersion in my research. Again, the equivalency is not exact, as some people could enact attitudinal compersion temporarily in response to punctual events—and not experience an *embodied* response. Nevertheless, Duma's research provides interesting parallels to my data and accurately conveys that compersion is not a one-size-fits-all experience.

Furthermore, the two main "flavors" of compersion—attitudinal and embodied—map quite well onto two of the main conceptual perspectives on the experience of empathy. As I noted in Chapter 2, the scholarly literature on empathy is vast and often debated;[7] however, there are three main scholarly perspectives on the experience of empathy:

- A cognitive perspective-taking process;[8]
- An emotional experience of being affected by someone else's condition—a phenomenon sometimes referred to as emotional contagion or sensate emotional resonance;[9]
- A combination of both resonance and perspective-taking (and most compatible with the data presented herein).[10]

Accordingly, evidence from neuroscience suggests two possible distinct systems for empathy: a sensate emotional system, and a cognitive perspective-taking system.[11] The basic sensate emotional system is thought to support the ability to empathize emotionally and share the sensate emotional feelings of others ("I feel what you feel"), while the second empathy system, termed cognitive empathy, refers to the cognitive process of understanding another person's perspective and mental states such as intentions, goals, and beliefs ("I understand what you feel"). These two distinct empathy systems rely on different neuronal circuitry. Sensate emotional empathy, or embodied empathy, relies on sensorimotor cortices as well as limbic and para-limbic structures, while cognitive empathy, also referred to as theory of mind (ToM) or mentalizing, relies on structures of the temporal lobe and the prefrontal cortex.[12]

Unsurprisingly, embodied empathy is linked to more intense emotions, and thus could be at the root of experiences of compersion that are described as more "high pitch" or akin to intoxication by participants; conversely, perspective-taking might be responsible for the compersion experiences described as more "low pitch" or attitudinal. That said, many participants provided accounts of experiencing both attitudinal and embodied compersion, which could occur and shift fluidly depending on changing circumstances. To this point, the experiential accounts of my participants are reflected most closely by the third conceptual approach to empathy—which refers to it as an experience that is both emotional and cognitive, either because the two elements are intertwined, or because the emotion results immediately from the cognitive state of perspective-taking. This perspective does not negate the distinction between contagion and perspective-taking, but it circumvents the pitfall of establishing a false binary between the two: it thus allows for many "flavors" of compersion to coexist within the same person or relationship in a way that is fluid and dynamic.

The contrast between attitudinal and embodied compersion I observed inspires avenues for further research. For example, it would be interesting to investigate how attitudinal versus embodied accounts of compersion correlate with other traits like personality, relationship status, attachment style, age, ethnicity, gender, and more. Neuroscientific studies with compersive individuals would also be a formidable way to determine whether compersion, both attitudinal and embodied, mirrors the same neurological circuits as those of cognitive and embodied empathy.

This chapter has established the distinction between the two main kinds of compersion that emerged from my interview data, and how each of them may show up in the lives of CNM people. The following chapter, "Spectrum of Compersion," situates attitudinal and embodied compersion on a spectrum that further illustrates the dynamism and fluidity with which CNM folks relate to compersion.

NOTES

1. Evita "Lavitaloca" Sawyers, personal communication, October 2, 2023. Reprinted with permission.
2. Thouin-Savard & Flicker, 2023.
3. Evita Sawyers, personal communication, October 2, 2023.
4. See podcast episode from *Multiamory* with Dr. Sharon Flicker and me discussing this topic: https://www.multiamory.com/podcast/386-compersion-is-it-necessary-with-dr-marie-thouin-and-dr-sharon-flicker.
5. Evita Sawyers, personal communication, October 2, 2023.
6. Duma, 2009.
7. For example, Batson, 2009.
8. Shamay-Tsoory et al., 2009.
9. Singer, 2006.
10. Pittinsky & Montoya, 2016.
11. Shamay-Tsoory et al., 2009.
12. Singer, 2006.

SPECTRUM OF COMPERSION

It was never like a hard switch. It's just at a certain point in time, the feeling slowly shifted. And at each point in time, there was less jealousy and slightly more compersion.

—Jenny, 26, software engineer

An erroneous myth about compersion is that it is an "on or off switch: you either have it or you don't." This is far from the truth. Instead, compersion exists on a fluid spectrum that encompasses different scopes, flavors, and intensities of experiences. For the sake of simplicity, I conceptualized this spectrum to include the broad categories of jealousy, neutrality, attitudinal compersion, and embodied compersion. Visually representing compersion on a spectrum facilitates the conceptual understanding that compersion is not a binary, and can show up in different varieties and textures.

However, there are many nuances to keep in mind when engaging with the concept of a compersion spectrum. First, CNM people tend to describe their experiences of jealousy and compersion as moving fluidly and nonlinearly along the spectrum, depending on their changing individual, relational, or social contexts; thus, folks are never "fixed" at one spot or another—although they might "hang out" at a certain spot more frequently.

Second, the spectrum is not meant to convey a hierarchy of emotions where embodied compersion is inherently "better" or "more evolved" than attitudinal compersion, neutrality, or jealousy—nor does the spectrum reflect a linear or temporal evolution of CNM people's emotional lives. While many participants reported that their capacity and tendency to experience compersion did increase over time, this was not an axiom: many people recalled experiencing bouts of intense jealousy, somewhat as a surprise, after years of having consistently enjoyed states of benevolent neutrality or compersion. This typically happened when their personal, relational, or social contexts changed in ways that created unforeseen triggers.

Third, jealousy, compersion, and other experiences are not mutually exclusive. Folks can situate themselves at more than one location on the spectrum at once, as I discuss in the next chapter, "Coexistence of Jealousy and Compersion." I describe these caveats and nuances in more detail, after an initial description of the spectrum, its origin, and its utility.

UNDERSTANDING THE SPECTRUM

I credit Hypatia from Space for first conceptualizing the concept of a spectrum of compersion. In her seminal book *Compersion: Polyamory Beyond Jealousy*, she proposed a "jealousy-compersion continuum" where she depicted jealousy, benevolent neutrality, and compersion on a horizontal axis:[1]

Jealousy	Benevolent Neutrality	Compersion

←—————————————————————————————————→

According to Hypatia, any one person's experience with a particular partner, and in a particular moment, would fall somewhere on the continuum. She portrayed this spectrum as fluid and dynamic, noting that people may experience different levels and flavors of compersion and jealousy at different times.

I wholeheartedly agree with Hypatia's contribution. Here, I expand and build upon her continuum to include the distinction between attitudinal and embodied compersion (see Chapter 4). Since my participants described a compersive attitude as a more cognitive, steady, and overall "lower pitch" type of compersion—and embodied compersion as a more spontaneous, sensory, and "higher pitch" emotional experience—I conceptualized a new spectrum with attitudinal compersion being closer to benevolent neutrality, and embodied compersion being at the far end of the spectrum:

Jealousy	Neutrality	Attitudinal Compersion	Embodied Compersion

←—————————————————————————————————→

This spectrum is representative of the different flavors of experiences described by my research participants in a simplified, straightforward way. As such, I believe it can serve as a tool to help CNM people and their counselors make initial sense of complex emotional experiences around non-monogamy, and dismantle the myth that a person is "either jealous or emotionally compersive." Identifying where one situate themselves on the spectrum at different times, given dynamic individual, relational, and social contexts, can provide a simple yet nuanced vocabulary to support self-understanding.

Since this is an intentionally simplified, two-dimensional representation of a complex and dynamic set of experiences, additional explanations are necessary to grasp its implications with adequate refinement. In particular, I address the questions of whether the spectrum is linear, and whether it is hierarchical.

IS THE SPECTRUM LINEAR?

For many participants, the spectrum mirrored their evolving experiences with jealousy and compersion over time. They described an overall progression from feeling "mostly jealous" about their partners' other relationships to "mostly compersive." For example, Jenny, a 26-year-old software engineer, explained how some CNM situations had become progressively less threatening, and come to evoke increased compersion for her—but that this was a gradual change: "It was never like a hard switch. It's just at a certain point in time, the feeling slowly shifted. And at each point in time, there was less jealousy and slightly more compersion."

This linear increase in compersiveness generally happened when a person's relational context did not change significantly for a while. When certain CNM dynamics were repeated and maintained over time—for example, if one's partner went out once a week for a date with a particular metamour, without significant changes in either relationship—initial anxieties could get defused as they realized that their greatest fears (for example, the fear of being abandoned in favor of a metamour) were not playing out. Additionally, for people initially transitioning from monogamy to non-monogamy, living outside of a mononormative paradigm would progressively get normalized, especially as they created increased self and relational security, better support systems, and more effective reassurance strategies within a CNM context. As long as no element in the relational ecosystem strongly inhibited gratitude or empathy, compersion would typically become more likely, frequent, and accessible as folks gained experience and habituation with CNM.

Additionally, most study participants reported having experienced attitudinal compersion before embodied compersion: once they had normalized CNM and soothed the sense of threat, they were more likely to experience compersion emotionally and sensorily. However, for some folks, the opposite was true—especially when embodied compersion was erotic. Some participants had entered CNM because imagining or witnessing their partner being sexually intimate with another person was an empathic turn-on, and they later developed a compersive attitude.

Other participants had very nonlinear experiences around the spectrum of compersion because of changing life circumstances. For example, Diane, an academic department administrator who was 54 years old at the time of the first interview, had been experiencing newfound challenges finding new lovers by the time of the second interview. This made it more difficult for her to experience compersion toward her husband James when he went out on dates. Meanwhile, James had the opposite experience: he reported experiencing more interest from other women than he had in years prior. Thus, at the time of her first interview in 2018, Diane typically experienced more compersion for James than he did for her, because she had initiated non-monogamy and enjoyed plentiful dating opportunities; in 2022, however, the tables had turned, and James then experienced more compersion toward Diane, as finding new partners had become easier for him than for her.

Bethanne—who was 29 years old at the time of the first interview and 34 at the time of the second—also had unexpected, nonlinear experiences with jealousy and compersion over time. In her second interview, she confided that she had unveiled new depths of jealousy in recent years due to her increased capacity to "hold" greater intensities of emotions. She attributed this change to her spiritual/meditation practice, as well as to the increased emotional maturity that came with her stage of life—a maturity that brought about greater acceptance, which in turn granted her newfound access to *all* emotions—not only pleasant ones. Thus, she situated herself on both ends of the spectrum at once—reporting that both her experiences of jealousy *and* compersion had grown deeper. I describe Bethanne's fascinating experience in more depth in Chapter 1 under the section, "The Malleability of Jealousy."

Similarly, Jo—a trans man who was a 29 years old cis-woman at the time of the first interview, and 33 and amid their gender transition at the time of the second interview—had been feeling less compersion toward their partners in recent years because of a combination of factors: the COVID-19 pandemic had thrown a wrench into their social life, the emergence of new disabilities and health issues had made dating and socializing more challenging, and their undergoing a gender transition at the time of the second interview had narrowed their dating pool compared to when they were a cisgendered woman. Thus, compersion had become less frequent for Jo, especially embodied compersion. They still experienced and expressed much attitudinal compersion toward their partners, but their emotional excitement had decreased due to these contextual changes.

These few examples show how evolving constellations of factors can cause CNM folks to situate themselves on the compersion spectrum in unexpected, dynamic, and nonlinear ways. As such, the spectrum is most helpful when used as a "snapshot" assessment tool rather than to create an expectation that jealousy should disappear over time, or that compersion should become more embodied than attitudinal in any permanent way. CNM ecosystems and the people in it are fluid and complex—and so are their emotional realities.

IS THE SPECTRUM HIERARCHICAL?

Just as this spectrum is not a linear representation of folks' lived experiences in long-term non-monogamy, it also does not represent a hierarchy of experience from the perspective of morality or competency. While compersion is typically sought after by CNM people and is a welcomed experience when it occurs, it is not a benchmark for a person's emotional, relational, or spiritual proficiency. Any rhetoric that elevates compersion as a "holy grail of polyamorous respectability"—considering compersive people as "more evolved" than those who regularly struggle with jealousy—should be met with suspicion. To make a parallel, experiencing joy is not "more evolved" than experiencing sadness; the feelings, events, and responses that spark and emerge from both emotions are unique and an integral part of the human experience. Certainly, most people would prefer to experience joy over sadness, but one does not supersede the other; besides, accessing deeper joy often means uncovering and processing painful emotions that could be blocking emotional well-being.

In addition, as I describe more thoroughly in Parts III, IV, and V of this book, the emergence of compersion often has more to do with the particular context of a person's relational ecosystem at any given time—especially as it pertains to inner and relational security—than with a person's relationship skills or personal qualities.

To this point, as Bethanne's story clearly showed in the last section (as well as in Chapter 1), the ability to "hold" great depths of emotions—including difficult ones like jealousy—can be a better marker of emotional maturity than the presence or absence of certain emotions. How a person responds to their emotions, and how they treat themselves and others as a result, is a more helpful focus than to label any particular emotion as desirable or undesirable. In other words, creating moral hierarchies between different emotional states can be gravely misleading.

Regarding the spectrum, I want to emphasize that just as compersion is not "superior" to jealousy or benevolent neutrality, embodied compersion is not "better" than attitudinal compersion, and that *it is no more possible to rid oneself of jealousy than it would be to rid oneself of fear or sadness forever.* These different experiences often occur simultaneously or in close proximity. For example, Sabrina, a 41-year-old dance artist, described attitudinal compersion as being "always there"—and embodied compersion emerging more sporadically when her partner was aroused by a new connection. She described attitudinal compersion as "always in the background, always there, even though we may not express it." In contrast, when her partner shared about a crush or pleasurable date, she described the experience as "titillating" and "bubbly"—which indicated a heightened intensity of experience. These two types of compersion were complementary, and she could find herself at two locations on the spectrum at once. Additionally, as we will explore more thoroughly in Chapter 6, jealousy and compersion can, and often do, coexist. In sum, like the spectrum of colors in a rainbow, each element of the compersion–jealousy spectrum is valuable and illuminating.

OTHER FLAVORS OF COMPERSION

Some participants reported experiences of compersion that did not fit the "traditional" definitions of the term, which added texture and nuance to my understanding of the dimensionality of compersion. The main themes were compersion for negative experiences and compersion in nonromantic life situations.

Compersion for Negative Experiences

A few folks used the term compersion to refer to sympathetic and loving support in the context of a partner's difficult or painful experience. While all participants emphasized that compersion was a source of joy and satisfaction in their relationships, they noted that the same empathic circuits allowing joyful compersion to take place also led to empathizing with their partner(s) when they experienced less glorious moments in their other relationships, such as disappointments, frustrations, even breakups. In other words, the expansion of personal boundaries to include one's partner not only allows participants to share happiness with their partner(s) but also challenging emotions. While these experiences do not fit the popular understanding of compersion, a few participants insisted that they were inseparable. This speaks of empathy being at the core of compersion.

For instance, Fred, a 75-year-old retired geneticist, described how he did not only experience compersion when positive events happened but also when difficult ones occurred. In these instances, he referred to compersion as a gentle and loving source of support:

> It occurred to me that compersion is usually sort of positioned as, you know, I just went out and spent three days fucking my girlfriend silly, and you come home and your wife is glad to see you, you know, how wonderful! I'm glad you're so happy, right? Also, like, I just broke up with somebody I had a lot of emotional investment in, and I feel awful, and your partner says, "Gee, that's too bad," and is gentle and loving with you. So, I think there's a compersion for the negative things that happen as well. . . . I think that's something even more important.

While compersion for negative experiences falls outside of what is typically defined as compersion, it is understandable that the enhanced closeness that makes positive empathy possible would not be confined to positive experiences. If muditā (sympathetic joy in Buddhism[2]) remedies the illusion of separation of the self from others, it logically ensures that one cannot pick and choose which experiences and emotions will be shared. In the same way as someone would feel saddened when hearing of a good friend's disappointing medical diagnosis, but rejoice at the knowledge of an encouraging one, it seemed that compersion for a romantic partner could not be isolated to one flavor of experience. Whether empathy for negative experiences should be labeled as compersion is up for debate—but this goes to show how the use of words can be fluid, dynamic, and very much dependent on individual expression.

Compersion in Nonromantic Life Situations

Similarly, my participants described instances of compersion outside the context of romantic or sexual relationships, woven into many aspects of their social lives. The lack of a different English word for the concept of sharing someone's joy in everyday circumstances made compersion an obvious choice to describe these situations. For example, Sylvia, a 49-year-old professor, described how she had recently begun to feel what she coined "aunty compersion" toward younger polyamorous people who have a chance at living in a better, less mononormative world:

> I was just at the solo poly conference, and there were these young couples, getting together or coming there together. I saw a triad, and then I saw this other couple . . . and you know, at a poly conference, people are not hiding anything. I just felt really a lot of compersion. I felt such joy that they were able to be so open. Because this gives me hope for the future. I started calling it *aunty compersion*, because I felt like an aunty or a mom, right? Really, I was very moved, almost to the point of tears by seeing this, there was a young woman in front of me with her female partner and her male partner, and they all had their arms around each other. I'm like, that's the kind of world that we should be able to live in. And thank God that these young people might have a chance at that, whereas my generation is just completely fucked up, you know? Really, I was just overjoyed, feeling joy for them and for what they get to experience.

Sylvia's "aunty compersion" was arguably an embodied form of compersion, even though it was platonic—as she was moved "almost to the point of tears" by her positive empathy.

For Simon, an 83-year-old retired professor, compersion expanded into a ubiquitous philosophy of life and relationships, a template for "letting people be who they are" by honoring their autonomy and releasing the tendency to control others:

> Dealing with diversity means learning to deal with other people without trying to be the controller, without being the boss, without being the white guy, the slave master, whatever you want to call it. You have to let people be

who they are. And that's what compersion really is, I think, letting people be who they are and not getting yourself all tied in a knot.

In other words, Simon described compersion as a general "vibe" or attitude of respect toward people and their authenticity—the opposite of control or dominance.

Several participants remarked that experiencing compersion (in the broader sense of sympathetic joy) in nonromantic life situations was no different than experiencing compersion in the romantic or sexual context of CNM. However, the former was considered "normal" in the eyes of mainstream culture, and the latter was generally viewed as a fringe phenomenon based on its defiance of mononormative cultural assumptions.

NOTES

1. Hypatia from Space, 2018, p. 23.
2. Coren, 2023.

COEXISTENCE OF JEALOUSY AND COMPERSION

They're always in the same jumbled space together . . . I'm mostly excited, especially because my thinking brain is almost always in the compersion zone, versus my unconscious is probably more often in the jealousy than I think. . . . I can think of many moments when it's like, "I am so happy for you!" but oh, there's some bad, ugly; I have a little bit of tenseness [*mimicking pain*].

—Bethanne, 29, nonprofit activist

Is compersion the opposite of jealousy? The answer is twofold. On the one hand, saying that jealousy and compersion are opposites is a helpful explanatory framework. They certainly are antonymic in meaning, as well as negatively correlated in the research.[1] Along the same lines, jealousy is considered the "far enemy" of muditā in Buddhism.[2] Far enemies refer to mental or emotional states that are opposed to, and incompatible with, the virtues that Buddhists seek to cultivate. Thus, the far enemy of sympathetic joy, or muditā, is envy or jealousy—because resentment, bitterness, or threat around someone's good fortune stands in opposition to genuine joy.[3]

On the other hand, my research showed that jealousy and compersion are not mutually exclusive, nor incompatible, as commonly assumed. Rather, they are unique sets of experiences that can, and often do, coexist—similar to how happiness and sadness are each complex emotions that can show up concurrently, as the expression "bittersweet" conveys so well. From this perspective, jealousy and compersion are not technically "opposites"—in fact, they can often be found entangled, and in dynamic tension, with one another.

PARTICIPANTS' ACCOUNTS OF JEALOUSY AND COMPERSION COEXISTING

Nearly all my study participants stated that they regularly experience jealousy and compersion in close proximity—either in quick succession or concurrently. Many pointed to instances where their cognitive minds would be in a compersive space while their body experienced some discomfort rooted in jealousy, fear, anger, or a sense of threat. For example, Bethanne, a 29-year-old nonprofit activist, reported that jealousy and compersion were always in the same "jumbled space together":

> I'm on the spectrum of both, like, usually it's high compersion and low jealousy, but they're always in the same jumbled space together. . . . I'm mostly excited, especially because my thinking brain is almost always in the compersion zone, versus my unconscious is probably more often in the jealousy than I think. . . . I can think of many moments when it's like, "I am so happy for you!" but oh, there's some bad, ugly, I have a little bit of tenseness [*mimicking pain*]. . . . It's about feeling mostly joy that they're feeling this thing, but also maybe there's a little voice on the side that's feeling jealous.

Although some may argue that any amount of jealousy would interfere with the quality or genuineness of one's compersiveness, my participants saw this differently. Tyrone, a 38-year-old facilitator, noted how a "tinge" of jealousy within an embodied compersive experience did not prevent him from being "fully in [his] joy":

> Being around your partner while they're being pleased, there's that compersion of, "you're getting the thing I can't give you. I can't give you that, and you are getting it and you are in bliss right now. Look at you squirm, look at you laugh, look at you cry, getting these things that you want. So yeah, I can't do that for you. And I can appreciate that you get the thing because that's what I actually want for you." And so regardless if there's a tinge of jealousy in my compersion, and the awareness that I can't provide that thing, I can still be fully in my joy.

Conversely, other participants reported being caught by surprise by feelings of compersion in situations that their conscious minds had labeled as threatening. For example, James, who delved into CNM after finding out his wife Diane was having an affair, advanced that a kernel of compersion had emerged from the moment he learned that Diane had been involved with another man. However, the compersion was juxtaposed with a host of challenging feelings stemming from the context of betrayal:

> In the first moment, in the midst of all this anger and shock over the discovery of her infidelity, I think I had elements of compersion because I understood what she did. I understood the need she had, and what her desire was about, immediately. She had sort of brought to life a desire that I had basically stuffed down and essentially ignored, sort of by fiat, and she acted upon it, so I understood that. I think I felt compersion immediately, and understood and appreciated that. It was just also combined with shock and anger and fear and a bunch of other things that weren't positive, that sort of shielded its presence.

In all of these examples, the ratio between jealousy and compersion was typically high enough in either direction to yield "mostly compersive" or "mostly jealous" experience. However, in some cases, the tension between jealousy and compersion could heighten to the point where it would cause an inner struggle, or a "*comperstruggle.*"

COMPERSTRUGGLE

Jealousy researcher Joli Hamilton and I recently coined the term "comperstruggle"[4] to refer to instances where a person feels pulled between jealousy and compersion. As relationship coaches, we regularly witness clients struggling with this tension. Being caught in a comperstruggle typically shows up as having a compersive attitude and a desire to feel compersion emotionally, but with the presence of jealous feelings. Because these feelings clash with a person's conscious intentions, the jealousy is often met with self-judgment, disappointment, or self-condemnation.

This self-recriminating response can in part be due to the countercultural nature of practicing non-monogamy within a monogamous culture, and the discrepancy of messages internalized from each environment. In wider society, there is an expectation or assumption that one should feel jealous when their partner engages intimately with another person. In CNM communities and networks, however, people typically view compersion as the most appropriate or desirable response to a partner's other relationships. As Deri conveyed in her work on compersion, CNM communities adopt very different "feeling rules" than the rest of society, and folks can feel caught between what they are "supposed to" feel, and what they *really* feel.[5]

Thus, when jealousy shows up in CNM contexts, there is often an internal conflict between "what I want or expect myself to feel" and "what I'm actually feeling." This contradiction may evoke shame, confusion, and embarrassment—which is then compounded with the personal pain of jealousy, fears, envy, grief, and/or other insecurities. Learning to work compassionately with these difficult feelings can be a powerful nexus of transformation and deeper intimacy for partners. I covered this process in more detail in Chapter 1 in the section "How CNM People Relate to Jealousy Differently: The Advent of Non-Mononormative Jealousy." Additionally, interested readers may find more information on working through comperstruggles on my website blog, or Joli Hamilton's site.[6]

FLUIDITY BETWEEN JEALOUSY AND COMPERSION

Although jealousy and compersion are antonymic to one another, the veil between them can be quite thin. Three participants (Lisa, James, and Alexis) expressed their perception that jealousy and compersion were "made of the same stuff," but took on their emotional meanings from different framing contexts. They invoked experiences where pangs of jealousy would shift into compersion, or vice versa—following shifts in personal and relational contexts at the levels of perceived safety versus threat, inclusion versus exclusion, buy-in versus powerlessness, consent versus nonconsent, perceived care versus carelessness, as well as other factors (see Chapters 7 and 8 for more detail on relevant factors). The shifts between compersion and jealousy seemed so fluid and dynamic that James alluded to them as "two sides of the same coin":

> I almost feel that they are two sides of the same coin. . . . I would say the difference is that one is strongly based on love, and the other is based in fear. Jealousy is based in fear and compersion is based in love. So now, if I look back to that original moment [the discovery of Diane's infidelity], I had the sense of fear but also had a sense of love for her in understanding the acts that she took initiating this.

This is congruent with philosopher Ronald de Sousa's perspective that compersion and jealousy are, in large part, socially constructed experiences that arise based on a particular person's beliefs, assumptions, and interpretations.[7] He used the concepts of emotional *valence* (whether an emotion is considered negative or positive) and *arousal* (emotional intensity) to explore the fluidity with which jealousy can shift into compersion, and vice versa, depending on how different contexts are interpreted at any given moment.

For example, witnessing a lover cuddling with another person can be ascribed a negative or positive meaning, or valence, depending on the thoughts and meanings that frame it. The stimuli from this witnessing can also vary in levels of arousal—from a low intensity to a high intensity. De Sousa proposed that "*a common core of arousal can sometimes elicit contrary emotional responses, depending on the framing story in terms of which it is construed.*"[8] These stories are rooted in social conventions and enculturated behaviors—which are deeply engrained, but not immutable.

In my study, this valence of emotions, with an emphasis on meaning-making, was perhaps most obvious in erotic contexts, as I explored in Chapter 2 under the section "Erotic Compersion." Sexualizing one's partner through a third-person gaze and playing with the taboo of nonexclusivity has long been a feature of otherwise mononormative contexts, as exemplified by role-play fantasies, cuckolding fantasies, allowances for an occasional threesome, or other occurrences of couples flirting with nonexclusivity in the sexual domain while remaining romantically exclusive. In such scenarios, people voluntarily introduce an element of jealousy, or potential for jealousy, in a small dose for its arousal potency—and thus flirt with the line between jealousy and erotic compersion. The attribution of a safe meaning to these situations (e.g., the intent of spicing things up sexually for the benefit of the primary couple) can establish what would be a jealousy-inducing situation into an edgy and erotic scene. However, if a different meaning is introduced—for example, a romantically exclusive heterosexual couple invites a woman to join them for a casual threesome, and this woman suddenly tells the husband, "I love you!" while engaged in intercourse with him—the emotional landscape of a situation can shift within an instant. In this case, a proclamation of love could have the effect of throwing the wife—who felt turned on and compersive a minute ago—into a spin of anger or jealousy.

In short: it is a fine, potentially exciting, and often fraught line between compersion and jealousy. Their proximity to one another, the speed with which people often oscillate between the two, and people's tendency to experience them concurrently, all demonstrate the fluid and dynamic nature of compersion.

EXPLANATORY FRAMEWORKS FOR THE COEXISTENCE OF JEALOUSY AND COMPERSION

A useful perspective to understand how a person may experience tension between compersive and jealous feelings in close proximity is the Internal Family Systems (IFS) model. IFS sees the mind as a conglomeration of "parts," or subpersonalities, that often come into conflict with one another—allowing for human beings' ability to hold opposite emotions, thoughts, and feelings concurrently. Furthermore, the model assumes that each part of the system plays a valuable role. It views people as "containing an ecology of relatively discrete minds, each of which has valuable qualities and each of which is designed to—and wants to—play a valuable role within."[9] This is a fitting lens to look at jealousy and compersion: jealousy often plays a protective role by warning people of possible threats to valued relationships,[10] while compersion plays a connective role by bringing people closer together.[11] It seems only natural that the two roles would coexist, and even compete, in a CNM context that challenges traditional expectations around attachment and relational safety.

Freud's structural model of the psyche, including the id, ego, and superego,[12] is also a fascinating lens to look at the proximal tension between compersion and jealousy. In CNM contexts where people are often enculturated into the idea of compersion as an ideal,[13] I would hypothesize that jealousy takes refuge in the instinctive shadow of the id, while the moralistic and critical superego may attempt to impose compersive behaviors and attitudes upon situations that trigger a threat response. In other cases, the id might experience arousal in relation to extradyadic scenarios, while the superego finds it morally dubious. The ego, on the other hand, fulfills its role as a mediating agent between the visceral desires of the id and the moral ideals of the superego—holding both compersion and jealousy together in a "jumbled space" or even a comperstruggle. Even though this may be an uncomfortable paradox to manage, it is not necessarily a bad thing: I would argue that CNM individuals often exert exceptional emotional intelligence, courage, and sophistication in their efforts to create love within riddles of opposites, in a rapidly evolving paradigm of human relationships.

It would be helpful for future research to investigate the nervous system correlates of both jealousy and compersion, using diverse lenses such as polyvagal theory[14] and theories of stress response.[15] Additionally, exploring how different therapeutic approaches, such as IFS and other modalities, may support folks in better understanding the roots and roles of jealousy and compersion would certainly be a captivating endeavor for scholars and practitioners alike.

NOTES

1. Flicker et al., 2021.
2. Kraus & Sears, 2009.
3. More complex are the so-called near enemies or qualities that can mimic a desired quality but are superficial renderings. The near enemy of mudità is exhilaration—which may appear as sharing another person's joy, but in reality, it is a self-centered, grasping emotion that grows out of insufficiency or lack, rather than an empathic one that grows out of sufficiency; see Tibetan Buddhist Encyclopedia, 2020.
4. Hamilton, 2023; Thouin, 2023.
5. Deri, 2015.
6. Hamilton, 2023; Thouin, 2023.
7. de Sousa, 2017.
8. de Sousa, 2017, p. 1, emphasis added.
9. Schwartz, 2013, p. 1.
10. Hamilton, 2020.
11. Flicker et al., 2022; Waugh & Fredrickson, 2006.
12. Freud, 1923.
13. Wolfe, 2003.
14. Porges, 2009.
15. For example, McCarty, 2016; Ursin & Eriksen, 2004.

A COMPERSION ROADMAP

Knowing the contexts that most impact the experience of compersion, both positively and negatively, can help CNM folks, as well as their therapists, coaches, and counselors, navigate the terrain of nonmonogamy with increased awareness and intention. As a dating and relationship coach, the roadmap I describe in the following chapters has been incredibly useful to myself and to my clients: when a person identifies their specific strengths and bottlenecks in the "compersion system" proposed herein, they gain a better understanding of what is going on in their relational ecosystem. With this map, they can pinpoint the elements that have most room for improvement, and thus clarify how to most effectively invite more empathy, gratitude, love, and security into the areas that are lacking it. Identifying and addressing the bottlenecks as they arise catalyzes coaching into a highly individualized and efficient process.

However, as I spelled out in the introduction, I reject the common assumption that everyone should attempt to feel compersion under every circumstance. Instead, what I have found is that not every situation lends itself to compersion. In some circumstances, folks may be better served aiming for benevolent neutrality (see Chapter 5) than compersion. In other cases, unhealthy relational dynamics must be addressed and transformed before compersion can be accessible. I refer readers to the section, "Should Compersion Always Be the Goal?" in the introduction of this book for a discussion of this important distinction.

OVERVIEW OF FACTORS THAT IMPACT COMPERSION

The following two chapters explore the factors that impact compersion in CNM relationships. Chapter 7 describes the elements that are most likely to enhance compersion, and Chapter 8 elucidates those most likely to hinder it. I broke down each chapter into three categories of factors: individual, relational, and social. Each chapter includes six factors in total.

The following tables offer a bird's-eye view of the main factors that promote and hinder compersion, and thus a preview of the next two chapters. Table III.1 outlines the main factors that promote compersion, and Table III.2 displays the factors that hinder compersion. Part IV then combines these factors with the elements described in Parts I and II into a comprehensive theoretical model of compersion.

Table III.1. Factors That Promote Compersion

Factors		Manifestations
Individual	Ideological commitment to CNM values	Pragmatism
		Ethics and politics
		Willingness to defy social conventions
		Sex positivity
		Non-mononormative stance toward jealousy
	Inner security	Personal autonomy and agency
		Self-confidence, self-esteem, and self-love
		Having one's personal needs met
Relational	Relational security, connectedness, and trust	Relationship health and satiation
		Open communication and transparency
		Reassurance strategies
		Going at the pace of the slower person
		Building tolerance
		Relationship agreements
	Positive integration of partner's other relationship(s)	Positive connection with metamours
		Positive regard toward metamours
		Boundaries with metamours
		Flexible sexual orientation
		Group sex
	Perception of benefits from partner's other relationship(s)	Richer emotional and sexual life
		Richer social life
		Authentic emotional expression
		Freedom from fear, emotional congruence, and pride
		Relief from guilt
		Growth
		Enhanced relationship satisfaction
Social	Community belonging	CNM/polypride and activism
		CNM social networks
		Media and literature
		Role models

Table III.2. **Factors That Hinder Compersion**

Factors		Manifestations
Individual	Obstacles to ideological commitment to CNM values	Internalized mononormativity Poly under duress Couple privilege
	Obstacles to inner security	Dependency/codependency Insecurity and comparison with metamour Sexual shame and sex negativity Unmet personal needs
Relational	Obstacles to relational security, connectedness, and trust	Betrayal Unmet relational needs Jealousy and deprivation
	Obstacles to positive integration of partner's other relationship(s)	Feeling excluded Not liking or trusting a metamour Weak boundaries with metamours and "cowboys" Disgruntled metamour and lack of consent
	Obstacles to perception of benefits from partner's other relationship(s)	Lack of perception of benefits from partner's other relationship(s)
Social	Obstacles to community belonging	Mononormativity and stigmatization of CNM relationships Lack of racial and cultural diversity in CNM communities

CHAPTER 7

WHAT PROMOTES COMPERSION?

There's no magic to all of this. Compersion is not an ability I was born with, far from that! I had to learn and develop this feeling from scratch, just as you probably will.

—Marie-Claude L'Archer (aka Hypatia from Space)[1]

Intentionally inviting more compersion into one's life starts with understanding what promotes it. My research yielded a trove of information in this realm. My interview data yielded six main factors that fell into three categories: individual, relationship, and social. Individual factors included (1) ideological commitment to CNM values, and (2) inner security. Relational factors included themes of (3) relational security, connectedness, and trust; (4) positive integration of partner's other relationship(s); and (5) perception of benefits from partner's other relationship(s). Finally, I found (6) community belonging to be the primary social factor impacting compersion.

In this chapter, I discuss these themes from the lenses of participants' stories, and at times weave those with supporting literature. In Chapter 8, I then explore the factors that hinder compersion. In most cases, themes from Chapters 7 and 8 mirror each other (for example, community belonging in this chapter mirrors obstacles to community belonging in Chapter 8), but there are important nuances in the ways they show up in the data. For example, the subthemes in the section on community belonging include specific ways in which participants have created a sense of community belonging—such as consuming CNM-affirming media and literature, joining supportive CNM social networks, and identifying positive CNM role models. On the other hand, obstacles to community belonging include two emphases, one on how widespread mononormativity and the stigmatization of CNM lifestyles can hinder compersion, and another on how the lack of racial and cultural diversity in many CNM communities has created challenges for BIPOC individuals to access a sense of belonging. Becoming aware of such specific challenges, ideas, and solutions can provide practical guidance to CNM people and their counselors in creating individualized strategies that support compersion and relationship satisfaction whenever possible.

GROUPING 1: INDIVIDUAL FACTORS

While compersion is a fundamentally relational experience, it begins within the individual. Participants noted that certain personal predispositions had nourished their propensity to experience compersion, while others had created blocks and challenges to it. In this section, I take a close look at positive individual predispositions from my interviewees' perspectives. Two main elements emerged in this category: (1) ideological commitment to CNM values, and (2) inner security.

Ideological Commitment to CNM Values

Full-hearted consent to a CNM relationship style was necessary for compersion to take place. One had to genuinely want to be non-monogamous in the first place and have self-driven motivations for doing so—as opposed to feeling pressured or coerced into CNM by a partner (also known as poly under duress, or PUD—see Chapter 8). My participants explained that if someone was not philosophically on board with practicing CNM, they would inevitably bring monogamous values and assumptions into their behaviors, and lack the necessary drive to "do the work" required for successful CNM: educating themselves about non-monogamy, conducting personal introspection, managing their emotions, and communicating their needs and desires proactively and compassionately within this new paradigm of intimate relating.

In other words, folks who lacked a strong and well-articulated buy-in to CNM would experience a lack of personal agency, which would restrict the possibility of experiencing compersion toward their partner(s) and metamour(s). This echoes psychotherapist Jessica Fern's assertion that having a clear *why* for being non-monogamous supports people in navigating their emotional experiences more successfully:

> My experience with nonmonogamous clients has shown me that the people who articulate their deeper purpose—that is, their *why* for being nonmonogamous—are then better able to navigate the ups and downs that lie ahead. When the waters of consensual nonmonogamy (CNM) begin to pick up and the emotional rapids of opening up your relationship begin, having

your *why* to remember and return to can serve as the needed life jacket that keeps you and your relationship afloat.[2]

From my research, people's whys spanned a wide spectrum of values and mindsets—including pragmatism, ethics, politics, willingness to defy social conventions, sex positivity, and holding a non-mononormative stance toward jealousy. I explore each of these elements next.

Pragmatism

For a vast majority of participants, adopting non-monogamy derived from a pragmatic realization that having more than one intimate relationship could enhance their lives by allowing them and their partners to get more of their needs and desires met. They typically considered the mononormative idea of expecting only one person to meet all their romantic and sexual needs to be unrealistic, and even damaging. They had examined the risks and benefits of CNM for themselves and concluded that the benefits outweighed the risks or hardships in their particular contexts. This concurs with Deri's statement that "polyamorists see having multiple loves as a more realistic, rather than idealistic, expression of love."[3]

Illustrating this pragmatic stance, Jenny, a 26-year-old software engineer, explained how having multiple partners was a logical solution to fulfilling her desires for both kink and domesticity—desires that she assessed could not be fulfilled with the same partner:

> I'm kinky—and, I really want a nesting mate. I want someone I can live a traditional life with, have kids with, merge our lives, live together, etc. But I have these other needs, wants, desires. I've learned over time that fundamentally, my nesting mate can't be my kink partner. Because in the kink dynamic, there has to be an intrinsic and inherent power imbalance. But in the nesting mate dynamic, I want an equal, someone who can be weak and small around me, that we are partners and that we will grow together, and they can be fallible. In the kink dynamic, that's not something that really works. So, it's kind of fundamentally impossible to have those two concepts, and those two needs within me be expressed with the same person.

Pragmatism also extended to a down-to-earth realization that one could not prevent their partner from being attracted to others, and that attempting to restrict how these attractions should be acted upon was unreasonable. Simon, an 83-year-old retired professor, stated,

You have to learn that people don't belong to you, that being married does not give you rights of ownership. You can't control somebody else's life, you can't stop them from finding other people attractive. It doesn't work!

Simon's comment bridged a primarily pragmatic concern—his assessment of the impossibility of monogamy for him ("it doesn't work!") with an ethical concern around refusing to "control somebody else's life." The ethical and political aspects of my participants' commitment to CNM values are where I focus next.

Ethics and Politics

For many participants, becoming consensually non-monogamous was primarily a result of an ethical and political stance around sexuality, love, and personal freedom. They felt that each person's sexual and romantic autonomy was sacred and that preventing one's partner from enjoying intimate connections with others would be unethical or selfish. Viewing people as fundamentally autonomous, self-directed, and whole was a premise for successful CNM. This philosophical viewpoint was mutually exclusive with mononormativity (although some participants would still consider monogamous agreements in noncompulsory contexts—see, for example, Ferrer's *Love and Freedom: Transcending Monogamy and Polyamory*[4] for an exploration of how monogamy may exist within a context of relational freedom). To this point, Laura-Lee viewed her engagement in polyamory "as a political act":

As a feminist, I see polyamory as a political act, like I'm making a statement about my power in the world and the control that I have over my body and my sexuality. So, having multiple partners is, for me, really empowering. And creating these ethical relationships with multiple people at the same time is incredibly empowering. I'm also modeling a certain kind of society that I want to live in, one in which we respect everybody, and don't treat our romantic partners as property, or as our inferiors, etc. . . . So I'm doing this not because I want to have multiple partners per se, but because I want to make ethical relationships with other people, and deconstructing a heteronormative marriage is one of the ways that I do that.

The idea of modeling a more mature society, free from patriarchal mores that view women's bodies as property, required a willingness to live outside of established conventions and normativities—often implying the loss of certain privileges and the work required to shift one's identity. This willingness is explored next.

Willingness to Defy Social Conventions

Showing commitment to CNM values, such as valuing one's partner's sexual and emotional autonomy as well as one's own, implied a willingness to defy and challenge the dominant mononormative paradigm. My study participants had to accept their status as a sexual/relational minority, along with the stigma and marginalization that typically accompanies CNM.[5] This required them to walk a path less traveled, and to "come out" to themselves and their partners (see Chapter 10 for a deeper exploration of the role of coming out in compersion). Participants who identified with other non-normative identities—such as LGBTQ+ folks—said they were predisposed to bend traditional rules in the relationship arena because they had already embraced an outsider status in other parts of their lives. Unsurprisingly, a large majority (77%) of my sample did not identify as heterosexual.

The few participants who identified as straight named other factors that may have predisposed them to embrace a non-normative relational path. Being generally open-minded, politically progressive, and open to challenging one's ideas had made the transition from monogamy to CNM possible for participants who did not otherwise view themselves as social outsiders. For example, Diane, a 54-year-old academic administrator, believed that her and her husband's intellectual curiosity and education had predisposed them to explore new ways of thinking around non-monogamy, although they did not otherwise lead particularly subversive lifestyles:

> I just think being highly educated helps. When we're reading books and talking about them, and listening to people like Dan Savage, that helps a lot too. James got a PhD, I have a master's degree, we read a lot, I mean, our marriage is long-lasting because we're always challenging each other and talking about new and interesting things.

Others pointed out that although they had grown up in traditional family settings, they had been raised with values around authenticity that had come into play in their journey of coming out as CNM. For example, Jenny noted that although her family of origin had "strong monogamous ideals," they also supported the idea of "believing in your own truth more than the societal truths":

I'm a quarter Chinese, a quarter Taiwanese, and half American. So my dad's lineage is, like, quite American. My parents are divorced and remarried. And my stepdad came into my life when I was five and his whole family's strongly Roman Catholic. And so I grew up in a Catholic community, which has very particular ideas about partnership. And I also grew up in a Chinese community that has also strong monogamous ideals. And both of my parents are monogamous, and have strong monogamous ideals. But at the same time, they also really supported the concept of believing in your own truth more than the societal truths, so I think that definitely had a large influence, because they always encouraged me to find my own personal way, rather than accepting what other people should tell me to do.

Jenny's account portrays meaningful intersecting elements of race, ethnicity, culture, and religion that at first sight, would have pointed her in the direction of monogamy—however, the value system that she learned in her family also carried a strong emphasis on personal autonomy, agentic thinking, and willingness to defy conventionality, which are linchpins of non-monogamy that also promote compersion. I explore sex positivity next as an adjacent manifestation of a commitment to CNM values.

Sex Positivity

A sex-positive attitude was intrinsic to CNM values and deeply intertwined with developing compersion. Since a core element of non-monogamy is the possibility of concurrent sexual relationships with more than one person, sex-positivity was essential to celebrating one's partner's other relationships. Sex therapist Chris Donaghue defined sex positivity as

> a perspective and a lifestyle of not perpetuating or creating "norms" or policing the borders of what is "acceptable" when sex is consensual, non-damaging, and pleasurable. Being sex-positive means you're open, flexible, and non-judgmental about your sexual preferences. It also means allowing your partners to feel the same way without shaming them.[6]

Since CNM lies outside conventional norms of sexual expression in the wider culture, sex positivity in this context went hand-in-hand with the willingness to question and defy social conventions. To mitigate living in a vastly sex-negative culture,[7] participants had to not only embrace their status as a sexual/relational minority but also endorse the idea that non-normative but consensual sexual expression should be celebrated rather than punished.

This mindset of celebrating, rather than stigmatizing, sexuality beyond the socially condoned dyadic structure was core to the experience of compersion. To illustrate, Fred, a 75-year-old retired molecular geneticist, described how his "career as a sex-positive activist" naturally lent itself to a CNM lifestyle:

> Because fear of sex and sex negativity is used in such a powerful way to keep people down, right into their graves. . . . There's an arsenal of ways to shame and put people down and denigrate people, and keep them from kicking them the hell out. The psychopaths that run things, they're adept at this. . . . There was a whole trope in the polyamorous community about people who don't want to have the word sex in the definition of polyamory in the description of it. And it's not all about sex, [just like] a car isn't just about the transmission but the transmission is a part of it. And guess what, the car doesn't go anywhere, if you don't recognize that a car with no transmission, and you really, you don't have polyamory without talking about sex. I try to be sympathetic with people, [but] the people I call the "I-am-not-a-swinger polys," it's so fucking stupid . . . these people who want to say that you can't be virtuous and ethical and serious if what you're doing is about sex. That is such a load of crap. And having healthy sex helps you be healthier physically in your body and mentally. You cannot be as healthy physically and mentally and be unhealthy about sex, and sex is fun, and you should have fun, you shouldn't, you shouldn't be put down for having fun. That's ridiculous.

Fred's account encompassed both personal and political aspects of sex positivity. His attitude toward sex allowed him to experience a sense of congruency between his philosophy and CNM relationship, which lent itself to compersion. Similarly, each participant expressed a sex-positive attitude that encompassed themselves, their partners, and their metamours, and verbalized a deliberate rejection of sex negativity and shame around their CNM relationship choice. This celebratory attitude toward sexuality was intrinsically linked to developing positive empathy and gratitude toward their partner's other relationships.

Non-Mononormative Stance toward Jealousy

In Chapter 1, I described how CNM people relate to jealousy differently than monogamous folks, and coined the term "non-mononormative jealousy." Adopting this stance toward jealousy and associated emotions like envy, possessiveness, and competitiveness is a crucial aspect of embodying a commitment to CNM values. I refer readers back to Chapter 1 to avoid repeating this information here, and I turn to the second element that promotes compersion in the individual category: inner security.

Inner Security

A sense of inner security strongly supports the occurrence of compersion. Inner security refers to the felt sense of having a strong, loving, and resourced relationship with oneself. Each of my study participants noted its central importance on the journey to successful CNM and as a pillar of their ability to experience compersion.

This theme parallels Jessica Fern's emphasis on the importance of secure attachment within self as a critical aspect of creating safe and secure bonds within CNM relationships. In *Polysecure: Attachment, Trauma and Consensual Nonmonogamy*, she explained how "the establishment of a secure relationship with our self is needed to fully embody healthy attachment with others."[8] While developing secure, loving, and restorative bonds with one's partner(s) is of course of utmost importance in the journey of developing securely attached relationships—particularly for those with insecure attachment patterns and histories of trauma—Fern noted that the relationship with self is the only relationship that is guaranteed to last forever and is therefore fundamental to one's broader sense of security with others and in life. She also insisted that secure attachment to oneself is particularly critical in CNM relationships, since non-monogamy is inherently less secure than monogamy as it invites more elements of unpredictability and change as a relational structure: "In polyamory, we need the internal security of being anchored in our inner strength and inner nurturer to navigate a relationship structure that is considerably less secure."[9] Therefore, a grounded sense of inner attunement, presence, self-love, reliability, coherence, and self-care is essential to navigating the choppy waters that CNM often offers. I highly recommend *Polysecure* for anyone seeking a practical framework for building secure attachment with oneself and others within CNM contexts.

For my participants, having a sense of inner security was twofold: as a trait, referring to the degree to which a person generally felt that a strong self-relationship was a constant in their lives, and as a state, which referred to the natural fluctuation of this inner sense of security depending on different circumstances. For example, if someone got fired from their job, had a health issue, or were hungry or tired, they might feel temporarily less secure or comfortable with themselves as a *state*—and this would lead to potentially feeling less compersive toward their partner(s) until their "personal cup" would be full again. When a person felt generally secure within themselves as a consistent *trait*, however, insecurities triggered by their partner's other relationship(s) would remain more tolerable during the ups and downs of life's fluctuations of comfortable and uncomfortable moments.

How did inner security show up in the interview data? The felt sense of having a secure relationship with oneself included the following elements: (a) personal autonomy and agency, (b) self-confidence, self-esteem, and self-love; and (c) having one's personal needs met.

Personal Autonomy and Agency

Being grounded in a strong sense of one's personal autonomy and agency, as opposed to feeling overly dependent on one's partner(s), came up as a crucial element in my participants' ability to experience compersion. While their intimate relationships were typically very interconnected and intertwined, they described how their own sense of inner connection, self-reliance, self-regulation, and resourcefulness was foundational to not only tolerating, but also celebrating, their partners' autonomy and agency. When they felt connected to their personal power, participants reported feeling equipped with greater risk tolerance and emotional resilience—necessary qualities in creating harmonious CNM relationships, which inevitably carry substantial opportunities for change, uncertainty, and jealousy. Conversely, folks who lacked self-reliance—whether psychologically, emotionally, or financially—would tend to form dependent or codependent bonds, and meet their partner's/partners' extradyadic connections with more fear. To illustrate, Laura-Lee described that she and her husband Martin had experienced successful CNM relationships because they had treated themselves, as well as one another, as autonomous individuals:

> Both of us have a strong sense of autonomy. So from the very start, there was this sense of, "Hey, we are doing this together, but the fundamental unit of action here is me as an individual, and Martin as an individual, so we're not acting as a couple." And we can make different choices, like, Martin has a different approach to polyamory than I do. And I recognize and value his approach even though he's making choices that I wouldn't make for myself. So, my sense is that because we came in consciously treating each other as autonomous individuals and asking questions about each other, that we wound up avoiding some of these pitfalls that I see other people falling into.

CHAPTER 7

Laura-Lee's attitude was to honor Martin's personal choices rather than attempt to change them—and she attributed much of their compersion to this dynamic. Indeed, honoring personal and erotic autonomy was a core value of CNM, which rejects the idea of possession and control over one's partner's sexuality. The practice of non-monogamy relies on a sense of personal power and agency over one's life and relationships, and positions each individual in a space of being at choice. Jamila, a 36-year-old program associate, described "loyalty to self" as a foundation for successful polyamory:

> Something that polyamory has taught me is that loyalty to myself! I think it's something you have to learn if you're gonna date more than one person. You know, it's just putting yourself a little bit first, so that you can drink from your full cup and then have a more well-rounded connection with people.

In this quote, Jamila described how she prioritized her own sense of personal power by drinking from her own "full cup." Looking at this theme through the lens of power dynamics, it is worth noting that feelings of jealousy and abandonment are typically intertwined with a sense of powerlessness. This explains why increasing one's psycho-emotional, as well as physical and financial autonomy can mitigate feelings of threat. For example, when someone financially depends on their partner, they may naturally feel threatened if their partner invests time and resources with another person.

However, there are exceptions. A partner who is dependent on their partner and who also receives support from their metamour may feel a lot of compersion because they are getting more of their needs filled through that relationship. Thus, financial autonomy may facilitate compersion but only as long as metamours are not contributing directly to filling one's needs. Conversely, instances where members of a polycule provide tangible support to one another may pave a path for gratitude, and thus compersion, in response to the perception of benefits from partner's other relationship(s) factor—which I dive into later in this chapter. Additionally, I explore the intersection between socioeconomic status and compersion more deeply in Chapter 11, "Social Positionality and Compersion."

For some participants, walking away from a traditional monogamous paradigm had been a meaningful step in their journey of personal empowerment and autonomy—and compersion had followed. Sylvia, a 49-year-old professor, spelled out how regaining complete autonomy over her body and emotions after ending a monogamous marriage had allowed her to become more nurturing, other-directed, and engaged with her partners. She explained,

> I am a lot more loving, forgiving and nonjudgmental than I used to be. And so I think it's because I don't feel smothered and trapped anymore. And when I felt smothered and trapped in a normative marriage, I got very emotionally and physically stingy. I just felt smothered, and I didn't want intimacy. I was like, "Get away from me." And since being non-monogamous, I am much more other-directed, I'm much more into being physically and emotionally nurturing, because I don't feel smothered anymore. And I realized that I'm actually a really giving person. I thought I was really self-centered, selfish . . . I'm actually not, I'm actually more generous than I've ever been in my life with my emotional energy.

Sylvia's noticing that a normative marriage had created a sense of scarcity for her was counterintuitive from the perspective of mononormative culture, which presents monogamy as the epitome of commitment. Conversely, mononormative narratives may characterize the expression of personal autonomy through non-monogamy as a lack of commitment or deep intimate engagement. This was not the case for my participants. In fact, in the second round of interviews (conducted in 2022 and 2023) I had with nine of my initial participants, each of the six participants who were in cohabitating partnerships at the time of the initial interviews in 2018 (Jo, Diane, Fred, James, John, and Natasha) were still with the same long-term non-monogamous partners four years later. While relationship longevity is certainly not the only, or best, measure of relationship commitment or quality, this is a notable data point that may contribute to rectifying false myths around romantic autonomy and commitment.

Self-Confidence, Self-Esteem, and Self-Love

Self-confidence, self-esteem, and self-love point to an additional layer of inner security. Indeed, since one of the main obstacles to compersion is negative comparison with one's metamours (see Chapter 8), having strong self-esteem and self-confidence was an asset when navigating CNM and mitigating insecurities. For Jamila, these qualities, and thus her ability to feel compersion, were rooted in self-love:

It would be more challenging to feel authentic compersion for someone if you didn't have a certain grounding of self-love in your heart, for just yourself to start. . . . I think people that have a certain amount of self-love often carry a certain amount of confidence. I would imagine it would be a lot harder to feel compersion for your partner if you're internally criticizing yourself.

Jamila evocatively voiced how self-criticism can impair compersion, and self-love promotes it. It seemed that self-love and self-esteem would mitigate the potential harms of negatively comparing oneself to one's metamours. As researcher Leanna Wolfe encapsulated, "If one can actually stand up tall and proud to all of those 'I'm not loved' demons, then they may truly emerge victorious from polyamory's dark night of the soul journey."[10]

Indeed, many studies have shown that jealousy often negatively correlates with self-esteem.[11] While compersion itself is not born from feeling better than one's metamours, having a healthy—rather than fragile—self-esteem helps mitigate potential fears of abandonment or rejection as well as negative comparison. In those lines, Ben-Ze'ev explored the comparative concern at the core of jealousy, envy, *Schadenfreude* (happiness for someone's misery), compersion, and admiration—and noted that compersion requires a "positive evaluation of the other's good fortune."[12] This demands that this good fortune not represent a threat to one's self-esteem. Thus, those with low self-esteem are more likely to struggle with experiencing compersion. Similarly, in a thematic analysis study I conducted with Drs. Sharon Flicker and Michelle Vaughan on factors that facilitate and hinder compersion in CNM individuals, a participant noted the importance of self-worth in accessing compersion: "If I don't feel good about myself, it's hard to feel good about other people. It is doubly hard to feel good about your partner having a good time with someone else when you're down."[13]

This quote speaks to the fact that inner security can show up both as a trait and a state. For example, someone having a generally high sense of self-worth (trait) may have more difficulty experiencing compersion when they are feeling down, tired, or hungry (state). Both sides of the coin are impactful on one's compersion roadmap and connect to the question of having one's own personal needs met.

Having One's Personal Needs Met

Several participants mentioned that having one's personal needs met and feeling resourced was a condition for them to experience compersion. Tapping into a sense of individual well-being and fulfillment was a foundation upon which they could enjoy their partner's/partners' other loves. In other words, feeling that their personal cups were full allowed them to tap into a sense of positive empathy and gratitude that constitutes compersion.

Alexis got their own needs met by practicing regular self-care: "getting enough sleep [and] feeling full or resourced" was one of the main factors contributing to them feeling compersion toward their partners' other relationships. Similarly, Sabrina's boyfriend could only experience compersion when he felt well-rested and had enough mental space to process extradyadic situations in a positive way:

> The psyche needs to be relaxed and have time to process. You know, his mind can take him all kinds of places. And he needs to have a lot of time to calm his mind down. [*laughs*] Yeah, so that's frankly a huge part of it. That spaciousness. Without that, he does not experience compersion. . . . If we're tired, if we're overworked, there's not enough space in the psyche.

The idea that physiological needs being met is directly linked to one's propensity to view a partner's other relationships in a positive light implies that self-regulation[14] may play a key role in the emergence of compersion. This makes quite a bit of sense, considering that empathy is a documented outcome of self-regulation. Eisenberg has shown how self-regulation is "an extremely important piece of the puzzle [of empathy] . . . [and that] self-regulatory capacities involved in empathy-related responding contribute broadly to prosocial and moral behavior."[15] In other words, a person's empathic capacity is enhanced when they experience embodied pleasure and well-being— which can be brought about by lifestyle practices and habits such as getting adequate rest. These findings may help explain my participants' accounts of fluidly moving between jealousy and compersion depending on how they felt at that particular time. To this point, it would be wonderful for future research to investigate the nervous system correlates of both jealousy and compersion, using diverse lenses such as polyvagal theory[16] and theories of stress response.[17]

While getting one's personal needs met is an intrinsic part of inner security, it is more likely to fluctuate with the ebbs and flows of life than the previous two themes of personal autonomy and agency, and self-confidence, self-esteem, and self-love. Getting adequate sleep and food, having a great day at work, feeling good about one's friendships and other relationships, were examples of events that could impact "state compersion" perhaps more so than "trait compersion."[18] Moreover, this contrast reinforces the fact that compersion is not an on or off switch: it may come and go, with different levels of intensity and flavors, depending on context. Knowing this, CNM folks and their counselors may demonstrate increased understanding and compassion toward themselves or their clients navigating the ever-changing landscape of emotions that come with the terrain of non-monogamy.

GROUPING 2: RELATIONAL FACTORS

Compersion is a fundamentally relational experience. One does not experience compersion in isolation but within ecosystems of relationships. Within these ecosystems, there are constellations of factors that can impact the interpersonal emotions, thoughts, and behaviors that arise. Given the complexity of intimate relationships in general, in addition to the dynamic and fluid nature of CNM polycules involving more than two individuals, the work of identifying the elements that may impact compersion in each situation is bound to be non-exhaustive. However, there were notable trends in my participants' stories, which I discuss next.

The three main themes that emerged in the relational category include: (1) relational security, connectedness, and trust; (2) positive integration of partner's other relationship(s); and (3) perception of benefits from partner's other relationship(s). These factors pertained to my participants' relationships with both their partner(s) and their metamour(s); accordingly, the compersion they experienced could be directed toward their partner, toward their metamour, toward the "metamour relationship," or toward a combination of those. Each one of these main themes also had associated obstacles, which I discuss in Chapter 8.

Relational Security, Connectedness, and Trust

All participants reported feeling more compersion and less jealousy toward their partners when they felt secure, connected, and trusting in their relationships with them. As Jo, a 29-year-old software engineer, put it simply,

"The more secure you are with a specific partner, the more happiness you can feel for them, because the threat has been diminished." Fittingly, relational security is emphasized in most books on CNM as a core element of successful non-monogamy.

In *Polysecure: Attachment, Trauma and Consensual Nonmonogamy*, Jessica Fern provided a roadmap for how CNM folks can create securely attached bonds with multiple partners. Remarkably, her framework circumvents couple-centricity and mononormativity—which is a pitfall of virtually all other adult romantic attachment literature. She emphasized that "adults do and can have multiple securely attached relationships"[19]—and that secure functioning promotes compersion among other benefits:

> When secure functioning is at play within CNM relationships, partners communicate well, trust each other, stick to their agreements and discuss wanted changes. They tend to have more compersion for their partners, they act respectfully towards their metamours and while they still do experience jealousy or envy, they are also able to support each other in the process. Jealousy becomes an opportunity for increased clarity and connection and it doesn't take them or their relationships down.[20]

Fern's quote confirmed that the presence of compersion does not imply that jealousy is absent—but that in secure CNM relationships, jealousy is handled in productive ways that do not cause irreparable harm to relationships. This echoes the concept of non-mononormative jealousy I proposed in Chapter 1, as well as the coexistence of jealousy and compersion I described in Chapter 6.

What is necessary for CNM folks to create secure relationships? Fern created the acronym HEARTS to outline the different conditions that generate and maintain security in multiple attachment-based relationships. HEARTS stands for: (a) *Here* (are you here and present with me?); (b) *Expressed delight* (am I special and valuable to you?); (c) *Attunement* (are you tuned into my world?); (d) *Ritual and routines* (do we have reliable structures and rhythms to sustain our relationship?); (e) *Turning toward after conflict* (do we successfully repair attachment ruptures and come back to one another after conflict?); and (f) *Secure attachment with Self* (do I have my own back?). The first five letters cover the relational aspect of CNM security, and the "S" refers to the individual aspect (I described this in the last section on inner security). I believe Fern's is an excellent model for CNM folks and their counselors to understand how to best cultivate security, connectedness, and trust within CNM relationships, and I consider it synergistic to the model of compersion I outline in this book.

From my participant interviews, several factors emerged as keys to establishing a sense of security, connectedness, and trust in their CNM relationships: (a) health of the relationship and satiation; (b) open communication and transparency; (c) reassurance strategies; (d) going at the pace of the slower person; (e) building tolerance; and (f) relationship agreements. Each theme is described and illustrated next.

Relationship Health and Satiation

Members of a relationship needed to feel that their relational cups were full, and that there was more than enough love to go around before they could experience the impulse of generosity at the root of compersion. In other words, feeling cherished and abundantly cared for by their partners was a condition for feeling supportive of their metamour relationships. If they felt deprived of love, time, or other meaningful resources, the idea of their partner connecting romantically or sexually with another person would typically be more threatening than joy-inducing, as it would feel as if their partner took away an already sparse amount of food from their plate to give it to someone else. When asked what promoted compersion for her, Lisa explained,

> I would say that the first factor would be the health of the relationship. I had times where I've had partners where as our relationship started to deteriorate or have challenges, they would try to use other relationships as sort of an escape, and there tended to be more jealousy and negative feelings than compersion because it is actually taking something away from our relationship, the energy or the time that they would devote to our relationship is now going someplace else. And that's not something I can really celebrate.

Indeed, the emergence of compersion depended on participants feeling emotionally fulfilled in their relationships. This sense of "satiation" would then create spontaneous feelings of generosity, or "giving desire." Michael epitomized this concept by explaining how grateful he was to his nesting partner Gisele for supporting him financially as he was earning a much lower income as a musician and artist. The experience of having been on the receiving end of sacrifices she made for him compelled him to want to do all he could to "make her happy," including enthusiastically supporting her intimate relationships with others:

> I had been incredibly lucky in that I partnered with someone who believed in my music so much that she would work a full-time job and let me stumble around trying to sell the music . . . from the start, she has always believed in it and thought that it was more important than us making a whole lot of money. So, how that relates to compersion, is in the sense that I want to do anything I can to make her happy.

Michael's sense of being deeply cared for and supported by Gisele elicited two sentiments: first, a sense of safety within the relationship, making it less threatening to witness her intimate engagement with someone else; second, it evoked gratitude for what he received, eliciting a desire to give back and see Gisele happy. The combination of these two sentiments created a fertile ground for compersion.

Feeling cared for in a relationship also revealed a perception of equity and shared power—a sense that both members of the initial relationship are on the same team, sharing power and responsibilities in a way that works for both of them. Hypatia from Space's and Deri's explorations of the role of power dynamics in the experience of compersion are helpful perspectives to bring into this discussion. Hypatia from Space asserted that each partner, to feel compersion, must rest assured in their own sense of personal power and agency.[21] A nonequitable relationship, or one that is perceived as such, would thus be infertile ground for compersion. This echoes Deri's explanation of how the perception of relational security in CNM dynamics is closely related to perceptions of power—which impacts one's propensity to experience compersion or jealousy:

> If you perceive that your partner is unconditionally committed to you, you may be less likely to experience jealousy. The reaction is based on one's perception of the power dynamics in one's relationship(s), possibly independent of the partner's behaviour. The reverse can also occur: one's insecurity can be based solely on one's perception of a lack of power, again potentially independent of the partner's actions.[22]

Deri emphasized how perceptions of power dynamics may not always coincide with a partner's actions, but still deeply impact one's embodied sense of relational security. To this point, people with insecure attachment styles and trauma may find it more challenging to feel secure and empowered, and therefore to access compersion in their CNM relationships. However, when partners intentionally team up to cultivate secure love and attachment, in big and small ways, their relationship can flourish and become "a competition of generosity" (a phrase attributed to pop singer Madonna), and thus become a fertile ground for compersion.

Open Communication and Transparency

Compersion is rooted in empathy—which fundamentally requires access to relevant information as well as a sense of emotional inclusion. All my participants named open, honest, and effective communication as a linchpin of compersion. A spirit of transparency—although enacted with different styles and preferences—promoted a sense of connection, security, and trust. Multiple popular and academic authors noted that while the clear, empathetic, and extensive communication necessary for successful CNM can be challenging and time-consuming, it is worth the effort.[23] My study participants would concur that open communication not only prevents misunderstandings or feelings of exclusion but also provides a necessary vehicle for compersion, as a form of positive empathy, to arise. To illustrate, Tyrone, a 38-year-old facilitator, explained:

> To me, transparency creates safety. I like to have partnerships where we get to experience ALL of each other. Like, I literally want you to tell me things that you feel that you shouldn't say. It allows me to see you more, and I want to see you and hold you as much as possible. So transparency has, I've learned, has even stopped my anxious attachment, when my anxious attachment start to boil up. What helps me is the clarity, I need to talk and be clear. I need to be transparent with you . . . transparency and communication is the key to having the level of compersion that's necessary in a romantic sexual relationship or commitment.

Similarly, Sabrina expressed that openness and honesty were necessary for her to experience compersion:

> I feel compersion when I'm feeling that he's sharing with me, that it's something that we're sharing, it's actually a very intimate thing that we are sharing together. If it was a situation that he was keeping from me, then I would feel very differently.

While my participants highly valued honesty and open communication across the board, it was very clear that intentional secrecy would lead to feelings of unsafety and exclusion.

However, not everyone needed the same type or amount of communication to feel safe and included. Some participants wanted to hear an abundance of details in regard to metamour relationships; others did not enjoy hearing many details. Furthermore, different members of the participants' polycules sometimes had different needs and preferences as it pertains to privacy—which makes it a complex task to establish guidelines of communication that take into consideration each person's safety and privacy needs. Thus, having intentional rules of disclosure was critical. For example, Lisa explained that because she liked to hear a lot of details about her partner's other intimate relationship(s), having a partner who did not like to communicate as much as she did was difficult:

> I tend to like to know a lot more details than some people do. . . . I want to know about everything in your life. So if I'm coming to the table with that expectation, and I'm sharing all these things, and my partner doesn't have that expectation or doesn't have that interest, it can be very challenging. . . . People who don't like to share much, it's harder for me to feel compersion for, because I don't know what is special and enjoyable about that connection. I need to feel it with you. So that, you know, to use the stereotypical "Oh, well, I just have my date," and then that's it, you know, "Oh, it was good." That's all I get? It's kind of harder to really get into it with them; a little level of detail or perspective that they're willing to share makes a big difference.

Lisa's reflection on the style of communication that would most stoke her compersion was evocative of Deri's research, who gave examples of communication agreements her participants shared, such as "tell me only the necessary details," "tell me before you do anything," "tell me within twenty-four hours after the act," and "tell me all the juicy details."[24] Whatever agreements folks made around disclosure, creating consensual rules and boundaries around that communication contributed to creating an atmosphere of emotional safety and mutual respect, which was critical for compersion to emerge.

Reassurance Strategies

Compersion was contingent on experiencing a felt sense of security within the relationship. Maintaining this sense of security, while diminishing any perception of threat to the relationship, could be enhanced by implementing intentional reassurance strategies. This was relevant whether participants had a hierarchical CNM relationship structure (primary versus secondary relationships) or a nonhierarchical one (solo polyamory, relationship anarchy, or nonhierarchical forms of polyamory and open relationships). Participants employed different strategies to foster a sense of security based on their unique relational dynamics and preferred ways to feel seen and loved.

For example, Michael, a 67-year-old musician, made an agreement with his partners that it was always okay to ask for verbal reassurance—and this was instrumental in fostering compersion:

> We learned that one of our rules through all of that is that we can always ask for reassurance, it's always fair and fine to ask for reassurance. And, you do that a few times, and people reassure you, and the fears kind of start to drop off.

For Tyrone, having "containers around emotions" to feel witnessed was also key to fostering relational security, even when jealousy, insecurity, or grief came up:

> The gift in that relationship was that he was so supportive, in that we had containers around emotions. I could be held and seen in my pitiful moments, in my grief. I'm not gonna do that all day. But I could have a container for five minutes where I'm holding eye contact with my lover and just crying and wailing and saying the things that I need to say. . . . It's just that I need to be able to be witnessed in the feeling that I have.

What these participant quotes reveal is simply that people have to feel loved by their partners before they can experience compersion. Reassurance strategies functioned to remind partners that love was still present—even amid challenging emotions.

Preferences for different reassurance strategies often correlated with the individuals' preferred "love languages" (LLs)[25]—thus, it may be helpful to know one's LLs as well as one's partner's to craft the most effective reassurance strategies possible. According to Chapman's model, people use five primary LLs: words of affirmation (loving messages), quality time (time spent engaged in shared activities), gifts (tokens of affection), acts of service (help with tasks, like cooking a meal), and physical touch (from hand holding to sexual intercourse). Furthermore, people tend to have one or two favorite LLs and often show love to their partners using their own preferred LL; however, partners who desire higher quality relationships—and in this case, more reassurance—need to express love according to their partners' preferred LLs. Accordingly, Chapman argues that romantic partners should fill one another's "love tanks" by speaking their partner's LLs. Although Chapman wrote this theory from a mononormative lens, it seems quite fitting in the context of creating effective reassurance strategies—and thus fostering security, connectedness, and trust within CNM relationships.

Going at the Pace of the Slower Person

For those who opened up a previously monogamous relationship, moving caringly and progressively from monogamy to non-monogamy was key to ensuring buy-in from all parties—which in turn was a prerequisite to all parties experiencing compersion. Within couples transitioning to CNM, there was often one person more eager to be CNM, or a "more poly" partner—and another person feeling more tentative or resistant. If the "more poly" person moved too fast without their partner's sincere consent, the "less poly" person's trust and sense of security could be diminished as they might feel excluded, unloved, or left behind.

Thus, going at the pace of the slower person aided many of my participants in cultivating the sense of safety, connectedness, and trust that was necessary for compersion to occur. This could take different forms. Some couples, for example, had begun their CNM journeys through swinging before entering polyamorous arrangements that included stronger emotional bonds with other partners, which had allowed them to ease into CNM progressively. For others, dating as a couple and/or having group sex had been a stepping stone toward both partners dating independently. For example, in the early stages of their move toward non-monogamy, Diane agreed to James' request to be present in the room when she would have sex with another man—which sometimes turned into group sex. They expressed that this course of action eased James' fear of the unknown and was instrumental in his process of initially feeling safe and included. They later started to date separately, and James' compersion blossomed. Diane explained how being patient with James in the early stages of CNM, as they progressively moved from monogamy to polyamory, had been necessary to create a fertile terrain for them to later experience compersion:

> I think for the partner who wants their partner to experience compersion for them, your job is to take baby steps and allow them to sit with things at their pace. I think I went to compersion pretty quickly. But he took a lot longer time, so I had to really manage my relationships at his comfort level to get where we are today. Because if I had just gotten full out, you know, I'm going to go find guys and fuck them, I don't know if we'd be here today.

Diane, as the "more poly" partner in this situation, had to withstand the frustration of not going at her own preferred pace to preserve the sense of being on the same team as James.

One caveat to going at the pace of the slower person, however, was that the "less poly" person had to be sufficiently on board with non-monogamy to allow gradual progress toward a common vision. In cases where the "less poly" partner is very resistant to the idea of CNM, perhaps "poly under duress" (PUD), the two partners' intentions and desires might be too far apart to bridge. As a relationship coach, I have often seen a "more poly" partner attempting to drag their CNM-reluctant partner into coaching, desiring compersion from them. I typically have to help the "more poly" person adjust their expectations in these situations, letting them know that as long as their reluctant partner does not genuinely get on board with CNM from a place of personal power and agency, they will most likely not experience compersion. This relates to the first factor in this chapter—ideological commitment to CNM values—where I explained how each partner has to buy into CNM from a place of fullhearted consent before compersion can arise. In other words, there is no "compersion pill"!

Building Tolerance

Hand-in-hand with the previous section of going at the pace of the slower person was the importance of progressively building emotional "tolerance," or habituation, vis-à-vis new non-monogamous behaviors. This process would happen over time and through exposure and repetition. Behaviors and activities that were initially unknown or scary, such as a partner going on a date or having sex with another person, became normalized as these occurrences would time after time prove to not cause negative changes to the preexisting relationship. This process generated a sense of trust and safety on which compersion could be built. When asked how compersion could be learned, Diane explained,

> It's like building a muscle. . . . It's being exposed to it, kind of to say, "Okay, James, I keep coming back home, I keep loving you, I keep reinforcing that you're number one," you just build that tolerance level up, like "hey, she's not going anywhere." She's gonna keep coming back. And I think that's all it is, it's just time. And reinforcing the relationship helps. That's all, it just takes time.

Colette, a 41-year-old sex and relationship coach, had a similar experience. She explained that her jealousy had "faded over time," and how certain CNM contexts that originally registered as threatening to her sense of security in her relationship—such as her husband taking a weekend away with another lover—now landed as normal, and even joyful, occurrences:

> In the beginning he had done a weekend away. That was harder because there wasn't a return home at the end of the evening. I'm much better with that now, like "Whoo! I got a whole weekend to myself!" At the beginning maybe there was bigger jealousy there. It's funny, it fades over time, the difficult moments.

These quotes about tolerance and habituation leading to compersion mirror much of the literature on CNM. In her seminal doctoral study on polyamory, Leanna Wolfe recounted witnessing a similar transformative process from jealousy to compersion where "[s]ometimes hot buttons simply get worn down. While initially the thought (and experience) of sharing one's lover with another person may be thoroughly revolting, eventually one has yelled and screamed and cried so much that the initial charge fades."[26] Similarly, well-known CNM author and counselor Kathy Labriola commented that in many long-term CNM relationships, simply staying the course typically yields a sense of safety and compersion over time—or at least a "feeling of neutrality":

> If I'm with a partner and they keep having other relationships, but they keep coming back, my relationship with them gets more and more stable and secure over time. It just would naturally engender more of a feeling of neutrality, at least, if not some amount of like, "well, I can see that my partner is really benefiting from being in this relationship so I can have that kind of generous feeling of love towards them having this."[27]

In sum, these quotes show that people's willingness and ability to tolerate the initial discomforts of CNM long enough to get used to a new paradigm of relating, as well as to gather evidence that their partner is not intent on leaving or demoting them, often softens their worst fears and paves the way to compersion. Next, I turn to the importance of relationship agreements.

Relationship Agreements

Having and respecting specific relationship agreements helped most participants mitigate jealousy triggers and manage the risks that came with CNM. Agreements would include parameters around safer sex practices, transparency about sexually transmitted infection (STI) status and disclosure, scope and timing of communication about other relationships and attractions, privacy, schedules, and other topics. In particular, the multistep process of identifying specific fear triggers, building agreements to contain those to a manageable level, respecting those agreements, and being open to renegotiating agreements over time helped my participants cultivate the quality of relational security, connection, and trust that was foundational to the emergence of compersion.

To illustrate, Jo explained how they and their husband came to develop agreements around safe sex but then modified them over time because of changing circumstances around ways to mitigate the risk of HIV:

> Yeah, we've actually changed agreements over time. When we first started dating, we were like, free for all, no rules! And then I was like, wait, some things are making me feel weird. So we did have safety rules, like using condoms unless otherwise agreed upon. And then we introduced a rule for a while, that before we had sex with someone, like anything beyond just touching, so oral sex or penetrative sex, we had to introduce the other person to our partner, so everyone felt comfortable. And we also just had to tell each other everything. So now, we've changed one rule, we don't have to introduce anymore, but we just have to introduce as soon as it's convenient. . . . And the reason why we changed that was is because we went on PrEP, which is a medication you can take that prevents you from contracting HIV. . . . Now we just feel a lot more safe because we have this pill.

As Jo demonstrated, CNM agreements often evolved according to participants' particular needs and circumstances. Respecting agreements, while also giving one another enough grace to go through trial and error when it came to finding agreements that would work for everyone—was a key part of the process of cultivating trust and security.

Kassia Wosick's research, which provided robust data on CNM relationship agreements, was echoed in my findings.[28] Her survey of 343 polyamorous individuals indicated that an overwhelming majority of polyamorists have some kind of relationship agreements about which extradyadic activities are or are not allowed with others—these agreements being either verbal (65%), case by case (15%), written (8%), or "don't ask, don't tell" (1%).[29] She argued that these agreements were an expression of agentic fidelity specific to polyamorists—a "more individualized form of loyalty [that] requires self-knowledge and the ability and choice to express one's needs, desires, and boundaries to a partner."[30] Wosick's research confirms what participants in the present study expressed: that relationship agreements are a necessary component in establishing closeness, cohesion, and a sense of security that is achieved by emphasizing a *"chosen* loyalty through knowing which rules to establish, choosing when and how to follow them, and effectively articulating among partners a renegotiation of the rules if they are broken."[31]

In sum, having clear agreements and respecting them was a foundational aspect of creating the level of relational security that made compersion possible for CNM folks. Fluidity, intentionality, and overtness in the creation and communication of these agreements were a feature of good CNM etiquette—which in turn enhanced trust and security among partners and metamours. These agreements often included how metamours would be integrated into the existing relational ecosystems—a topic I turn to next.

Positive Integration of Partner's Other Relationship(s)

Having a positive outlook toward metamour relationships was a crucial element that facilitated compersion for my participants. The multifaceted experience of "feeling good" about those relationships—the multiple facets of which I explore next—allowed my participants to gain a sense of positive integration of these connections into their lives, as opposed to feeling that these metamour relationships stood in opposition, competition, or disjointedness vis-à-vis the rest of their lives and partnerships. This positive integration facilitated the emergence of genuine care, love, empathy, and compersion—attitudinal and embodied—toward metamours and their partner's connections to them.

The integration of metamour relationships had a lot to do with feeling positively connected—rather than disconnected—vis-à-vis these relationships. Feeling disconnected often indicated a sense of exclusion, judgment, mistrust, jealousy, negative comparison, envy, or other dynamics that worked against a sense of connection. Conversely, compersion is based on positive empathy: at its core, it relies on trust, collaboration, gratitude, and a sense of being on the same team.

My use of the words "integration" and "connection" in this section should not be taken to mean that my participants needed to be physically present on their partner's dates, hear every detail of their connection to their metamour, or even be friends with their metamours to be compersive. Compersion could arise without having personally met a metamour. However, one had to have a sufficiently positive *interpretation* of a metamour relationship to foster positive empathy and gratitude.

What specific factors led my participants to positively integrate their metamour relationships into their minds, hearts, and lives? Interviewees reported five main factors that fostered this: (1) positive connection with metamours, (2) positive regard toward metamours, (3) boundaries with metamours, (4) flexible sexual orientation, and (5) group sex.

Positive Connection with Metamours

My study participants associated a positive connection to their metamour(s) with increased compersion. Trust and friendship toward a metamour created a sense of being on the same team with them, rather than viewing them as rivals. These positive connections also promoted a sense of safety and reduced threat—first, in mitigating the fear of the unknown, and second, in fostering trust that their partner was not going to get hurt or snatched away by a metamour relationship. For example, Michael said that although he could feel some degree of compersion when he didn't personally know a metamour, it was much easier to experience it, and to a higher degree, when he knew, respected and trusted a metamour:

> We've been with people that we didn't know very well. And I've been fine with it. And knowing that she is happy about it makes me happy to a degree, right? On the other hand, I would much rather know the person, and have some sense of what they're about.

Similarly, Jo felt a lot of compersion for their husband and metamours when they felt emotionally included and built friendships with them. They described a relationship with such a metamour:

> I feel really included. And that's how I like it to be. If I didn't feel included, then I'd feel a little weird. I don't need to be, like, part of every date or anything like that. But, you know, he's dating a woman right now, and we're texting a lot. And that's really fun. And we're going to go to a movie on Saturday night together because we both like horror movies, and he doesn't.

Both of these quotes show that having a positive connection and a sense of closeness with a metamour promotes security, trust, and connection—which then turns into compersion toward that particular metamour relationship.

Having a genuine connection with one's metamour, in combination with a lack of perceived threat, was one of the main ways that emotional closeness and integration would manifest. To this point, researchers Flicker and Sancier-Barbosa recently found, in a quantitative study with 255 participants seeking to identify the main predictors of compersion, that "the desire to be close and closeness to one's metamour were two of the most powerful predictors of compersion."[32] This stood in contrast with most other factors analyzed in their study—factors that previous qualitative research had identified as relevant, but that when put to the quantitative test, only correlated weakly with the occurrence of compersion. This new data emphasizes the critical importance that metamour relationships carry in the "compersion equation." However, Flicker and Sancier-Barbosa also noted that "the causal nature of this relationship is unclear and likely bidirectional":

> Although being close to one's metamour could facilitate the experience of compersion, it also likely that the experience of compersion facilitates close relations with one's metamour. Part of this relationship may be accounted for by the fact that some participants were intimately involved with their metamours and intimate involvement predicted high levels of compersion.[33]

While some participants in my study brought up their erotic involvement with metamours as a factor facilitating compersion in the context of group sex (a theme I explore later in this section), this was not very common. Most of the time, interviewees named a sense of emotional comfort and trust toward particular metamours or metamour relationships as the more determinant factor in their propensity to experience compersion. Having a positive regard toward one's metamour was also an important piece of the puzzle.

Positive Regard toward Metamours

How my participants viewed their metamour(s) would impact how they felt about their partner's relationship with them, and therefore, be a significant predictor of compersion. On the one hand, admiring one's metamour typically enhanced compersion, but only in contexts that were also low threat. In other words, participants would evaluate metamours along the axes of worthiness (e.g., likeability, trustworthiness, admirability, maturity, positive contribution to the relational ecosystem) and threat (e.g., "might this metamour snatch away my partner or otherwise cause harm to the relational ecosystem?").

The evaluation of each metamour along these two axes would greatly impact one's propensity to experience compersion. Everything else being equal, I found the outcomes of metamour perception to follow these general patterns as shown in Table 7.1.

In other words, if the metamour was seen in a favorable light, and did not seem to pose a threat, they would more easily be met with compersion by my participants. A "threat assessment" of one's metamour could include questions such as,

- Does this person seem competitive or collaborative in this CNM context?
- Is this person versed and experienced with CNM etiquette and philosophy, or do they come from a completely monogamous background or apply a mononormative lens to this relationship?

Table 7.1. Perception of Metamour Worthiness and Threat's Impact on Compersion

Perceived Worthiness/Threat	Level of Compersion
Metamour perceived as high worthiness/ low threat	Highest compersion
Metamour perceived as high worthiness/ high threat	Less compersion due to high perceived threat
Metamour perceived as low worthiness/ low threat	Less compersion due to low perceived worthiness
Metamour perceived as low worthiness/ high threat	Lowest compersion

- Does this person appear to wish that my partner were single and could give them more time, attention, and resources?
- Is this person treating me with respect and warmth, or are they avoiding me, snubbing me, or competing with me?
- Is this person in love with someone else, or are they directing their entire romantic and sexual attention toward our hinge partner?
- How in love is my partner with them, and how do I perceive the quality and intensity of this love in comparison to their love for me?
- Does my partner express more excitement or admiration about my metamour than they express about me?
- Is my partner spending more time or resources with them than with me, or doing activities with them that I have been wanting to do with my partner?
- Does this person trigger a particular sense of comparison or insecurity for me—for example, gifted with certain attributes that I perceive myself lacking?
- Does this person carry certain social privileges (at levels such as race, age, socioeconomic status, or gender) that I don't?

This list is not exhaustive, but it paints a picture of how CNM people might assess whether or not a metamour could pose a threat to an existing relationship—the result of which would impact how much and what type of compersion one may have, and how easily it may arise. There is a complex map of factors at play determining whether a person may have "positive regard" toward a metamour—but in short, the best-case scenario is when a metamour appears likable, trustable, compatible to the polycule, and respectful of boundaries—while also not representing a threat given the earlier questions.

A wonderful illustration of these complex dynamics was provided by Laura-Lee, a 32-year-old anthropologist. When I asked her about how she felt about her metamours, she contrasted her sense of admiration for Rose, one of Martin's partners whom she considered very mature and worthy of respect, with another metamour, Katalina, whom she did not feel brought positive value to the table. I quote Laura-Lee at length to show why Rose elicited more compersion than Katalina for her:

Martin's very first significant partner was someone named Rose . . . she was a lot older than me, and very mature and experienced. And, frankly, I felt flattered that Martin wanted to date this older, more mature person, that she and I were equals here in this relationship, that there was something in her that Martin also sort of recognized in me, because we're both very mature people. I'm a very mature person. And so it was like this sort of mirror moment where I recognized some of my skills and abilities in this other woman and I recognized how we were both contributing positively to Martin's life. . . .

    Katalina is the only partner of Martin's I have felt uncomfortable about. We still had tabletop poly, where we would have dinner together and hang out, and whatever. But I was really concerned about her. Because she was so much younger than Martin, and was not very experienced, and seemed really kind of emotionally immature. And I was concerned about what this said about the way Martin was relating in his private life. And it kind of hooked into a worry that I had that Martin wants me to be his inferior because this woman, Katalina, was clearly Martin's inferior. And so I had trouble . . . I had trouble having compersion with her. I mean, I still really valued what she brought into the relationship. And I absolutely valued that she and Martin cared for each other so deeply. But because I didn't see her as my equal, it was hard for me to cultivate those feelings of compersion with her. So as compared to Rose, for example, where I saw her as being my equal, I saw her as being this, powerful, mature woman. And so it was really easy for me to sort of relate to her with value and joy.

In this instance, Laura-Lee contrasted two metamours, Rose and Katalina, under a few lenses: first, the way that each of their personal qualities and relational dynamics with Martin shaped her meaning-making of those situations, impacting favorably or unfavorably her self-esteem (which feeds into the previously explored theme of inner security) and her esteem for Martin; and second, the perception of these relationships as being additive (Rose) or subtractive (Katalina) to Martin's life and her life—which feeds into the upcoming theme of perception of benefits from partner's other relationship(s). Therefore, she had more compersion toward Rose than toward Katalina. It is worth noting how several themes, as well as the intersectional factor of age, interweave in this situation. I explore my participants' evaluation of whether metamours represent a threat to a valued relationship in more length in Chapter 8.

Boundaries with Metamours

Developing trust toward metamours implied having consensual boundaries with them—which would create a sense of safety, mutual respect, and being on the same team. Communicating and respecting one another's boundaries was a central feature of good etiquette when dating non-monogamously, and as a prerequisite for compersion. Often, partners created boundaries in the spirit of protecting the needs of preexisting relationships, and my participants viewed the failure to honor boundaries as a symptom of a zero-sum monogamous ideology. To illustrate, James described that his compersion toward one of Diane's lovers was enabled by an embodied sense of this metamour's respect for their existing boundaries, as well as an agentic sense of his own boundaries, which fostered trust and safety:

> I never felt that he was trying to push me out of the way. . . . I think the issue that provides the basis for compersion is people who seem to have a good sense of boundaries, that their boundaries are clearly defined, and they adhere to those boundaries, as not something they're just telling you, but something that they actually embody and provide, sort of active support for the boundaries that they described.

The opposite experience—having a metamour disregard boundaries and/or attempt to pull someone away from their preexisting relationships in the attempt to become monogamous with them—was colloquially known as the "cowboys" phenomenon. I describe this attitude in Chapter 8.

Flexible Sexual Orientation

Having a "flexible sexual orientation" (bisexuality, pansexuality, homoflexibility, or heteroflexibility) made developing a sense of intimacy, trust, and connection easier for some participants when polycules included individuals of different genders. A vast majority (77%) of my sample did not identify as hetero or homosexual, and some of them expressed that this flexibility fostered their ability to feel compersion. For example, Michael explained,

> I don't know how straight people do this. [*laughs*] . . . The fact that Cedric and I can make out sometimes, and have fun, makes it a lot easier. . . . Part of the compersion is the sense of wanting to dive in with them, even just having the choice of that, you know, and not feeling like I'm being denied something. . . . I just think that there's an element of the way American straight men relate to each other . . . that makes that difficult.

Indeed, it is well documented in the CNM literature that polyamory is more common among bisexual and pansexual people.[34] In a study of the intersectional coming out processes of bisexual polyamorists in Italy, Gusmano related one participant's account of considering bisexuality as a driver for polyamory: "Bisexuality is something that already leads you to wonder more about exclusivity, basically. And so this not a causal link but rather a driver."[35] This statement echoes accounts from some of my own participants, such as Teresa, a 54-year-old nanny:

> I was married for a long time, 18 years. And then, when I was divorced, I had said to myself, well, I figured I was always curious about being with women. I decided to explore that part of me, so I dated a few women. And then when I wanted to have a relationship, I was like, well, I don't really want to not have women, but I really like men. So I got in a relationship with a man and said, "Hey, well, for getting in this relationship, you need to know that I'm going to want to date women as well."

Teresa's first experience of compersion was while being involved in a sexual situation with both a man and a woman—a situation in which the sense of expansion of personal boundaries may have been enhanced by her fluid sexual attraction that included both genders. Tyrone had a similar experience:

> I think my bisexuality has been one of my biggest "whys," I feel that non-monogamy has been a natural way of being. I've always been aware of being attracted to men and women. The story of ownership has never clicked for me, because I was always desiring two things. I always wanted to have both. And I can see that there's things that I cannot give someone because I don't have all genders in my body. So, immediate awareness that if I were to date someone that desired that, I can't provide those things and I would like them to have those things.

While it seems clear that being bisexual or pansexual is a strong predictor for CNM and compersion, being anywhere else on the LGBTQ+ spectrum (gay, lesbian, trans, genderqueer, etc.) also appears to facilitate compersion because coming out as a sexual minority of any type paves the path to questioning mononormativity, which in turn, promotes compersion. I further explore the intersection of sexual orientation, gender, and compersion in Chapters 10 and 11.

Group Sex

Group sex was a way some participants felt included and positively connected with their partners and metamours together, which could be a compersion catalyst. While group sex certainly promoted erotic compersion (as described in Chapter 2), my participants also emphasized the effects of group sex on emotional intimacy and empathy.

For some people, group sex had been a stepping stone to more independent forms of non-monogamy. For example, Diane and James had begun opening their relationship by having group sex, which had set the stage for becoming more comfortable having separate lovers. This promoted a sense of inclusion and safety before approaching the deeper layers of sexual disentanglement that individual dating required.

For others, group sex was a regular practice that promoted compersion. Tyrone emphasized the stimulating role of group sex in his compersive journey by promoting "intimacy and connection":

> I live a life of ethical hedonism. I have a lot of group sex. . . . I will plan a day to be, like, we're just gonna have a group sexual experience where you get to have sex with these people, or get tied up with these people. I've done that for my partners. For me, it's a level of intimacy and connection.

Similarly, for Michael, who is part of a "fourple," group sex was a common occurrence with his three partners. He reported that the practice made compersion blossom among them. Michael credited his bisexuality and the sense of "wanting to dive in" with his partners' other relationships: "As they're making out in the next room, it makes me smile. It makes me want to go in and join them, and sometimes that's fine too." For both Michael and Tyrone, the proximity, emotional closeness, and erotic turn-on that group sex provided could facilitate empathy and trust building among members of a relational ecosystem—thus facilitating compersion.

In sum, the positive integration of metamour relationships could take many forms—and it was a highly significant factor that facilitated compersion. Next, I turn to the perception of benefits from a partner's other relationship(s).

Perception of Benefits from Partner's Other Relationship(s)

Gratitude was one of two significant components that answered my original research question, "What is compersion?" Gratitude was derived from the perception that a partner's other relationship yielded benefits—whether for them individually, for their partner(s), or for their relationship(s). This perception of benefits would be a source of positive regard about a particular metamour relationship, and yielded gratitude, which was a significant component in compersive attitudes and feelings. When the gratitude was greater than any sense of threat, compersion would be the dominant experience. As CNM counselor and author Kathy Labriola eloquently stated, "Compersion grows in those situations where everyone benefits . . . where the benefits outweigh whatever fears and insecurities the jealousy is being sparked by."[36]

In Chapter 3, I described each of the themes my participants emphasized as sources of gratitude: (a) richer emotional and sexual life; (b) richer social life; (c) authentic emotional expression; (d) freedom from fear, emotional congruence, and pride; (e) relief from guilt; (f) growth; and (g) enhanced relationship satisfaction. These were the main ways in which interviewees perceived benefits from their partners' other relationships, bringing about gratitude and, thus, facilitating compersion.

For the sake of space, I thus refer readers to Chapter 3 for these descriptions and relevant participant stories. In Chapter 8, I describe the opposite theme that blocks compersion—the lack of perceived benefits from a partner's other relationship(s). Now, I turn to social factors that promote compersion.

GROUPING 3: SOCIAL FACTORS

Human beings do not conduct their intimate relationships in a vacuum. They are deeply influenced by the communities and cultural contexts that surround them, through which they learn about what are "normal," "expected," or "valid" behaviors and feelings. Because CNM folks conduct their relationships within the larger societal context of mononormativity (except for very few exceptions around the world), they greatly benefit from associating with subcultures of CNM-inclusive people who can validate and normalize their own identities as non-monogamous.

This happens through participation in social networks where CNM is normalized rather than stigmatized, having role models, consuming CNM-positive media, and celebrating one's identity through pride. These elements were significant factors in my participants' accounts of developing compersion. Thus, the last major grouping of factors impacting compersion was social, and one overarching theme emerged in that category: community belonging.

I expand further on the social category later in Chapter 10, and I explain how the process of coming out as non-monogamous plays an important role in the emergence of compersion. In Chapter 11, I explore how the social positionality variables of age, disability, gender, sexual orientation, race, and socioeconomic status impact compersion. Here, I describe how community belonging functions to allow CNM folks to construct social identities that validate their relational styles and philosophies within mononormative societies—and how this process facilitates compersion.

Community Belonging

Given a societal context where only 4–5% of people engage in CNM relationships (in the United States)[37] and these relationships are still highly stigmatized,[38] it was extremely valuable for my participants to have strong CNM social networks and role models, as well as literature and media, to support their identity development and validation as CNM.

Indeed, CNM resources and communities (e.g., formal interest groups, activist groups, informal social networks, literature, and media that portray CNM as a valid relationship style) were critical to help normalize CNM and support pro-compersion narratives. This process enabled CNM pride to emerge, and this pride was conducive to compersion. Many participants noted that compersion emerged from a process of unlearning monogamous myths and assumptions, which was facilitated by community belonging. Four elements composed this category: (1) CNM/polypride and activism, (2) CNM social networks, (3) media and literature, and (4) role models.

CNM/Polypride and Activism

People involved in CNM relationships constitute a socially marginalized minority group, and as with any other minority group, CNM-identified individuals can benefit greatly from bonding with and being exposed to other similarly identified people. Connecting with CNM community reinforced participants' CNM sense of identity and pride, which helped them unlearn monogamous conditioning and in turn created a more fertile emotional terrain for compersion to emerge.

Similar to the gay pride movement in the 1970s, the CNM/poly community served to reduce shame and marginalization for CNM-identified individuals by supporting and validating non-monogamy as a valid and healthy relational orientation. Participating in the CNM community normalized and celebrated the freedom and ability to have multiple simultaneous emotional and sexual connections outside the couple-centric paradigm. Having to overcome the obstacles of mononormativity and stigmatization to be true to oneself and one's sexuality seemed to have a dual effect: on the one hand, it could make it more difficult for people to embrace their identity fully, but on the other, it could reinforce a sense of accomplishment, strength, and radical commitment to one's truth and convictions—leading to a sense of individual and collective pride.

As I explore more deeply in Chapters 10 and 11, compersion could then become part of someone's strategy of resistance from oppressive normativities. Not only would CNM folks exercise their agency to not *do* what was expected of them in the relational field, they would also not *feel* what was expected of them. The idea that one could live outside normative realms and withstand social marginalization while also growing into a more generous and fulfilled version of themselves was a hero's journey of sorts for many participants—yielding deep pride which in turn catalyzed compersion.

There was also a political flavor to many participants' narratives of CNM identity development, especially those over 60 years old. Most of them had grown up in conservative and sex-negative environments and generally faced greater obstacles than their younger counterparts to become openly non-monogamous. For example, Simon, who was 83 years old at the time of his first interview (and 87 at the time of the second), had been involved in CNM activism at the national level, an activity that was intertwined with his sense of identity:

> I'm part of a national poly coalition, national poly leaders who are trying to figure out how to make it an overriding umbrella organization to work for polyamory and work toward legal acceptance. . . . We're 20 years behind the gay rights movement for gay marriage.

While not every participant was a CNM activist, I discerned a tangible sense of excitement for greater societal, political, and legal acceptance of CNM lifestyles in a vast majority of participant interviews. Being on the fringe of socially acceptable mores, while experiencing joy and gratitude in their relationships, fostered solidarity, bonding, and pride—which were significant vectors of compersion.[39]

CNM Social Networks

Interviewees frequently mentioned that engaging with the wider CNM community, beyond one's personal relationships or polycule, supported compersion. For one, many participants relayed learning compersion "by example," by virtue of observing other CNM folks behaving compersively toward their partners (see Chapter 12, "Can Compersion Be Learned?" for more detail). Belonging to a subculture of non-monogamy would typically engrain the concept of compersion as a normal desirable way to feel and act, and thus counter the normative narrative of monogamy being the only valid way to love.

Additionally, friendships were often central to my participants' experience of CNM, as these affirmed and normalized their non-monogamous identity and provided support on their relationship journeys. By centering friendships, non-monogamists often challenged *amatonormativity*—the elevation of romantic relationships as more important than all other types of relationships.[40]

For CNM folks, friendships were often deeper, almost family-like, when a sexual connection had either been present in the past, was currently ongoing, or was not out of the question—in contrast to monogamous contexts where intimate partnerships and platonic friendships are viewed as separate categories that should never overlap. Providing mutual aid and support among friends in a CNM paradigm would promote compersion by creating special bonds outside "normal categories" according to mainstream society. This type of solidarity among folks who stand in resistance to mononormative pressures would create opportunities to enrich each other's lives, and thus evoke gratitude and further empathy.

Being part of a strong CNM community was especially important for aging individuals, as the focus of their interpersonal relationships became less about sex and more about friendship. Fred, a 75-year-old retired geneticist who had been polyamorous for almost five decades, explained that two of his lovers had become too physically ill to have sex—but that as far as he was concerned, "it isn't that big a deal. I've had lots of sex. [*laughs*] I wouldn't not have sex, but it isn't the most important thing on my radar. Staying in touch, being friends and being helpful is on my radar."

While CNM social networks were particularly valuable in upper age ranges, they were highly valued for folks at different life stages. For example, Natasha, who had a two-year-old child at the time of her second interview (2022), described her appreciation for being part of a community of other moms who live outside of the monogamous paradigm—the "hot mamas gone wild":

> I have this group of mom friends. And we're all in, like, we wouldn't all call ourselves poly, but we're all in semi-non-monogamous relationships, and we have a Marco Polo channel all together and we call it the "hot mamas gone wild." We all went to a play party, early on in our relationship, and it just turned into this great forum where we vent our struggles with parenting, but then also, it'll be like, "Oh, there's this party going on, and oh, I went on a date with this guy . . ." We're all older moms, in our late thirties, and so it's just like, wow, I love that I have this very niche group of women who really feel what I'm experiencing right now. So I've been really, really grateful for that community.

Having one's "very niche" experience of motherhood while non-monogamous be seen, normalized, and supported by other women in the same situation would facilitate compersion for Natasha by fostering the sense that the paradigm she had chosen was something to be celebrated rather than ashamed of. I explore the intersection of age, stage of life, and compersion in more detail in Chapter 11.

In sum, the majority of participants considered their participation in the CNM community as vitally important. Much like for LGBTQ+ folks, values-based communities of like-minded people often took the role of chosen family. This experience of belonging was instrumental in identity development, which in turn promoted CNM-supportive narratives and behaviors, and made compersion more likely to arise.

Media and Literature

CNM media and literature (including online and social media resources) were particularly helpful with identity development and validation; additionally, they provided a roadmap for folks transitioning from monogamous to CNM lifestyles. For Michael, Robert Heinlein's *Stranger in a Strange Land* had been formative.[41] Natasha had been greatly inspired by Dan Savage's podcasts discussing CNM. Diane and James had read several books such as

Janet Hardy and Dossie Easton's *The Ethical Slut*[42] and Tristan Taormino's *Opening Up*.[43] James explained,

> There was a whole raft of books that we read that helped us. I think it provided a good sort of narrative element for us to sort of center our thoughts around, so it did help to provide basic grounding and various models and various forms of thinking.

Indeed, according to philosopher Ronald de Sousa, even though the culture we grew up in vastly impacts how we respond to different situations, it is possible to reshape our psycho-emotional habits through cultivating new understandings of the world as adults—understandings that are greatly facilitated by art and literature:

> Our repertoire of emotions is learned on the basis of early experience of "paradigm scenarios." These are built up out of simpler responses that are weaved into stories, and are triggered in adult life by situations similar to those in which they were learned. But our acquaintance with art and literature, as well as our general knowledge of the world, is able to reconfigure some of those stories.[44]

Thus, exposure to CNM-supportive narratives was normalizing for my participants, which helped them anchor their sense of identity in CNM values and provided practical advice to overcome challenges specific to their relationship configurations. This helped create a fertile terrain for compersion.

Role Models

Having CNM role models toward whom one felt kinship and admiration was key for many individuals in developing community belonging. For example, Alexis, a 26-year-old professional cuddlist and events program director, explained that they had thought polyamory was not for them until they met healthy role models. When asked when and why they became consensually non-monogamous, they answered,

> It was in the summer of 2015. It was the first time that I came in contact with healthy polyamorous role models. Before that, I was monogamous. At this event called New Culture Summer Camp East I attended, I saw some people like Max Rivers and Elise Rivers who are a married couple who go around and give poly workshops. They attended, and Elise shared about

their third partner. Her name was Jill Sarah. Elise said, "Jill Sarah, I'm so glad that you are in my husband's life. You light him up, he goes to visit you and comes back full and joyful and energized. And I'm so glad that you're in my life too." And that struck me like, wow, I want that. That's amazing. And I saw other healthy poly role models for the very first time. I had seen unhealthy polyamory, and thought, that's not for me.

When Alexis saw compersion being modeled, they understood that it was available to them, and that was the starting point of their CNM journey. This echoes other stories from participants, who recalled that they did not experience compersion until they spent time with other CNM folks who modeled ease around positively integrating different partners' connections in real time.

In sum, having access to supportive CNM resources and community was extremely important for the vast majority of participants' ability and propensity to experience compersion. These accounts confirmed what de Sousa astutely remarked upon:

> Whether you are able to achieve the re-gestalting of a jealousy-triggering scenario into one that instead evokes compersion, will depend in part on what is expected by those around you. It will be a good deal harder if you are surrounded by traditional monogamists . . . who cannot conceive of any possibilities beyond indifference and entitled possessiveness. In that case, you might do well to heed an anecdote involving Charles de Gaulle. Told by an aide that all the latter's friends opposed his plan for Algerian independence, de Galle replied, "Change your friends."[45]

How does community belonging support the individual experience of compersion? Meyer's conceptualization of LGB minority stress processes can help explain this connection.[46] Meyer, who proposed the term minority coping to refer to a "group-level resource, related to the group's ability to mount self-enhancing structures to counteract stigma,"[47] later emphasized the importance of community support in providing sexual minorities with in-group appraisal and validation, as well as access to role models and other resources that support meaning-making and identity-building.[48] This is very congruent with the interviewees' data presented here.

Additionally, Peace found through her examination of polyamorous identity development that connecting with the polyamorous community represented a distinct and critical stage of development.[49] Community was an important source of finding support, information, and dating partners for her participants—with their sense of belonging to a larger community catalyzed by their participation in virtual and in-person interaction with other poly people. To this point, Witherspoon later found that connection to polyamorous/CNM community was a factor of strength and resilience in CNM individuals.[50] Connections to a community of peers conferred added benefits beyond general social support from family, friends, and coworkers by disseminating supportive cultural norms, values, and wisdom. Witherspoon explained that

> in a monogamist culture which devalues CNM and those who practice it, polyamorous or CNM-identified individuals must seek sources of in-group connection and support in order to counteract the negative societal appraisals of their lifestyles. . . . Becoming involved with polyamorous community, such as via reading popular press books,[51] attending community functions, or engaging in online poly/CNM communities, allows access to a wealth of helpful knowledge and terminology.[52]

Witherspoon also found that greater outness about one's CNM practices was positively correlated with both connection to a supportive CNM community, as well as having a positive sense of CNM identity. Having a positive sense of CNM identity seems to positively contribute to participants' experiencing compersion.

In sum, one of the most impactful things CNM folks can do to promote compersion is to join communities where CNM is normalized and celebrated—and where they can feel free to be their full selves through "being out." I explore the relationship between coming out, identity development, and compersion in more depth in Chapter 10.

NOTES

1. Hypatia from Space, 2018, p. 16. Reprinted with permission.
2. Fern, 2020, p. 73.
3. Deri, 2015, p. 46.
4. Ferrer, 2021.
5. For example, Witherspoon & Theodore, 2021.
6. Donaghue, 2015, p. 5.
7. For example, Barratt, 2010.

8. Fern, 2020, p. 197.

9. Fern, 2020, p. 199.

10. Wolfe, 2008, p. 1.

11. For example, Buunk, 1982; Mathes et al., 1985.

12. Ben-Ze'ev, 2022, p. 129.

13. Flicker et al., 2022, p. 3039.

14. For example, Vohs & Baumeister, 2016.

15. Eisenberg, 2010, p. 129.

16. Porges, 2009.

17. For example, McCarty, 2016; Ursin & Eriksen, 2004.

18. See Duma, 2009, for an exploration of trait versus state compersion.

19. Fern, 2020, p. 127.

20. Fern, 2020, p. 127.

21. Hypatia from Space, 2018.

22. Deri, 2015, p. 98.

23. For example, Anapol, 1997; Conley & Moors, 2014; Conley et al., 2017; Hardy & Easton, 2017; Sheff, 2014; Wosick, 2012.

24. Deri, 2015, p. 49.

25. Chapman, 2009.

26. Wolfe, 2003, p. ix.

27. Kathy Labriola, personal communication, October 10, 2022.

28. Wosick-Correa, 2010; Wosick, 2012.

29. Wosick-Correa, 2010, p. 47.

30. Wosick, 2012, p. 150.

31. Wosick, 2012, p. 151.

32. Flicker & Sancier-Barbosa, 2024.

33. Flicker & Sancier-Barbosa, 2024.

34. For example, Barker & Langridge, 2010; Bauer, 2014; Klesse, 2007.

35. Gusmano, 2018, p. 21.

36. Kathy Labriola, personal communication, October 10, 2022.

37. Conley et al., 2013, p. 3.

38. Moors & Ramos, 2022; Witherspoon & Theodore, 2021.

39. On the flipside, it is worth noting that *polypride* often comes hand-in-hand with *monophobia* (Ferrer, 2018)—creating competitive tension between monogamous and polyamorous folks. Conversely, *monopride* usually comes together with *polyphobia*, which has been defined as (conscious or unconscious) fear of or disgust toward non-monogamy. A detailed discussion of polypride was introduced by Halpern (1999) and then extended upon by Ferrer (2018).

40. Brake, 2011.

41. Heinlein, 1961.

42. Hardy and Easton, 2017.

43. Taormino, 2008.

44. de Sousa, 2017, p. 11.
45. de Sousa, 2017, p. 15.
46. Meyer, 2003a, 2003b, 2015.
47. Meyer, 2003b, p. 677.
48. Meyer, 2015.
49. Peace, 2012.
50. Witherspoon, 2018.
51. For example, Easton & Hardy, 2009; Labriola, 2013; Taormino, 2008; Veaux & Rickert, 2014.
52. Witherspoon, 2018, p. 21.

WHAT HINDERS COMPERSION?

Your task is not to seek for love, but merely to seek and find all the barriers within yourself that you have built against it.
—Helen Schucman, *A Course in Miracles*[1]

The previous chapter highlighted the individual, relational, and social factors that promote compersion. The present chapter follows the same organization, and describes the elements that hinder the occurrence of compersion. Becoming aware of common challenges to compersion can support CNM people in understanding, anticipating, and addressing them, whenever possible—as well as develop compassion and empathy toward people who may struggle to experience it. Those challenges mirror the factors described in Chapter 7. They include: (a) obstacles to ideological commitment to CNM values; (b) obstacles to inner security; (c) obstacles to relational security, connectedness, and trust; (d) obstacles to the positive integration of partner's other relationship(s); (e) obstacles to perception of benefits from partner's other relationship(s); and (f) obstacles to community belonging.

GROUPING 1: INDIVIDUAL FACTORS

Participants noted that certain individual dispositions hindered their propensity to experience compersion. In this section, I describe the two main factors that emerged in this category: (1) obstacles to ideological commitment to CNM values, and (2) obstacles to inner security.

Obstacles to Ideological Commitment to CNM Values

Adopting a CNM mindset was a starting point for folks to experience relationship satisfaction in non-monogamy. If they lacked a genuine desire to make it work, or did not have strong enough motivations to go against the grain of mononormativity, compersion would be much less likely to come by. Put simply, lacking a personal commitment to CNM values would inhibit compersion. This obstacle showed up in three main ways: (1) internalized mononormativity, (2) poly under duress (PUD), and (c) couple privilege.

Internalized Mononormativity

Unanimously, participants expressed that mononormative beliefs and narratives (e.g., a sense of entitlement to possessiveness of one's partner and jealous behavior, couple-centricity, believing that "real love" cannot be shared among many) presented roadblocks to compersion, whether they noticed these beliefs within themselves, in a partner, or in another member of their polycule. As Fred, a 75-year-old retired geneticist, explained,

> One of the things that's a struggle in polyamory is that people come to it with a monogamous mindset, whether they like it or not. So, monogamy myths are still there rumbling around in their heads. If you let go of those myths, you can have more fun and live more productive lives. I mean, I think it's the monogamy stuff that poisons polyamory.

Similarly, Lisa, a 41-year-old faculty counselor, pointed to the fact that many people are held back from experiencing compersion because of internalized mononormativity:

> The core of [experiencing compersion] is being able to get in touch with a level of intimate empathy that has some of the cultural expectations removed. I think it is possible for anyone to experience compersion, but that many of us are held back from it because of these prejudices and social expectations.

Deri's study on polyamorous women's compersion echoed this theme. One of her participants described "how she had internalized a sense of shame in her desire to have more than one lover."[2] In her personal reclamation of "slut pride," she had grown determined to become "really conscious that if I ever do feel ashamed to really look at it and pull it away from me and see that again it's about oppression of people and silencing of love."[3] This testimony shows the importance of actively and consistently disentangling one's inherited mononormative belief system from one's chosen mindset and values.

Indeed, CNM folks regularly took inventory of their thoughts, beliefs, and assumptions, especially when emotional triggers would arise, to discern which thought patterns were at the helm of their emotional life. The careful work of dismantling a lifetime's worth of mononormative conditioning was not always easy, but it would typically be rewarded by greater access to compersion.

Poly Under Duress

Being pressured by a partner to be non-monogamous (a dynamic also known as poly under duress, or PUD) was seen as antithetical to compersion by several participants. Individuals needed to choose CNM from a place of full-hearted consent, personal power, agency, and freedom if they were to experience positive empathy toward their partner's other relationship(s) at an emotional level. If someone did not genuinely embrace a CNM ideology, and somewhat resented being non-monogamous, they would unavoidably bring monogamous values and assumptions into a CNM relationship—and would lack the self-generated motivation necessary to do the hard work, as described in the previous section, of dismantling mononormativity within themselves. To illustrate, Jo, a 29-year-old software engineer, explained:

> I think you can experience compersion if you really wanted CNM in the first place. There's some people who are trying to be poly because their partners are poly and they like them. Or, they feel like they should be able to be poly, or something like that. And maybe those people will never, never feel compersion.

Indeed, without sufficient buy-in, folks would uphold a level of inner resistance that would generate a sense of contradiction, rather than congruence, between their relationship structure and their mindset—and hinder the potential emergence of compersion.

There was nuance to this, however: not every "yes" needed to be a "hell yes" for healthy CNM relationships and compersion to take place. As Fern conveyed in *Polywise*, a "yes to consenting" or a "yes for now"[4] was sometimes sufficient to get started. For some participants, CNM had not initially been their first choice, but they had agreed to try it in good faith. Fern described the difference between PUD and someone who went into CNM reluctantly but uncoerced:

> There are numerous times in our lives when, because of another commitment—be it to a partner, child, work or significant personal goal—we

are willing to do things we're not 100% excited about or potentially wouldn't have decided to do on our own. We accept taking on the inconveniences and discomforts associated with the decision because we know it's important to the relationship or goal that we value. Perhaps there is no direct payoff for us, but we recognize the benefit the decision has for the relationship, and thus, for us, it's worth it. This is often the starting point for many partners who would not have chosen nonmonogamy on their own. They love their partner so much they're willing to try it, even in the face of uncertainty and apprehension. In cases like these, the important thing is that the choice be conscious, clear and uncoerced.[5]

Some participants who were initially skeptical of CNM "bought into" it more fully after realizing that it could in fact work for them, and did experience compersion down the line.

Couple Privilege

Couple privilege refers to the entrenched priority and advantages that society gives to cohabitating couples, and that single people or non-nested partners do not receive. An increasing number of authors have denounced this social elevation of the couple as the most valuable relational unit, also known as *couple-centrism*, as a harmful form of normativity that often gets overlooked within CNM contexts.[6] Although CNM allegedly seeks to liberate love from oppressive normativities, some manifestations of couple-centrism can unwittingly make non-primary partner(s) feel undervalued, or robbed of their uniqueness and complexity—which constitutes an obstacle to experiencing compersion.

While prioritizing one's "primary" relationship above all others was a form of reassurance for some of the folks I interviewed (Colette, James, and Diane), others specifically warned that some forms of relationship hierarchy may create relational ecosystems that fail to promote each member's well-being. In their view, giving a higher status to one partner in comparison to another was bound to make the other partner(s) feel dehumanized, disposable, or unseen—which in turn would prevent them from experiencing compersion toward their partner's nesting relationship. Laura-Lee, a 32-year-old anthropologist who was married to Martin, explained:

> I think there's a lot of couple privilege in our culture. And that if you're moving into a nonmonogamous space, if you're not able to recognize the privileges that you're bringing into that space, you are inevitably going to make your other partners feel bad. Or, one of your partners is going to feel

like they have special privileges that the other partners don't get . . . both of us place a high value on treating everybody like a complex human being, whose feelings are just as valuable as mine, or as are Martin's.

Similarly, Sylvia, a 49-year-old professor who practiced solo polyamory, spoke of feeling excluded and devalued by her partners who were part of established heteronormative marriages. She commented on being emotionally deprioritized, or treated as the "disposable" party in the relational ecosystems she took part in—which of course limited the possibility of experiencing compersion toward her partners' other relationships.

This was not the case for all participants in "secondary" partner roles, however. Teresa, a 54-year-old nanny who also practiced solo polyamory, did not feel devalued by her married partner Calvin and his wife. She felt a lot of compersion toward them and their relationship:

> I certainly don't ever feel jealous around him and his wife. I actually am a cheerleader for them spending more time, I'll volunteer to babysit. I'm like, go out, go have fun, you know, because the happier they are, as a couple, I benefit from their happiness. Their healthy relationship makes it possible for me to be with him. I want to feed that.

The contrast between Teresa and Sylvia's experiences seems to have to do with how much respect, dignity, and love they received from their partners and metamours within the context of hierarchical CNM. Nurturing and caring relationships that honored every person's full humanity and complexity—even though the scope of these relationships was very different—would pave a path for compersion. Matching the types of relationships with each person's needs and desires was also key: some folks desired coparental, spousal, cohabiting partnerships, while others preferred less entangled relationships—possibly shorter term or geographically distanced. When everyone in a relationship ecosystem was getting their needs and desires met, and did not compete for each other's roles, compersion was more likely to occur.

In other words, there seemed to be two conditions for compersion to emerge within de facto hierarchies: (1) having a sense of mutual care grounded in the recognition of all partners' complexity and uniqueness as individuals; and (2) a lack of competitiveness between partners, requiring that each person feel comfortable in their particular role. These elements made it possible to create safety and inclusion for many partners in a way that promoted compersion and also mitigated the potential dehumanization of couple privilege. Balzarini and colleagues have also explored these patterns in their research, which interested readers may want to explore further.[7]

Obstacles to Inner Security

Just as a sense of secure attachment with oneself was key in enabling compersion to flow in participants' intimate relationships, a lack of inner security hindered compersion. This obstacle showed up in the interview data under four themes: (1) dependency/codependency, (2) insecurity and comparison with metamour, (3) sexual shame and sex negativity, and (4) unmet personal needs.

Dependency/Codependency

As discussed in Chapter 7, it was clear from participants' accounts that a strong sense of personal autonomy and agency was required for compersion to occur. The opposite was also true. A lack of autonomy and agency—which translated into dependency or codependency between partners—was an obstacle to experiencing positive empathy. When a person was dependent (whether financially, emotionally, or otherwise) on their partner, the threat of losing them to other relationships became greater, and the need for predictability was more dominant. Because CNM requires a certain level of comfort with unpredictability,[8] the enhanced threat that dependency introduced made compersion much less likely to arise.

Insecurity and Comparison with Metamour

In instances where participants compared themselves negatively to their metamour(s), compersion was less accessible. On the one hand, negative comparison could spark painful personal insecurities, and/or the fear of losing one's partner to an imagined "higher-value" metamour: this would trigger folks' competitive response and hinder the possibility of genuine love, empathy, and support toward metamours. Colette, a 41-year-old sex and relationship coach, depicted how her comparative mind operated when her husband dated other women:

> There's always a little, like, whenever I've met the other women, sometimes I'll do this whole comparison thing, like is she thinner or prettier? Or, he'll be describing a sexual experience where she does something that I don't do,

you know, there's always a little tinge of like, "Oh, is he gonna want that more than he wants what I have to offer?"

While negatively comparing oneself to a metamour hindered compersion, intense *positive* comparison (e.g., seeing oneself as dramatically "better" than a metamour) could also trigger a shutting down of love and empathy. In these cases, a metamour's perceived "low-value" would negatively reflect on one's self-esteem and respect for one's partner, from the meaning-making around one's partner intimate association with a person one looks down upon. I explored this phenomenon in Chapter 7 under "Positive Integration of Partner's Other Relationship(s)." The following quote from Carmi and Sadeh-Saadon helps illustrate the bidirectional nature of comparison's impact on compersion. In this story, a polyamorous husband described his wife's requirements for compersion:

> Sometimes, Talia [my wife] wants to compare. On the one hand, that the other woman's not better than she is, that she's not a threat, and on the other hand that she's not a few degrees below her because that creates a certain disdain.[9]

Indeed, comparison is a complex psycho-emotional phenomenon that, when activated to a certain threshold, creates a barrier to love and empathy—and therefore has the power to hinder the flow of compersion.

Furthermore, research studies have found that rejection hurts more when a person is rejected *for someone else*. Examining the effect of this distinction on emotional reactions across four studies ($N = 608$), Deri and Zitek have found that

> for those who are rejected, one important difference is whether they are rejected for someone else (comparative rejection) or no one at all (noncomparative rejection). Our results show that comparative rejections feel worse than noncomparative rejections and that this may be because such rejections lead to an increased sense of exclusion and decreased belonging.[10]

Additionally, Deri and Zitek found evidence that, by default, people react to rejection as though it were comparative: "In the absence of any information about whether they have been rejected for someone or no one, they react as negatively as if they were rejected for someone."[11] This may help explain why many monogamous people experience immediate anxiety when being presented with the possibility of CNM—because the comparative nature of potential rejection in situations that include other lovers can seem more unbearable than rejection for other reasons. Anticipating or imagining this level of pain can be enough to keep many people away from exploring non-monogamy.

That said, since humans are viscerally "wired" to compare, it is unrealistic to attempt not to compare at all. To mitigate the potential negative effects of comparison, cultivating inner security and intentionally viewing each person as unique and incommensurable—which is often aided by cultivating intentional connections with metamours—can serve as antidotes.

Sexual Shame and Sex Negativity

While my study participants named sex positivity as an ally to compersion, sexual shame and sex negativity were a clear hindrance. For compersion to flourish in their CNM relationships, participants had to not only accept but also celebrate the unconventional idea that sexuality can be explored consensually with more than one person. This celebratory mindset would mitigate the sex-negative beliefs that most people inevitably inherit from their upbringings, as well as a wider culture that validates only a narrow lane of sexual expression as healthy and normal.[12]

Fredrick Zal refers to this traditional and narrow view of human sexuality as the "cis-hetero-monogamous-ableist kyriarchy"[13]—a set of sex-negative attitudes that shames and marginalizes any erotic expression that fails to match the model of a cisgendered, heterosexual, monogamous, and able couple. Zal argued that these attitudes can be reassessed, by sexuality professionals and others, through the Sexual Attitude Reassessment (SAR) process, to "stop the perpetuation of sexual shame, stigma, and other harms" and move into a space of "embodiment, loving kindness, compassion, compersion, and equanimity" around sexuality.[14]

Blocks to compersion would be intensified if layers of personal sexual shame were at play following sexual trauma and abuse, which robbed people of their sense of safety around sexuality. For some communities, trauma and sexual shame had been systematically ingrained. Sylvia, a Dakota participant, gave a poignant example of this dynamic. She pointed out the widespread pedophilia and sexual abuse of Native children throughout the 20th century as a direct cause for deeply engrained sexual shame, which she argued played into her community's inability to embrace CNM as a legitimate lifestyle today—although their ancestors were non-monogamous, and they felt pride in virtually every other aspect of their culture. She explained,

> I think for us, because the rest of the boarding schools, the residential schools, the boarding schools in the US and residential schools and Canada, children were forcibly removed from their homes, my grandparents' generation, especially, were forcibly removed from the home from the time they were five until they were eighteen. They were made to go to boarding schools, often church-run, they were forbidden from speaking the language, they had to convert to Christianity, they had to cut their hair. They were deeply shamed. And one of the major forms of abuse in residential schools was sexual abuse—there was emotional, physical, and sexual abuse. And so there are a lot of testimonies now. The Catholic Church has been highlighted as having all this pedophilia, and everybody's all shocked. Well, we already knew that; the Catholic Church has been subjecting Native children to pedophilia throughout the twentieth century. And so out of that, then comes a lot of conservatism around sex, right? And a lot of sexual shame. We don't talk openly about sexuality. I mean, in the multiple generations of my family, you know, my great-grandmother, who was in a Catholic convent school, to my grandmother, who was in boarding school to my mom, who was kind of halfway between boarding and public school. You don't talk about sex, you just don't talk about it. You know, there was no talk about the birds and the bees, there was not even a talk about what happens when you start to menstruate. Everything was whispered and quiet. And we have high rates of teenage pregnancy because of that, right?

Indeed, embracing CNM required a revisioning of sex-negative patterning that could invoke self-judgment, shame, or fear around breaking mononormative rules. Fortunately, CNM communities and adjacent communities of learning and practice—for example, classes on sexual consent, kink events, erotic embodiment workshops, communication classes, and more—would often become sites of healing and transformation, helping turn shame into pride, joy, and a celebratory attitude toward all forms of consensual sexuality.

Unmet Personal Needs

Many participants reported that they and/or their partner(s) had difficulty feeling compersion when their personal needs were not met. For example, Alexis explained that their propensity to experience compersion was intrinsically connected with their getting a good night's sleep. Asked about instances when they might have struggled to experience compersion, they replied, "Anytime that I'm sleep deprived, or tired." Similarly, Sabrina, a 41-year-old dance artist, noted that her partner was not likely to feel compersion "if he's working a lot and feeling stressed." On a light-hearted note, Martin, a 33-year-old software engineer, also pointed to the fact that compersion was more elusive when his needs for sleep and personal space were not met:

> We have a one-bedroom place, because this is the Bay Area, and everything's very expensive. So sometimes, Laura-Lee will bring somebody over and they will have a date here. And since I live here, I'll also be here. I've definitely had some times where I'm like, "Well, I kind of want to be happy for her, but on the other hand, I want to go to bed, which means I really wish that they would just stop having sex and I could go to bed." [*laughs*] . . . I want to be happy for my partner and I want to be happy for their partner, but I can't, because God damn it! I want to go to bed and they're having sex in bed!

A thematic analysis study conducted by Drs. Sharon Flicker, Michelle Vaughan, and I on factors that facilitate and hinder compersion in CNM individuals corroborated this theme.[15] In a survey administered to 44 CNM individuals, respondents commented on how they needed to have their personal needs met to experience compersion—and that unmet needs would conversely hinder compersion. One person mentioned that being in a "good headspace [and] keeping my own mental health in check" was essential; another reported that "people with no other outside support struggle [with experiencing compersion]. It's important to have a full life when your partner is away." Yet one more mentioned, "When I only have one partner and my partner has many I feel less compersion."[16] This last participant quote seems to point to comparative insecurity around one's self-worth, as compared to one's partner, but it could additionally indicate that this respondent felt they would get more of their needs met if they had many partners—and that their partner may have been less available to fulfill their needs when they had many other partnerships.

In sum, when CNM folks come to their intimate relationships with personal cups that are more empty than full, they are less likely to experience compersion toward their partner's/partners' other relationship(s). This also applies to monogamous partners—as having a sense of well-being and fulfilling life outside of one's intimate partnership typically provides a sense of emotional resiliency, abundance, and generosity, where people have more to give—and the lack thereof may create a sense of scarcity and undue pressure on one's partnership.[17] Thus, counselors and therapists working with folks of all relationship styles should keep in mind that supporting their clients' needs in all aspects of their lives will deeply impact the quality of their intimate relationships—including their ability to access positive empathy.

GROUPING 2: RELATIONAL FACTORS

The three main themes that emerged in the relational category included: (1) obstacles to relational security, connectedness, and trust; (2) obstacles to the positive integration of partner's other relationship(s); and (3) obstacles to perception of benefits from partner's other relationship(s). These factors pertained to my participants' relationships with both their partner(s) and their metamour(s); accordingly, the obstacles to compersion they experienced could be toward their partner, toward their metamour, toward the "metamour relationship," or toward a combination of those.

Obstacles to Relational Security, Connectedness, and Trust

Participants expressed how obstacles to security, connectedness, and trust within a relationship would hinder compersion. Three elements were noted as common obstacles: (1) betrayal, (2) unmet relational needs, and (3) jealousy and deprivation.

Betrayal

A breached agreement with one's partner rendered compersion improbable. James, a 54-year-old scientist engineer who delved into CNM with his wife, Diane, after experiencing the betrayal of her having an affair, explained that even though a seed of compersion was present from the moment he knew that Diane had cheated on him, it was camouflaged among a host of negative feelings—which had to be processed, and their relational context transformed, for compersion to grow and eventually take prevalence. James described how the emotions associated with betrayal shielded the presence of compersion:

I think [the compersion] was always there. It was always there but it wasn't, it was always confused with a lot of other feelings. So it felt like it was shielded or it was buffered by a lot of other negative feelings. And so, it was difficult to feel it in its more pure form. My sense was that it always was something that was an element. You know, I always want [Diane] to feel good and enjoy herself. And so there's always an element, I think I had compersion. In essence, in the first moment, in the midst of all this anger and shock over discovery of her infidelity, I think I had elements of compersion because I understood what she did. I understood the need that she had, and what her desire was about, immediately. She had sort of brought to life a desire that I had basically stuffed down and essentially ignored, sort of by fiat, and she acted upon it, so I understood that. I think I felt compersion immediately, and understood and appreciated that. It was just also combined with shock and anger and fear and a bunch of other things that weren't positive, that sort of shielded its presence.

This section highlights, once again, how consent and agency are at the core of people's ability to experience compersion. When someone's trust is betrayed, their power and ability to choose is taken away—which creates a breach in relational safety and connection, rendering positive empathy and gratitude out of reach. Ruptures that ensue can be healed when folks who broke agreements take responsibility and members of a relationship rebuild trust. However, insult is sometimes added to injury when a breached agreement turns into gaslighting. In *Polywise*, Jessica Fern and David Cooley described how broken agreements—compounded with the failure to take responsibility for one's actions—can tear CNM relationships apart:

> For example, eschewing our personal accountability for breaking a mutual agreement to not sleep with someone new on the first date by suggesting our partner's hurt is a product of their own attachment issues rather than an actual broken commitment is unethical and highly problematic. It creates an acute sense that the relationship is not safe by undermining the foundations of trust. In order to maintain a legitimately secure attachment in any relationship, we have to explicitly recognize that our behavior can have negative consequences on other people, even when we had no intention of harming them.[18]

In other words, members of a relationship could heal from betrayal and eventually foster compersion as long as folks in that relationship had healthy enough power dynamics, transparency, and accountability to warrant a genuine restoration of trust.

Unmet Relational Needs

When participants were experiencing a lack of love, connection, or security within their relationship(s), it made it difficult to access compersion when their partner enjoyed other connections. As stated earlier, members of a relationship needed to feel that their "relational cup" was full before they could experience the senses of gratitude and generosity that were at the root of compersion.

For Sabrina and her partner, spending plenty of quality time together, including sexual contact, was the primary way in which reassurance was cultivated—and therefore, a failure to fulfill this need would result in the sore absence of compersion:

> If we don't have time to connect, if we're busy working, and we don't have time to go on a date, or have personal time together, or have sex, or take a couple days off in wine country or something, which we're doing this weekend before I go on a date next week, then it's not going to work out.

Similarly, in Flicker and colleagues' study on factors that facilitate and hinder compersion, a participant noted the importance of getting enough time with their partner: "I don't feel compersion when it feels like it's been too long since I've seen my partner. I also don't feel compersion when I feel like a partner doesn't have time for me."[19] Having unmet relational needs often led to jealousy and deprivation, to which I turn next.

Jealousy and Deprivation

Feeling deprived of love, time, or attention was especially challenging when these resources were being offered to another partner. This would lead to difficult emotions of jealousy, negative comparison, feeling "unchosen" and "less than." Evita "Lavitaloca" Sawyers, author of *A Polyamory Devotional,*[20] encapsulated this theme into a single sentence: "It's really hard to be at ease about somebody serving someone else a plate when you're hungry . . . very, very hard."[21] Similarly, Tyrone, a 38-year-old facilitator, remembers experiencing jealousy and insecurity vis-à-vis a male partner who did not display as much adoration toward him as he did toward his fem-presenting partners:

> There was one relationship where he, I was his first male partner, he had two fem-presenting partners, and *he loved women.* He did not *love* men. He loved me, but I just could see the difference when he looked at me and when he looked at his other partner. His body would light up. I knew that wasn't the case for me. There were times where I would really fall into a deep hole of sadness and grief around this thing that I wanted that I couldn't have . . . there was a lot of desire and wanting and yearning of the thing that I saw him give.

Jealousy and deprivation sometimes intensify when one's partner is experiencing new relationship energy (NRE),[22] the emotional rush associated with getting to know a new partner that one feels excited about. One respondent in Flicker et al.'s survey noted that NRE "between their partner and a metamour could result in a dip in attention toward them, which undermined their ability to experience compersion."[23] While jealousy and compersion could coexist (as I described in Chapter 6) the result of this coexistence was sometimes a state of inner struggle that made one's expression of compersion more difficult.

Obstacles to the Positive Integration of Partner's Other Relationship(s)

Participants expressed that the lack of positive integration of a partner's other relationship(s) would hinder compersion toward these relationships and metamours. Four types of blocks to compersion emerged in this category: (1) feeling excluded, (2) not liking or trusting a metamour, (3) weak boundaries with metamours and "cowboys," and (4) disgruntled metamour and lack of consent.

Feeling Excluded

Participants had different preferences in terms of how much information they wished to receive about their partner's other relationship(s): some preferred hearing a lot of details, and others, not as much. However, all of them wanted a sense of transparency—that is, they wanted to know and feel that their partner was not deliberately concealing information from them. When they sensed or learned that their partner was being secretive, they would feel excluded, upset, and deprived of their own sense of power and agency; this would prevent them from feeling grateful and empathic, and therefore, compersive. Jo described how in the early days of dating their current husband, the latter's lack of sharing sufficient information about his other relationships prevented them from experiencing compersion:

> When we first started dating, it was really my first time doing polyamory. And at first, he didn't know how much to tell me. So he'd just be like, "I'm going out." I'd be like, "Where are you going?" And he'd be like, "Hmm a date?" And I'd be like, "Tell me about it." And he wouldn't automatically. . . . I didn't want to pry, since sometimes he wouldn't tell me a lot about it. And I'd feel weird about it. That was a real jealousy trigger for me, like, not knowing what was going on. Basically, I don't want to feel like something's happening behind my back in any way. And even though it's allowed, I want to know everything about the situation. And if I don't, then I don't like it, and I feel uncomfortable. And I want to eventually meet the person and if they're not okay with meeting me, then I feel really weird about it and I don't like that. Because then it makes me feel like I'm not, like, they don't actually want me to exist or something. . . . And that feels a lot like cheating . . . anything that feels similar to cheating in any way, I don't like that situation.

In this case, Jo spoke to both the experience of feeling excluded from their partner's emotional life through a lack of communication, and also having the sense that a metamour "does not want them to exist"—which connects with the theme of not trusting a metamour, which I describe next.

Not Liking or Trusting a Metamour

When my participants did not like or trust a metamour, compersion was much less likely to occur. Alexis, a 26-year-old professional cuddlist and events program manager, gave the example of a metamour whom they perceived as not being "worth their resources":

> Jules has a partner who I've decided . . . I used to have a desire to connect with this other partner, but I don't anymore. Partially, they don't see each other very often. It's an unequal power dynamic where Jules sort of mentors and is sort of a therapist for this other partner, and I have limited time with other people. So I've devalued that other partner. . . . It's been harder to feel compersion, partially because I've decided that the other partner's worth less of my resources.

Sylvia conveyed a similar situation, as she was feeling triggered by her partner dating a younger, emotionally volatile woman who she viewed as "not of [her] caliber":

> I'm really judgmental about people that I perceive as weak, and emotionally insecure and troubled, because I think of myself as a very strong person and dignified person. And so when I see somebody being what I would call weak, and undignified and needy, it really turns me off. And she was like that. And I remember thinking, why are you wasting your time on an idiot like that? When you've got me and Leah and we're like, quality people, you know, and I knew his other girlfriend, Leah. I was kind of insulted. I'm like, I wouldn't waste my time with some joker of a guy when I have you. And you're amazing. I'd better spend time with you. And eventually, he broke up with me and Leah to be with this younger woman because he was kind of having a monogamy hangover.

Here, Sylvia described how she had vastly different amounts of compersion for different metamours, depending on whether or not she perceived her metamour to be trustworthy, a positive addition to the relational ecosystem, a valuable allocation of their partner's time and energy, and/or a threat to their own relationship with their common partner.

In some instances, embodied feelings of disgust, disdain, or repulsion could arise—toward not only the metamour but also toward their hinge partner—which is an opposite reaction to compersion, but is also different from jealousy. A participant in Flicker and colleagues' study conveyed this vividly:

> Disliking one's metamour can sometimes undermine one's own relationship with one's partner, "Once my partner crushed on [someone] I found strongly unsympathetic [sic]. I felt disgusted. A lot. [A]fter them telling me about their kiss or anything [sic]. I lost being attracted to my partner for a while then, feeling disgusted from their body too."[24]

Participants in Flicker et al.'s study also noted the importance of trusting their metamour, and that a lack of trust undermines their capacity to feel compersion. This was noted numerous times, as illustrated by the following two quotes from CNM individuals reporting on factors that hinder compersion for them: "Red flags with metamours. Dishonesty or lack of consideration," and "a lack of trust regarding the other person (they throw up a red flag or push a boundary)."[25] Indeed, a sense of threat would show up when a metamour disrespected established boundaries, or had weak boundaries themselves. I explore this topic next.

Weak Boundaries with Metamours and "Cowboys"

As I explained in Chapter 7, having good boundaries with metamours—as well as metamours showing sincere respect and appreciation for preexisting relationships and associated agreements—promoted a sense of trust, and therefore compersion. On the flip side, having the suspicion, real or imagined, that a metamour wanted to "snatch away" one's partner ("cowboys" in CNM jargon) engendered mistrust and the sense of not being on the same team with one's metamour. This caused a strong hindrance to compersion. Colette had this experience with one particular woman her husband dated:

> Generally, I can have a pretty good dose of compersion. A strong exception to that is when he has seen a woman who I feel doesn't respect my place in the relationship. So, he was dating this one woman in particular, who he found on Tinder, and she was not exposed to open relationships before. So she didn't really have any concept of it. And I think it was really difficult for her to understand that he was happily married, and that this was something he could do with her from time to time and have a really enjoyable time, but then that was going to be it. And . . . I don't need to meet all of the women he sees, it's not important, but she actively did not want to meet me, even if I was, like, near the coffeeshop she worked at, which I liked going to before I knew her, you know, and I would write to my husband like, "hey, I'm right next to the coffeeshop, let me message her!" And he would say, "oh no, don't go in, she's super freaked out!" I was just like, "What the heck." I had very little compersion for that relationship. Like, almost none.

Furthermore, when a participant sensed that a particular metamour wished to occupy more of one partner's time or other resources—more than their partner could comfortably offer without shifting pre-existing relationship dynamics—a sense of competitiveness could arise. Colette contrasted this experience with the compersion she felt when her metamours showed appreciation, connection, and generosity toward her. Elaborating on the metamour relationship described earlier, she recounted:

I definitely felt like she wanted more from him than he would be able to give her. And that made me kind of not trust her. Whereas, like, some other women that my husband dates, like, he's out on a date, they'll send home a chocolate croissant to me, and, we'll message each other and thank each other for sharing, and it's just really sweet . . . with some of our other partners, there's a couple that I see, I'll invite them over for dinner, and we'll all hang out and have dinner, or like, the woman that he sees, we get the families together for a weekend, like, lots of it is good—but not that woman. [*laughs*]

Put simply, participants wanted to feel that their metamours were on the same team with them, rather than in competition. A sense of threat was typically compounded when a metamour had little or no prior experience with CNM. In these cases, the metamour was thought to be more likely to carry monogamous intents—that is, to wish that the hinge partner would leave their existing relationship(s) and become monogamous with them. There would be little room for positive empathy or gratitude in these situations. Thus, perceiving a metamour as a potential "cowboy" easily shifted the compersion dial to zero.

Disgruntled Metamour and Lack of Consent

When a metamour in one's relational ecosystem was displeased, the positive relational feedback loop I described in Chapter 2 would break, resulting in difficulty experiencing compersion. Jo explained how they often ended relationships with people when they realized a metamour was made "severely uncomfortable" by their connection:

I've broken up with a number of people because their partner was clearly not experiencing [compersion]. And it made it feel similar to cheating. Like, that I was dating someone, and it was making someone else severely uncomfortable. And I would, most the time, unless it was like, the very beginning of a relationship, if it was like date two and they told me their partner is not comfortable, I'm like, let's just not do this, you know. But if I found out, like a month in, then I'd reach out to the partner and be like, "Hey, is there anything I can do to help with the situation?" Like, "Do you want to ask me questions or anything like that?" and if it just still seemed like it wasn't working, then I would get out of the situation.

Several participants expressed the same sentiment. Michael, a 67-year-old musician, stated that "if everyone is not having a good time, then it's not working." Disgruntled metamours would represent an obstacle to maintaining the sense of openness and transparency necessary for compersion to blossom. This finding showed how a sense of inclusion across the polycule or relational ecosystem was central to compersion. If one person in the CNM network was distressed by their partner's/partners' other relationships, this would impact everyone's ability to enjoy those connections. The presence of a disgruntled metamour could indicate the presence of interactions that were not truly consensual; and compersion thrives in an environment of enthusiastic consent.

Obstacles to Perception of Benefits from Partner's Other Relationship(s)

In Chapter 7, I explained how the perception of benefits from partner's other relationship(s) significantly promotes compersion—because it directly feeds into the gratitude component of compersion (see Chapter 3). When people perceive metamour relationships as additive to their own life, their partner's life, and/or to their relationship, it typically leads to thankfulness.

Conversely, the perception of a metamour relationship as not bringing any benefits, or worse, taking away precious resources, energy, or enjoyment—from one's life, one's partner's life, and/or from one's relationship—presents an obstacle to compersion. In other words, when someone perceives a particular metamour to be a liability rather than an asset to the relationship ecosystem, it becomes more difficult to show full-hearted support for that metamour relationship.

In my research, when a participant felt that their partner's relationship was somehow unhealthy or detrimental to the overall harmony of the polycule, compersion was less frequent, less intense, or nonexistent. For example, Laura-Lee expressed discontent and difficulty experiencing compersion toward one of Martin's ex-girlfriends, Katalina, who "just kind of turned into this emotional sink [and] bottomless pit of need, where she . . . wasn't taking care of herself. She just wanted Martin to take care of her." In this situation, Laura-Lee felt that Katalina was taking more than she was giving to Martin, and by consequence was draining energy from her own relationship with Martin and other more "healthy" metamour relationships—rather than adding to them. As I described in Chapter 7 under positive integration of partner's other relationship(s), Laura-Lee experienced much more comper-sion for another metamour, Rose, whom she perceived to add positive value to Martin's life, and thus to the polycule as a whole.

Alexis had a similar experience with one of their partner Jules' other part-ners, with whom he had "an unequal power dynamic where [he] sort of men-tors and is sort of a therapist for this other partner." Alexis perceived that this other partner was not "worth their resources." Seemingly, attempting to cul-tivate compersion did not present any advantage for Alexis in this situation.

Kathy Labriola also noted that compersion sometimes emerges as CNM people get older and have more to gain from metamour relationships in terms of sharing caregiving responsibilities. She recounted a situation where a woman had experienced serious jealousy toward her metamour for years until her husband became disabled and needed a lot of care. Her metamour stepping in, and providing clear value to the relational ecosystem, shifted this woman's jealousy into compersion quite rapidly—even provoking the envy of her monogamous friends.

> Her husband was injured in a car wreck and became somewhat disabled from that. She was the only caregiver for him, and luckily, he also had a girlfriend and they were in an openly poly situation. And the girlfriend really stepped up and was coming over and providing respite care so that the wife could rest and go out and see her friends and see the grandchildren and all of that. Even though she had had a lot of jealousy before this happened, she became very grateful and compersive toward that girlfriend.
>
> She said all the women in her caregiver group, they were always com-plaining about it, they were always upset about how they're the only one taking care of their husbands. They have no help and they're exhausted, and it's like a 24/7 thing. And if they can't do it, they end up having to hire someone to help, and that's super expensive, and then they're under financial stress, too. So she said, "I have my metamour and she comes over a couple days a week and taking care of him so I can get some rest. And the women in the room were like, wooooow, why don't I have *that*?" [*laughs*][26]

This instance provides a clear example of how compersion becomes much more accessible when there is a mutual benefit—something valuable to be grateful for. Before her husband's accident, this woman might have seen no practical advantage to this metamour relationship. However, when the dynamics shifted and the benefits of this metamour relationship became clear, compersion strongly surfaced.

GROUPING 3: SOCIAL FACTORS

The last major grouping of factors negatively impacting compersion was social. One overarching theme emerged in that category: obstacles to community belonging. I expand further on the social category in Chapters 10 and Chapter 11, where I explain how obstacles to coming out as non-monogamous can impact the emergence of compersion, as well as how the variables of age, disability, gender, sexual orientation, race, and socioeconomic status may play into this picture. Because community belonging enables CNM folks to validate their relational identities within mononormative societies, obstacles to this belonging are likely to hinder the emergence of compersion.

Obstacles to Community Belonging

I described in Chapter 7 how community belonging plays a major role in CNM people's identity development and likelihood of experiencing compersion. However, access to this belonging is not always easy—or equally easy for everyone. Due to the widespread stigmatization of non-monogamy, as well as intersecting factors like racism, ageism, sexism, classism, heteronormativity, and ableism (see Chapter 11), many participants felt restricted in their ability to be fully "out" as non-monogamous and thus benefit from the advantages of connecting to like-minded people and communities. While I dive deeper into these themes in Part V, "Social Lenses on Compersion"—I include the descriptions of two notable obstacles my participants voiced in that realm: (1) mononormativity and stigmatization of CNM lifestyles, and (2) lack of racial and cultural diversity in CNM communities.

Mononormativity and Stigmatization of CNM Relationships

Participants in my study had to mitigate widespread mononormativity and stigmatization of CNM relationships.[27] The practical and socioemotional impacts of mononormativity would hinder their freedom of expression, often "forcing them to live in the closet," as polyamory activist Caroline Rose Giuliani recently wrote in *Vanity Fair*. She described some of the workings of compulsory monogamy in enforcing monogamy as the only "acceptable" relationship structure:

With the recent exception of residents in the progressive city of Somerville, Massachusetts, all other polyamorous people in America currently have zero protection from being blatantly discriminated against. They can be denied housing, prevented from advancing at work, and even fired, all without any legal recourse whatsoever. Relationship structure does not yet qualify as a "protected class" like gender, religion, race, or sexual orientation do. This lack of social and legal acceptance has compelled many polyamorous people to hide their true identity from their coworkers, family, and even closest friends.[28]

Indeed, many of my participants did not feel that they could be "out" to their broader communities beyond their partners. Natasha, a 34-year-old physician, explained:

I don't like to feel I'm keeping a secret from the rest of society. . . . The biggest challenge about CNM would probably just be that it's not more universally accepted. I still feel that if I was to openly tell everyone, I would have one or two friends who would be like, "oh, that's disgusting, that's gross."

Similarly, Simon, an 83-year-old retired professor, expressed that the majority of his polycule had to maintain absolute privacy for professional reasons:

It's a real problem, because the other four people have to maintain absolute privacy. We're all PhDs. We all have prominent jobs. And I'm the only one who can really be out. And my wife, who was out with me, doesn't want to make a big deal of it. She was a college professor, she's got a lot of friends in the college and she's a part of the emeriti society.

In other words, many people would stand to lose a lot by being outed as CNM. On the personal level, not being able to freely disclose one's relationship status in meaningful social contexts can reinforce internalized mononormativity and shame, or a sense that there is something deviant to hide about non-monogamy. This would reduce people's ability to normalize and celebrate CNM, and thus hinder the flow of compersion. Not being "out" would also restrict the psycho-social benefits of feeling authentically supported within one's communities.

Despite these obstacles, participants in my study (given that they were a self-selected group of people who were eager to discuss compersion—not necessarily a representative sample of everyone who practices CNM) had found their own ways to defy mononormative conventions to foster authentic self-expression in their intimate relationships in ways that made the most sense for them and their partners. Some participants who identified with other marginalized statuses, such as being queer, said that embracing an "outsider" status in other parts of their lives had predisposed them to question and bend traditional rules in the relationship arena. In other cases, however, being part of a marginalized group in more than one area compounded into greater difficulty finding inclusive communities. This was the case for most of my BIPOC participants.

Lack of Racial and Cultural Diversity in CNM Communities

Several participants brought up the lack of racial and cultural diversity in CNM communities as a barrier to experiencing a sense of community belonging, which in turn presented an obstacle to compersion. BIPOC participants who lived in geographical areas where CNM networks and communities were overwhelmingly White generally reported feeling out of place in these groups. Not feeling "home"—that is, feeling inhibited from showing up with one's full freedom of expression—within local CNM subcultures would then hinder their ability to meaningfully connect with other CNM people in those spaces. This obstructed access to the kind of mutual support that would otherwise come from these connections—mutual support that would otherwise foster compersion. This discomfort was not strictly based on racial identity: it also varied depending on individuals' cultural values. For example, Sylvia, a Dakota participant, commented on the clash between her local polyamorous community and her cultural roots:

> You know how polyamory communities are. There's a lot of New Age people, there's a lot of people into Renaissance Fair stuff and kink. And I think none of that resonates with anything to do with my culture. I kind of just thought they were weird.

Furthermore, Sylvia was keenly aware that monogamous marriage had been enforced on her cultural lineage as a part of systematized assimilation—and she wanted her practice of non-monogamy to be anchored in defiance to the systems of oppression she saw at play. However, she did not feel that her authentic thoughts on compulsory monogamy and settler colonialism would be well-received, or even understood, by most polyamorous men in her area or at a "polyamory meetup":

For me, the central problems are not jealousy and time management. The central problems are that compulsory monogamy is so deeply tied up with private property in a sense of ownership, and the settler colonial state and who gets benefits. So for me, it's all about settler colonialism. And those are not conversations I can have at a polyamory meetup. I mean, polyamorous people don't know that they are oppressed by settler colonialism. They think it's religion, or, you know, religious mores left over. They don't get the nature of their own oppression. Because settler colonialism oppresses all of us, not just Native people. It has so deeply structured the state, and the state is invested in marriage and private property.

Sylvia commented further on the fact that men of color face an even greater stigmatization than women, due to the stereotypes of Native and Black men being "players." This highlights the intersection between gender, race, sexual orientation, and relationship orientation. She paraphrased an Indigenous man who confided in her about his feelings toward CNM:

"I can't be openly non-monogamous, I can't be viewed as a player. That's not going to work in my community, you know. . . . Native men are viewed as running around and cheating. And we get stigmatized, like, I'm not going to do this. . . . " He's right. I [Sylvia] can be open as a non-monogamous [woman], whereas if a Native man tried it, it's like Black men, they get kind of stigmatized in the same way as Black men do. "Oh, you have a bunch of children, you don't take care of them, you just run around and cheat," like that.

Bethanne, a White participant active in social justice movements, also commented about why CNM communities are generally not ethnically or racially inclusive:

My anecdotal kind of perception is that it is primarily in White communities that this is practiced. I am often in POC communities and it's hilarious how many times I'll be with POC friends and the shit or rap on White culture using some metaphor about poly, like just a hippie thing, whatever. . . . I think it's really interesting to think about the ways that, because it has that, like, hippie stereotype. . . . It excludes or alienates people from different cultures, and different racial backgrounds specifically, and then also, in ways that that's like, problematic or not. And then it's also interesting to think about ways that trauma and suffering in Black America, specifically, creates specific barriers to other types of family structures, let alone that the patriarchal kind of family unit is a product of capitalism. . . . Brown and Black families, specifically, that overlaid is an intersection issue around how these families are being, or how the dominant narrative, in those spaces around, like, you must reproduce, must be a fit, a unit, so it doesn't threaten the State. It's a whole other kind of baggage.

These participant accounts show that the coming out process into CNM is often more challenging for BIPOC individuals—an assertion that is supported by previous literature.[29] These challenges, in turn, may hinder those folks from reaping the benefits of being intimately connected to CNM networks or openly expressing polypride.[30] I discuss these themes in more detail in Chapter 10, "The Role of Coming Out and Pride in Compersion," and Chapter 11, "Social Positionality and Compersion."

Conversely, as I explore later in this book, compersion may also function as a strategy of resistance, solidarity, and collective healing for folks with marginalized identities who have access to supportive CNM communities. For these individuals, openly defying mononormativity may go beyond rejecting the *structural rules* of compulsory monogamy, and include the rejection of its *feeling rules*. Thus, compersion may become an expression of resistance to internalized oppression, and a path to reclaiming power over one's body and heart. I describe this in depth in Chapter 11, "Social Positionality and Compersion," under the section "Compersion as Resistance."

NOTES

1. From *A Course in Miracles*, the Foundation for Inner Peace, T-16.IV.6:1. Copyright © 2007 by the Foundation for Inner Peace, copyright holder and publisher, 448 Ignacio Blvd., #306, Novato, CA 94949, acim.org. Used with permission.

2. Deri, 2015, p. 81.

3. Deri, 2015, p. 81.

4. Fern & Cooley, 2023, p. 39.

5. Fern & Cooley, 2023, p. 40.

6. For example, Klesse et al., 2022; Tallbear, 2014; Willey, 2018.

7. Balzarini et al., 2017, 2019.

8. Fern, 2020.

9. Carmi & Sadeh-Saadon, 2021, p. 51.

10. Deri & Zitek, 2017, p. 1.

11. Deri & Zitek, 2017, p. 1.

12. For example, Barratt, 2010; Donaghue, 2015.

13. Zal, 2022, p. S30.

14. Zal, 2022, p. S30.

15. Flicker et al., 2022.

16. Flicker et al., 2022, p. 3039.

17. For example, Perel, 2006.

18. Fern & Cooley, 2023, p. 138.

19. Flicker et al., 2022, p. 3040.

20. Sawyers, 2023.

21. Evita Sawyers, personal communication, October 2, 2023.

22. Stewart, 2001; Sheff, 2014.

23. Flicker et al., 2022, p. 3040.

24. Flicker et al., 2022, p. 3042.

25. Flicker et al., 2022, p. 3042.

26. Kathy Labriola, personal communication, October 10, 2022.

27. For example, Moors & Ramos, 2022; Witherspoon & Theodore, 2021.

28. Giuliani, 2023.

29. For example, Patterson, 2018; Rambukkana, 2015; Schippers, 2016; Sheff & Hammers, 2011.

30. See Ferrer, 2018, and Halpern, 1999, for descriptions of polypride.

A COMPREHENSIVE MODEL OF COMPERSION

In Parts I and II of this book, I described how participants in this study construed their experiences of compersion. In Part III, I outlined the most significant factors that promote and hinder compersion based on interview data—yielding a compersion roadmap. In Part IV, I now incorporate the factors outlined in Parts I, II, and III into an integrative theoretical model that bridges what compersion *is* with the *contexts that impact it.*

This section includes only one chapter: "A Proposed Theory of Compersion." It provides a description and schematization of the proposed theory and explains how this model may support CNM individuals in understanding how their unique life contexts interact with different aspects of compersion. Then, I introduce the Dual Control Model of Compersion—a model based on the idea that compersion can be accelerated or inhibited. Inspired by language from the Kinsey Institute's Dual Control Model of Sexual Response,[1] I use the analogy of break and acceleration pedals in a car—which makes it easy to grasp how some contexts "accelerate" compersion, while other factors act as a "break" to its occurrence.

While I geared my research toward CNM individuals, I believe this model could be adapted to inspire and guide people to cultivate more positive empathy and gratitude in many other types of relationships—from intimate monogamous partnerships to collegial and family relationships, to platonic friendships, and beyond. I hope that other researchers will test and build upon this model to further the understanding of compersion in CNM, as well as in other types of relationships.

NOTE

1. Bancroft, 1999; Bancroft et al., 2009; Bancroft & Janssen, 2000; Janssen & Bancroft, 2007.

CHAPTER 9

A PROPOSED THEORY OF COMPERSION

The two research questions I set out to answer in my original study,[1] "What is the experience of compersion?" and "What factors impact compersion?" yielded the information I described in the previous chapters of this book. My investigation of the first question, "What is the experience of compersion?" yielded the *components* of compersion described in Part I and its *dimensions* described in Part II. The second question, "What factors impact compersion?" led to the factors that promote and hinder compersion described in Part III.

Inspired by the participants' stories, I soon realized that these two groupings of data did not function as separate silos—but as an interconnected system of factors at play in people's ecosystems of relationships. I then synthesized the findings from my two research questions into an integrative model that highlights significant relationships between the elements that constitute compersion and the factors that impact it. I offer this model as a first theoretical attempt toward a holistic understanding of how compersion functions in CNM relationships. I portray it visually in the following schema (Figure 9.1) and explain these relationships in more depth in the next pages.

At the crux of this "compersion system," tying all of the aforementioned themes together, are two main elements that determine the occurrence of compersion:

1. *CNM meaning-making*, which refers to the CNM-supportive, and therefore compersion-supportive, narratives a person applies to their extradyadic experiences; and
2. *Lack of threat*, which refers to a favorable ratio between individual and relational security and perceived threat from a partner's relationship with another person.

The first element, CNM meaning-making, occurs through one's ideological commitment to CNM values and community belonging. It pertains directly

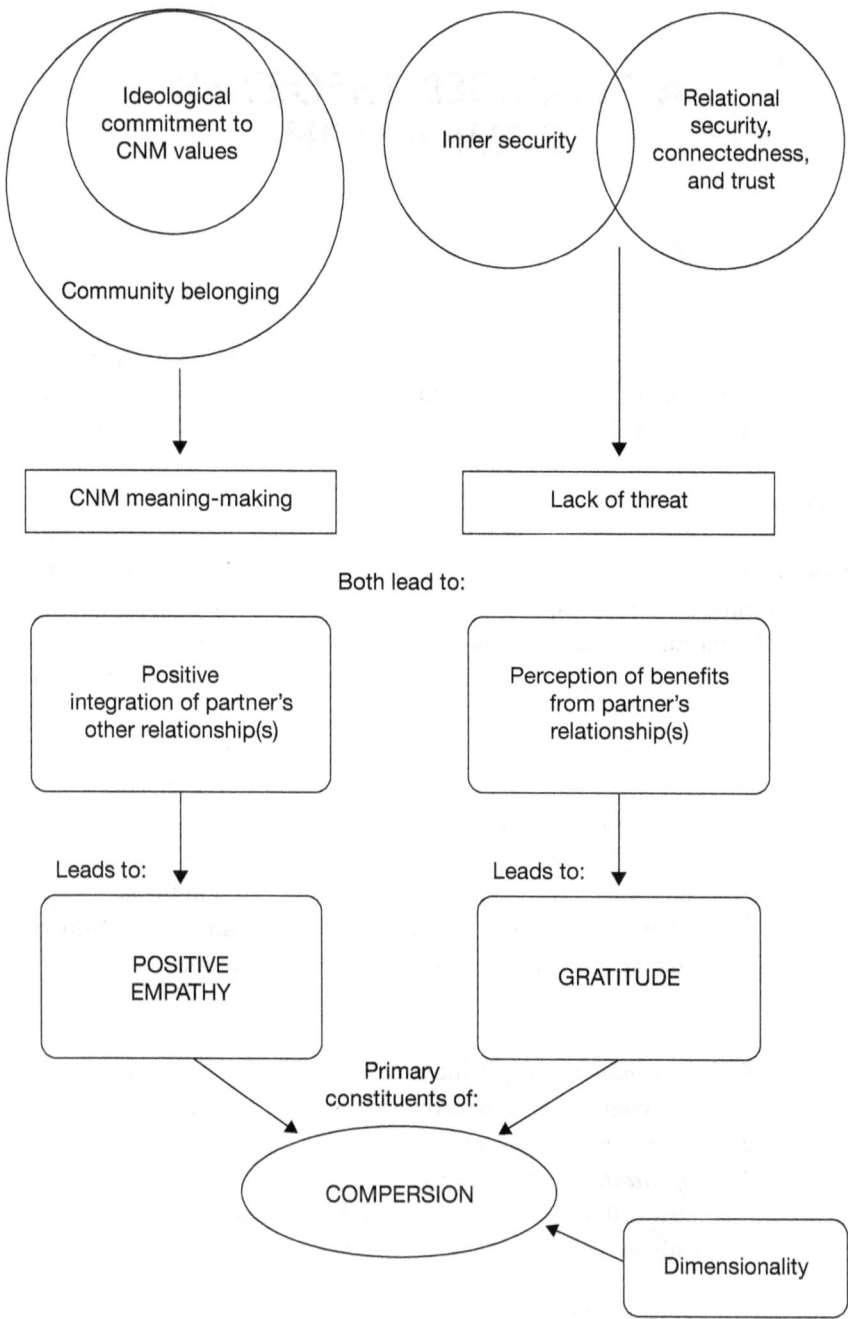

Figure 9.1. Compersion Model

to the process of coming out as non-monogamous, both to oneself and to others, on which I elaborate in chapter 10. The second factor, lack of threat, derives from inner security and relational security, connectedness, and trust, which has to do with attachment security to self and others. The combination of these elements catalyzes compersion through the "compersion system" I describe here.

The presence of both CNM meaning-making and lack of threat together facilitates the occurrence of the (a) positive integration of partner's other relationship(s), and the (b) perception of benefits from partner's other relationship(s). The positive integration of partner's other relationship(s) leads to an ability to experience positive empathy for one's partner's other relationship(s) and metamour(s)—which is one of the main structural components of compersion. The perception of benefits from partner's other relationship(s) leads to gratitude for those benefits, which is the second main structural component of compersion. The perception of benefits from other partner's relationship(s) also facilitates the positive integration of these relationship(s)—because when these relationships are seen in a positive light, the desire to include (rather than exclude) metamours from one's "circle of care" paves the path for positive empathy. Finally, the dimensions of compersion (as described in Part II) qualify the experience in its uniqueness and complexity, reflecting the diverse ways it can show up: attitudinal versus embodied, on a spectrum, and at times, coexisting with jealousy or other challenging emotions. This model visually demonstrates the interconnectedness of the elements at play in people's compersion experiences—and helps visualize how fluidly the outcomes can shift when any of these factors get impacted.

CONGRUENCY AND EXCEPTIONS

The vast majority of my interviewees' accounts of compersion portrayed each of the elements shown in the model. However, there were a few exceptions—situations where a participant would describe a version of compersion that did not include all the elements of this model. Indeed, because compersion is such a fluid and dynamic concept, some people may define it using outlier interpretations of the term.

For example, George, a 53-year-old professor, saw compersion as a chosen behavior rooted in a "sense of duty." He recounted how he used to drive his ex-wife, who was bisexual, to meet her female lovers—not because it was particularly joyful for him, but because he believed that supporting her in getting her needs met was the "right thing to do" as a husband. George's compersion was primarily rooted in his ideological commitment to CNM values, while the other elements of the compersion model were in the background for him. As I described in Chapter 4, his experience exemplified an extreme version of attitudinal compersion.

Sabrina, on the other hand, experienced a high level of embodied compersion—but one of the main factors was missing: community belonging. She and her partner had barely ever connected with any CNM community or media, and in fact, Sabrina had never heard the word "compersion" before encountering my study. Nevertheless, she had developed a proud CNM identity without relying on wider networks and had internally created pro-CNM and pro-compersion narratives that had allowed her to positively integrate her partner's other relationships and perceive those relationships as yielding great benefits. Thus, the CNM meaning-making factor had been met for her, even without the community belonging piece—showing that a personal commitment to CNM values could be enough to create and maintain positive CNM meaning-making, even in the absence of supportive community.

Sylvia's story was another outlier, as she experienced much more compersion in her platonic connections than in her romantic and/or sexual relationships. While she clearly adhered to the individual factors of ideological commitment to CNM values and inner security, she encountered many obstacles at the relational and social levels—which prevented her from experiencing compersion in her intimate relationships. She did, however, experience compersion in other aspects of her life, especially witnessing younger folks thriving in their non-monogamous lives—which she affectionately called "aunty compersion." Her account shines light on the potentials of compersion in nonromantic life situations.

A DUAL CONTROL MODEL OF COMPERSION

The present theory of compersion includes not only a qualitative description of the experience of compersion itself but also a map of its contextual excitatory and inhibitory factors, based on participant data. It appears that the interaction of these factors determines whether or not, and to what degree, compersion occurs in a given situation.

This model structurally mirrors the Dual Control Model of Sexual Response.[2] Going beyond previous models of sexual response,[3] the Dual Control Model did not simply describe the phases of a "normal" sexual response (e.g., desire, arousal, orgasm, resolution),[4] but also took into consideration the impact of the individual psychology of sexual desire by proposing that sexual responses involve an interaction between a sexual excitatory system (SES; i.e., "accelerator") and a sexual inhibitory system (SIS; i.e., "brake"). Thus, each lived experience of sexual stimulation reflects a complexity of factors that either promote or inhibit sexual desire—the combination of which leads to a specific sexual response outcome.[5] The model also postulates that individuals vary in their propensity for both sexual excitation and sexual inhibition, and that these variations may help explain much of the variability in human sexuality.[6] It is an example of a state-trait model,[7] which proposes that the weighing of excitatory and inhibitory processes determines whether or not a sexual response occurs within an individual in a given situation. At the same time, it assumes individual variability in the propensity for these processes. Thus, every person has a more or less sensitive SES (or "accelerator") and a more or less sensitive SIS (or "brake")—creating a spectrum between folks whose sexual desire is very easily aroused, and not so easily tampered (high SES and low SIS), and at the other end, those whose sexual desire is difficult or rare to stoke, and easily extinguished (low SES and high SIS).[8]

The compersion theory herein structurally emulates the dual model of sexual response, as it reflects how a variety of contextual factors are at play in a person's likelihood to experience compersion, each factor promoting or hindering its occurence. It is thus helpful to adopt similar language—that of a *compersion excitatory system* (CES) and *compersion inhibitory system* (CIS). Just like the dual control model accounts for individual variability in the propensity for SES and SIS, the compersion model proposed here also assumes such variability.

The dual model of sexual response also accounts for two different types of SIS: (a) SIS1, a chronic, low-level SIS that keeps the brakes on all the time, such as a general sexual performance anxiety (similar to a "hand brake" in a car); and (b) SIS2, a circumstance-based SIS that can be activated sporadically when an external threat to desire arises—such as fear of unwanted pregnancy, an unpleasant smell, and the like (comparable to a "foot brake").[9]

I categorized the inhibitory factors of compersion similarly. The factors that hinder compersion from an ideological standpoint (e.g., internalized mononormativity, marginalization) can be compared with SIS1—a low-level, chronic block to experiencing compersion. In contrast, the circumstantial factors, such as a breach of trust or temporary lack of sleep, are comparable to SIS2, being more readily changeable. I thus coined these interactions of compersion inhibitory factors as CIS1 and CIS2.

While the dual model of sexual response does not propose a distinction between two types of "accelerators," such a distinction could be discerned in the compersion model: a general predisposition toward compersion (a positive attitudinal orientation toward a partner's other relationships, or trait compersion), versus a circumstantial accelerator that is activated when specific, punctual circumstances are met—a great connection with a metamour, an abundance of security and reassurance within a specific relationship, stellar communication, and so on (state compersion). These interactions of compersion excitatory factors could thus be coined CES1 and CES2.

For example, a person could have a high general predisposition toward compersion (CES1) because their CNM meaning-making is very positive—they wholeheartedly *want* to be non-monogamous—but they may find themselves in a circumstance that inhibits compersion (CIS2), such as disliking a particular metamour or feeling particularly insecure because they just lost their job or suffered a romantic rejection. Conversely, someone may have a low general predisposition toward compersion (CIS1)—perhaps they were "dragged" into CNM reluctantly by a partner—but find themselves experiencing high levels of compersion when they find themselves in a favorable circumstance (CES2), for example, by benefiting greatly from a particular metamour's presence, or getting sexually turned on by their partner's other relationship.

These distinctions mirror the idea of trait versus state compersion,[10] where trait would refer to CES1 and CIS1, and state, to CES2 and CIS2. This model also resonates with the distinction between attitudinal (CES1) and embodied (CES2) compersion discussed in Chapter 4. While these delineations are still tentative and theoretical, they map quite well onto my participant data and can be quite helpful in predicting how certain contexts will impact someone's compersion experiences.

APPLYING THE MODEL IN PRACTICE

Understanding how one's compersion "brake" and "accelerator" function can go a long way toward supporting folks to create the circumstances they need to invite more compersion into their lives. I learned from coaching CNM individuals that when one becomes aware of the specific circumstances that inhibit and accelerate compersion for themselves and their intimate partners, they gain a deeper sense of agency within their relational ecosystems.

Furthermore, understanding why someone would *not* experience compersion can facilitate compassion for oneself and others. As I emphasized in the introduction to this book, a lack of compersion can serve to illuminate the areas where one's personal or relational needs are not being met, or where folks may not be acting in fullhearted consent. I urge readers to practice compassion, trust, and acceptance across the variety of their relational experiences, as to avoid the common pitfall of pressuring themselves or others to feel compersion. In my experience, heartfelt curiosity and openness toward emergent relational realities are more conducive to inclusive and authentic love than the expectation that one *should* experience more compersion (or any other state). *Toxic positivity*—the mandate that one should only experience "positive" thoughts and emotions and get rid of "negative" ones[11]—will cause more harm than good in any type of relationship, as it stifles curiosity and can prevent folks from acknowledging and dealing directly with issues at hand. Treating one another with respect and care as a foremost relational commitment should always take priority over "being the most compersive person around."

In closing, I also want to note that while this chapter offers a congruent theoretical map of compersion in CNM relationships, this is a first attempt at such a project based on a relatively small sample of qualitative data—and therefore has limitations. It would certainly be helpful for future research to test this model with larger samples of participants to further understand how compersion functions in different contexts. Additionally, the reality on the ground is by no means linear: relationships—let alone CNM ones—are constellations of complex systems (human beings) with other complex systems (other human beings), within ever-changing, fluid, and multifaceted environments. Given the complexity of the topic and the novelty of this research, I encourage readers to treat this model not as a prescriptive or definitive guide, but rather as a point of reference and assessment tool as they conduct their own explorations.

NOTES

1. Thouin-Savard, 2021.
2. Bancroft, 1999; Bancroft et al., 2009; Bancroft & Janssen, 2000; Janssen & Bancroft, 2007.
3. For example, Kaplan, 1979; Masters & Johnsons, 1966.
4. Basson, 2000.
5. Janssen & Bancroft, 2007.
6. Bancroft et al., 2009.
7. See Duma, 2009, for a state-trait understanding of compersion.
8. Nagoski, 2015.
9. Nagoski, 2015; Bancroft & Janssen, 2000.
10. Duma, 2009.
11. Goodman, 2022.

SOCIAL LENSES ON COMPERSION

One of the main takeaways of this book thus far is that compersion is *contextual*. People may experience compersion with different flavors, intensities, and frequencies, depending on their particular individual, relational, and social contexts. Furthermore, as I demonstrated in the last section, these various contextual elements do not function in isolation: they are highly interconnected, and intersect dynamically to create environments that promote or inhibit the emergence of different components and dimensions of compersion.

The influence of social and cultural contexts in which people are immersed as they co-create their intimate lives is still under-researched in the CNM literature. Yet, these basic influences deeply impact whether and how compersion emerges. I dedicate this next section of the book to exploring these significant dynamics.

In Chapter 10, "The Role of Coming Out and Pride in Compersion," I investigate the connection between compersion and CNM identity development, meaning-making, and the process of coming out as non-monogamous within a mononormative society. I hypothesize a parallel between the role of pride in LGBTQ+ communities and compersion in CNM, and explore how the perception of CNM as an orientation versus a choice may impact one's propensity toward compersiveness. In Chapter 11, "Social Positionality and Compersion," I look at compersion from the lenses of age, disability, gender, sexual orientation, race, and socioeconomic status. Using participant stories as well as several additional interviews with trusted colleagues in the field of CNM education, I show how nuanced and often counterintuitive the impact of these factors can be.

To my knowledge, the next chapters are a first-ever attempt at connecting the dots between compersion, identity development, and social positionality in the CNM literature. While many possible angles of inquiry will not be covered here, my goal with this section is to begin an expanding dialogue that will be helpful to CNM folks, therapists, and health professionals alike, as well as inspire other researchers to further investigate these questions.

THE ROLE OF COMING OUT AND PRIDE IN COMPERSION

I decided to become consensually non-monogamous when I found the language around relationship practices. It was just always a natural state of who I was.

—Tyrone, 38

A great majority of participants in my study contextualized their experiences of compersion as intrinsically linked with their process of identity development and coming out as non-monogamous. Because CNM lies outside mononormative templates, all participants had to transform their inner and outer paradigms[1]—both behaviorally and feelings-wise—to embrace non-monogamy and experience compersion. The process of defying established social conventions to live a more authentic life is well known to members of the LGBTQ+ community and is thoroughly documented in literature on coming out. As members of a sexual/relational minority, CNM folks typically go through a similar process of integrating and claiming their identity—which is key to developing a healthy sense of self when creating a life outside the norms.

In this chapter, I explore how the *CNM meaning-making process* in my model of compersion (see Chapter 9) is inherently a process of identity development. From there, I hypothesize a parallel between pride in queer communities and compersion in CNM relationships. In similar ways that joy and pride can serve as a counteragent to shame and marginalization for LGBTQ+ folks, compersion may play an integral role in emancipating oneself from mononormative norms and reconciling dissociated aspects of the self. The emphasis on shared joy, solidarity, and pride functions as an antidote to the shame, repression, and isolation that can come with being an outsider vis-à-vis ingrained social norms. Compersion, like pride, is antithetical to shame.

As I described in Chapter 3, one of the main elements that promotes gratitude in CNM relationships, and therefore leads to compersion, is *freedom from fear, emotional congruence, and pride*. CNM individuals tend to feel pride when they create harmonious CNM ecosystems despite the widespread social expectation that those relationships are bound to fail and the stigma surrounding them. This sense of pride and alignment becomes a source of deep gratitude for the opportunity to "be oneself" openly, and live in emotional congruence with one's authentic sense of self, values, and ideologies—which is often a linchpin of people's compersive experiences. In other words, coming out as CNM may generate pride—which is a factor of gratitude, which then leads to compersion.

In the next pages, I explore notable parallels between the processes of coming out for LGBTQ+ and CNM folks. I survey the literature on CNM identity development and discuss the mixed impact of CNM being a *hidden target identity*. Then, I explain how resilience plays into coming out and compersion, leading to the finding that compersion can serve as a strategy of resistance against inner and outer oppression. Finally, I elaborate on how one's perception of innateness versus choice around non-monogamous identity formation may impact compersion, as well as how these dynamics may show up differently for members of established couples versus solo polyamorous or uncoupled CNM people.

WHAT IS COMING OUT?

The journey from shame to acceptance and pride for members of sexual minorities is most often associated with homosexual,[2] bisexual,[3] and transgender[4] models of coming out and identity formation. It is also—however more sparsely—documented in some CNM literature.[5] According to research, the process of coming out is one of the most crucial elements in the development of a healthy sexual identity.[6] Indeed, studies show negative physiological outcomes among folks who remain "closeted,"[7] as well as psychosomatic symptoms that may reduce quality of life.[8]

Typically, research in the LGBTQ+ field breaks down the process of coming out into two main phases: (a) coming out to oneself, which means internally discovering and accepting one's true identity or orientation; and (b) coming out to others, the process of revealing one's authentic self to other people—usually starting with one's most trusted loved ones, and progressively enlarging the circle toward an integrated public identity.[9] For example, psychoanalyst Jack Drescher described this distinction in the context of coming out as gay. Although in a different context, the process of coming out as non-monogamous is analogous for many people:

> Coming out to oneself is a subjective experience of inner recognition . . . a realization that previously unacceptable feelings or desires are part of one's self. It is, in part, a verbal process—putting into words previously inarticulated feelings and ideas. It is a recapturing of disavowed experiences. Coming out to oneself may precede any sexual contact. Sometimes, the moment of coming out to oneself is sexually exciting. Some gay people describe it as a switch being turned on. "Coming home" or "discovering who I really was" are how gay people frequently describe coming out to themselves. . . . Coming out to oneself may be followed by coming out to others.[10]

In my study, the processes of coming out to oneself and coming out to others found parallels in the themes of ideological commitment to CNM values and community belonging, respectively. As a whole, the process of coming out as non-monogamous mirrors the theme of CNM meaning-making, which is a crucial element of my compersion model (described in Part IV) and includes both intrapersonal and social elements. Positive meaning-making around non-monogamy is essential for CNM folks to experience the sense of self-actualization (i.e., authenticity, acceptance, and integrity with oneself) that is a marker of any coming out process.[11] Self-actualization is a cornerstone of the propensity to experience compersion and pride.

For both LGBTQ+ and CNM individuals, celebrating an identity that has been shamed and ostracized is a defiant act that has both personal and social ramifications. Although the coming out process can be fraught with challenges, its purpose is one of emancipation. Coming out represents a journey of liberating one's true self from hiding, a transformation of shame into pride, of fear into joy, of social isolation into community belonging, and of reclaiming one's true gender, sexual, and/or relational expression from the shadows of dominant social norms. As such, there are undeniable parallels between the process of coming out as LGBTQ+ and CNM. While still in its infancy, a growing body of research addresses the specificities of CNM identity development—which I turn to next.

CHAPTER 10

IDENTITY DEVELOPMENT AND COMING OUT
FOR CNM PEOPLE

A few significant studies[12] have highlighted markers of meaning-making and identity construction when embracing a CNM identity. In *"There Aren't Words for What We Do or How We Feel So We Have to Make Them Up": Constructing Polyamorous Languages in a Culture of Compulsory Monogamy*, Ritchie and Barker highlighted the importance of language in the process of constructing a CNM identity.[13] They documented how polyamorous individuals have had to invent new words to reflect and validate their unique experiences of extradyadic intimacy and create new cultural narratives of relationship and sexuality. Arguing that the conventional mononormative language that saturates mainstream media is constraining the potentials of polyamory, they indicated that "alternative languages seem to enable new ways of experiencing as well as expressing sexual stories"[14]—in a similar way that the

> emergence of the label "gay" in the early 1970s was important in terms of the public expression of homosexuality as a legitimate sexual identity . . . by [establishing] a clear social identity, which offered a previously unavailable sense of security and community.[15]

In the same way, the word compersion holds the potential to normalize non-monogamy by rebutting the myth that jealousy is the only valid, or even possible response to extradyadic intimacy—and that this response is both inflexible and inevitable. As such, simply learning the word compersion can be greatly validating on one's journey of coming out as CNM and reorienting oneself to a new socioemotional paradigm. I can personally testify to this, having received countless messages from people who stumbled upon my research on compersion and gratefully expressed that learning about this word helped them reclaim a disowned or ostracized part of themselves.

What developmental tasks and stages are most common in CNM folks' coming out processes? Pioneering CNM identity development research, Weitzman documented common milestones and growth tasks she observed in her therapy clients who were coming out as CNM.[16] These included: (a) coming out to oneself, (b) coming out to a monogamous partner, (c) negotiating how "out" to be in different spaces (such as at work or among relatives), and (d) including additional partners in the primary bond. Later, Peace identified several more developmental stages marking the transition from a monogamous to a polyamorous identity.[17] From her qualitative data analysis, nine identity development steps emerged: (a) unaware of polyamory, (b) attempt to conform to monogamy, (c) failed monogamy, (d) introduction to polyamory, (e) acceptance of polyamory, (f) engaging in polyamorous relationships, (g) coming out as polyamorous, (h) insulation in the poly community, and (i) self-identify as polyamorous. These steps were similar to other identity development models, such as Cass's theory of homosexual identity formation.[18]

Both Weitzman's clients and Peace's research participants started as monogamous. Thus, as Witherspoon noted, "it remains unclear whether or to what extent such models of poly identity development would apply to those who are exposed to CNM relationships from an early age."[19] It is also unclear where this leaves individuals who do not identify as either monogamous or polyamorous, but instead adopt in-between statuses such as "novogamous" or "monogamish." Jorge Ferrer characterized novogamy as a "fuzzy, liminal, and multivocal semantic-existential space"[20] that circumvents the binary of monogamy versus non-monogamy. Simply put, novogamy represents the freedom to adopt any relationship structure that suits a person and their partner(s), at any given point, without being bound to a rigid identity or set of beliefs. Novogamy presents a challenge to the narrative of the CNM coming out process as a straight evolutionary line between monogamy and CNM. Similarly, the expression "monogamish"—originally coined by popular author and columnist Dan Savage[21]—refers to the liminal space between monogamy and CNM. It is a "third option" of sorts that is still widely absent from the intimate relationship literature, although it is compatible with the values of fluidity and agency guiding CNM individuals when creating relationship agreements "by design"—based on partners' specific needs and desires at a particular time.

For both novogamous and monogamish folks, it may be easier to retain social privilege based on the appearance of adherence to mononormativity— analogous to BIPOC people who can "pass" as White, or folks with invisible disabilities. While this may yield a certain social advantage, it can also make it more difficult to reap the benefits of coming out to a supportive community and access a sense of belonging, which would support compersion and overall wellbeing. This relates to a phenomenon that most CNM individuals encounter on their coming out journey: the paradox of embodying a *hidden target identity*.

CNM as a Hidden Target Identity

The fact that CNM people can hide their non-monogamous identity from immediate recognition—a phenomenon known as a hidden target identity—offers an awkward trade-off.[22] On the one hand, CNM folks can employ passing as monogamous to maintain the privileges that come along with it, such as avoiding serious social and legal consequences like the loss of housing, jobs, child custody, or important relationships.[23] As such, many people who identify as CNM do not share their identity with immediate family members, friends, and colleagues, to retain social status and privilege.

However, this "advantage" may also create difficulty in accessing a culture of positive validation and mutual support. CNM folks often live a double life between the social environments where they can be "out" and those where they cannot. As Peace explained, embodying a hidden target identity may perpetuate a fragmented sense of self and reduce quality of life:

> If someone who is in a target group can hide their identity and *pass* as a member of the non-target group (i.e., people with hidden disabilities or LGBT people), this strategy may be employed to escape discrimination or persecution. However, like shifting, hiding important aspects of one's identity causes psychological distress. Research has shown this hidden target group membership is a particularly salient issue for bisexual people.[24]

To this point, Rambukkana observed commonalities between coming out as polyamorous and coming out as bisexual:

> I believe that, to a certain extent, the politics of polyamory can be seen as similar to those of bisexuality. Both "polyamorous" and "bisexual" are particularly difficult social mantles to take on, partially due to the fact that their liminal nature—their position between conditions that many conceive of as mutually exclusive (i.e., gay/straight, radical/mainstream)—makes them uncomfortable bridges between discourses that, at the best of times, resist being bridged, and at worst, want nothing to do with each other.[25]

In the case of CNM folks, not coming out to others may not bode well for compersion because it prevents the possibility of connecting to a supportive community, which is the best catalyst for CNM people to uproot and transform internalized mononormative values. The need to hide one's CNM identity within a mononormative society generates intrapersonal and interpersonal friction, and often a level of tension between one's private and public identities. This is, in part, why dismantling mononormativity and cultivating a culture of acceptance around sexual and relationship diversity is such a worthy pursuit. Meanwhile, CNM people must adopt strategies of resilience that counteract the effects of mononormative pressures, to invite compersion.

CNM RESILIENCE, COMING OUT, AND COMPERSION

A significant component of coming out as CNM is rooted in resilience and strength vis-à-vis the tension engendered by going against the grain of mononormative culture. Indeed, a majority of CNM-identified folks have experienced a need to "conceal their true sexual identity for fear of disapprobation, discrimination, and even violence."[26] Witherspoon looked at how polyamorous individuals invoke resilience and strength to alleviate the negative mental health outcome from minority stress and stigma, as well as discrimination, harassment, and violence (DHV).[27] He found four constructs as potential resilience and strength factors: (a) mindfulness, (b) cognitive flexibility, (c) a positive CNM identity, and (d) connection to a supportive CNM community. Greater outness about one's CNM practices was positively correlated with a connection to a supportive CNM community, as well as having a positive sense of CNM identity.

These two last constructs—a positive CNM identity and connection to a supportive CNM community—coincide with the results reported in my study on the themes of ideological commitment to CNM values and community belonging. These two themes constitute the CNM meaning-making component of the compersion model I described in Chapter 9, showing a clear correlation between factors of CNM resilience and strength and factors of compersion. This helps explain why the process of coming out to oneself and others is such a critical context for compersion to arise.

Of course, connecting to a supportive community is easier in some circumstances than others. As Rambukkana astutely remarked, CNM individuals are "located along multiple axes of privilege/oppression [and therefore] cannot be seen collectively as an oppressed class."[28] Indeed, there are many factors that influence how challenging one's coming out process might be. For example, as I described in Chapters 8 and 11, Black, Indigenous, and people of color (BIPOC) folks often have greater difficulty seeing themselves represented in CNM communities than White folks in a vast majority of geographical areas. Without inclusive representation, sharing a sense of pride and trust with other CNM folks can be challenging. There can also be obstacles to coming out for people with less socioeconomic advantage, as they may not be able to afford the risk of losing certain privileges—for example, work or housing—by rejecting mononormativity.

That said, some folks introduce a counterintuitive narrative by utilizing CNM pride and compersion as a strategy of resistance vis-à-vis an interconnected system of oppression—mononormativity being one cog in a machine sustaining several other vectors, such as patriarchy, sexism, colonialism, racism, capitalism, and more. I expand on this more in the next chapter, "Social Positionality and Compersion," but I give an overview of this concept here since it is deeply relevant to the intersection of CNM identity development, pride, resilience, and compersion.

Compersion as Strategy of Resistance

Compersion can function as a strategy of resistance and agentic empowerment for folks who openly defy mononormativity. In adopting compersive attitudes and behaviors, they not *only* reject compulsory monogamy, they also transform the psycho-emotional narratives associated with it. While the process of coming out as CNM can be more fraught for marginalized folks, rejecting non-monogamy can go hand-in-hand with resisting other vectors of oppression. For example, when describing how her racial identity as a Black woman intersects with compersion, Evita Sawyers described,

> I think that the intersection of compersion and race has to do with what we are told is available to us, and what we're capable of having as people of color, and how sometimes, our partners can engage in relationships that challenge those notions and cause us to have to really look at that. And I think some people's response to that is to react very strongly. They don't feel the compersion or they feel a lot of fear. They feel a lot of scarcity. They feel a lot of threat, because of those internalized beliefs. And then for some people, I think their response to it is to figure out how to go in the other direction. It's like, "I don't want to hold these beliefs and carry them around because they limit me, or it's something that was given to me by colonization, racism, white supremacy, whatever. And I don't want any part of anything that's been laid on me unconsensually because of these things." And so their response is, "Oh, no, I'm gonna go in the completely opposite direction. Because of all this scarcity and all of this fear and all of this threat, all those things have tried to embed into my beliefs about myself and my existence, I'm going to

completely revolt against that by going in the other direction and embracing this thing and celebrating it, because that's a part of my resistance."[29]

Sawyers described how the effects of compounded discrimination can play out for different folks in CNM—bringing some people to feel more threatened and less compersive, while inciting others to adopt a stronger stance of defiance by bringing compersion forward. Many mitigating factors influence which direction a person may take—including the stage of one's CNM identity development and coming out process, and access to supportive community. I elaborate further on compersion as a strategy of resistance in Chapter 11.

In both LGBTQ+ and CNM coming out processes, pride and celebration can function to resist dominant narratives and overcome shame. CNM people may transcend internalized mononormativity by practicing a defiant stance of inclusive love, even against the odds.

CNM IDENTITY DEVELOPMENT BASED ON PERCEPTION OF INNATENESS VERSUS CHOICE

There is no consensus in the literature about whether CNM is an innate way of being akin to a sexual orientation,[30] or a chosen strategy of sexual and relational expression.[31] The subjective experience of participants in my study reflected this duality of perspectives, as some considered themselves innately and irrevocably non-monogamous, while others felt they had selected a CNM lifestyle through a rational decision or specific circumstances that were subject to change.

A CNM individual's perception of innateness versus choice most likely has consequences on the nature of their coming out process. Anecdotally, one participant, Jo, suggested that having CNM as an orientation was a good predictor for compersion, because it facilitated identity development around CNM. Self-identified as "polyamorous by orientation," Jo reasoned that compersion would be less likely for people who are choosing CNM from the desire to please a partner, or because they came to a logical conclusion that they *should* be CNM. While the CNM literature does not yet address the impact of CNM individual's perception of innateness versus choice in the coming out process, it appears that those who identify as innately non-monogamous have no difficulty creating positive CNM meaning-making, which in turn facilitates compersion.

Indeed, for my study participants who had previously felt stifled within the mononormative paradigm, and sensed that their "true" identity was non-monogamous, actualizing CNM with intimate partners as well as being part of a broader community had brought particularly potent relief, gratitude, and joy—joy from no longer needing to suppress one's authentic emotional or sexual expression to access love and belonging. Pride, exaltation, and renewed aliveness were often byproducts of this felt sense of congruence and alignment between their authentic self and their external relational reality—leading to the emergence of *polypride*.[32] These emotions were, in themselves, a constituent of their experience of compersion.

"More Poly" versus "Less Poly" Partners

The perception of innateness versus choice sometimes translated into a difference in levels of enthusiasm for members of established couples transitioning from monogamy to CNM. In my study, this difference in perception of innateness had a notable effect on compersiveness. In cases where a person initiated non-monogamy with a more reluctant partner, the initiator typically felt more strongly non-monogamous at the identity level. When this "more poly" partner (or the initiator) witnessed their "less poly" partner developing other intimate relationships, they were more likely to experience relief and joy—as this was a sign that non-monogamy would be feasible for them, and that they could keep both their valued relationship and their authentic sense of self as a CNM person.

Those instances would bring gratitude for the perception of benefits from a partner's other relationship(s)—benefits connected to the fact that a more authentic and richer life had become possible for them. Thus, the "more poly" partner of an initial couple opening up would *typically* (depending on the other contextual factors at play) meet the "less poly" party's new relationships with compersion.

For the more reluctant partners, however—especially those who had initially been poly under duress, or PUD (see Chapter 8)—the socioemotional journey from monogamy to CNM was fraught with more challenges. As I discussed in Chapter 7 under the section "Ideological Commitment to CNM Values," these folks needed to eventually choose CNM from a place of sufficiency, personal autonomy, and agency before compersion could arise. Otherwise, they could remain caught in a disempowered space of inner friction between their monogamous beliefs and values and their CNM behaviors, and this would block the possibility of compersion.

When a "less poly" or more reluctant partner stepped into nonmonogamy, their developmental journey was less about coming out—as they may not have previously harbored non-monogamous desires or identities—and more about buying into the creative possibilities of non-monogamy. Deliberately abandoning monogamy and choosing a new identity and mode of relating was a significant development in a person's sense of self, and without the emergence of a positive interpretation of this transition, compersion would typically remain elusive. As an analogy, if one member of a couple who has lived together in California for several decades were to suggest that they move to Europe, the more reluctant partner would have to find enough advantages about living in Europe (including, but not limited to, making their partner happy) before they could full-heartedly participate in their partner's joy of moving to a different continent.

In sum, compersion has a lot to do with how enthusiastic each person feels about their newfound CNM identity and relational prospects. However, there are also instances where things take a surprising turn: a "more poly" partner who originally initiated CNM with a more reluctant partner sometimes encounters greater difficulty finding dates and other relationships than the "less poly" person—which can result in the initially "less poly" person experiencing more compersion.

This was the case for my participants Diane and James when comparing their first and second interviews: while Diane had initially initiated CNM and identified as the "more poly" partner in 2018, she had experienced more difficulty than James finding new partners when they were last interviewed in 2022. At the time of the more recent interview, James was experiencing more compersion for Diane than she did for him—because their circumstances had changed. Thus, as with every factor of compersion I explored in this book, personal realities on the ground are complex and dynamic—and are always subject to change.

CNM Identity Development of Uncoupled and Solo Polyamorous People

Uncoupled or solo polyamorous participants typically had more similarities to the "more poly" folks described earlier than with the "less poly" or reluctant parties. Because being single inherently carries less social privilege than being coupled (see section "Couple Privilege" in Chapter 8 for a discussion of couple-centrism), and CNM carries less privilege than monogamy, a person had to carry a more assertive CNM sense of self in order to renounce monogamous social privileges and accept the realities of compounded discrimination. Most often, these folks (as well as their "more poly" coupled counterparts) identified as "poly by orientation"—which would be favorable to compersion, other variables being equal.

However, solo polyamorous folks often encountered other obstacles to compersion. Partnering with members of established couples, for example, could sometimes bring about hierarchical dynamics where they were treated as "more disposable" than their metamours—a situation that would make it quite challenging to access compersion. While one's meaning-making process around CNM identity is a large part of the puzzle as it pertains to compersion, it does not erase or outweigh the need for other factors to be in place—particularly as it pertains to inner security, relational security, and lack of threat.

In sum, this chapter has focused on how coming out to oneself and to others is core to the CNM meaning-making process that favors compersion. This tends to be easier for folks who perceive CNM as an innate orientation versus a circumstantial choice. Yet, many other variables at play impact compersion outcomes—including inner security, relational security, the perception of benefits from a partner's other relationship(s), and the positive integration of partner's other relationship(s). In Chapter 11, I explore more social factors that impact compersion by diving into the connections between social positionality and compersion.

NOTES

1. For an exploration of the paradigmatic transition from monogamy to CNM, I highly recommend Jessica Fern's and David Cooley's *Polywise* (2023).
2. Cass, 1979, 1984a, 1984b; Coleman, 1982; Falco, 1991; Lewis, 1984; Sophie, 1982.
3. Brown, 2002; D'Augelli, 1994; Harper & Swanson, 2019; Reynolds & Hanjorgiris, 2000; Rodríguez Rust, 2007; Weitzman, 2007.
4. Bockting, 2014; Bradford & Syed, 2019; Kuper et al., 2018; Levitt & Ippolito, 2014.
5. Barker, 2005; Manley et al., 2015; Peace, 2012; Ritchie & Barker, 2006; Table et al., 2017; Weitzman, 2006; Witherspoon, 2018.
6. For example, McLean, 2007.
7. Cole et al., 1996.
8. Weinberg & Williams, 1974.
9. For example, Guittar, 2013.

10. Drescher, 2004, p. 14.

11. Samuels, 2003.

12. Barker, 2005; Manley et al., 2015; Peace, 2012; Ritchie & Barker, 2006; Table et al., 2017; Weitzman, 2006; Witherspoon, 2018.

13. Ritchie & Barker, 2006.

14. Richie & Barker, 2006.

15. Richie & Barker, 2006, p. 585.

16. Weitzman, 2006.

17. Peace, 2012.

18. Cass, 1979, 1984a, 1984b.

19. Witherspoon, 2018, p. 121.

20. Ferrer, 2018, p. 3.

21. Savage, 2014.

22. Peace, 2012.

23. Ravenscroft, 2004.

24. Peace, 2012, p. 40.

25. Rambukkana, 2004, p. 144.

26. Weitzman et al., 2009, p. 22; see also Conley et al., 2013; Ravenscroft, 2004; Witherspoon & Theodore, 2021.

27. Witherspoon, 2018.

28. Rambukkana, 2015, p. 24.

29. Evita Sawyers, personal communication, October 2, 2023.

30. For example, Tweedy, 2010.

31. For example, Klesse, 2016; Robinson, 2013.

32. Ferrer, 2018; Halpern, 1999.

CHAPTER 11

SOCIAL POSITIONALITY
AND COMPERSION

Our love and relationships and how we choose to participate in them, or
NOT participate in them, are political acts. . . . I don't only want systems
like colonialism and capitalism and heteronormativity and white supremacy
to not dictate what I do, I also don't want them to dictate how I think and
feel, which influences what I do. It's going deeper than the surface to uproot
those ideals within myself, to get them out of my mind, body, heart, and
soul, not just out of my external behavior.

—Evita "Lavitaloca" Sawyers[1]

A central finding of my research is that compersion emerges from a gestalt
of individual, relational, and social contexts. Individually, a person brings a
nuanced canvas of predispositions to the table—mindsets, values, personal
trauma, relationship history, and much more. At the relational level, each
connection between two or more individuals contains its own undercur-
rents, patterns, structures, and power dynamics. Then, from a social perspective, people's intimate lives are impacted by environments defined by
the broader culture, as well as *social positionality*—that is, where someone is
located in relation to their various social identities, such as gender, race, class,
ethnicity, ability, sexual orientation, immigration status, religious affiliation,
marital status, geographical location, and more.

These *social identities* deeply impact our worldviews and perspectives,
how we perceive and treat each other, how we assess our own worth, how we
interpret other people's actions, and how much social risk we are willing to
take. Becoming aware of the ways these social identities shape our engagement with the world is an important step in cultivating deep understanding
and empathy toward ourselves and others—which is highly relevant to the
study of intimate relationships, and therefore, of CNM and compersion.

CNM studies have notoriously been criticized for portraying CNM
communities as homogenous—stereotypically White, highly educated, and

socioeconomically privileged. This stereotype is also prevalent in the popular media, with most TV shows, documentaries, and books on CNM featuring those same identities at the foreground. This was a central critique of a 2024 article in *The Atlantic* provocatively titled "Polyamory, The Ruling Class's Latest Fad[2]"—where the author commented on how a recent uptick in CNM exposure in popular media has been led by White, wealthy, heterosexual representatives of non-monogamy. While these folks have indeed garnered a lopsided share of public visibility, is it reasonable to conclude that CNM people are a homogenous bunch, as they are portrayed?

According to research, these stereotypes do not reflect the actual diversity present in folks who practice non-monogamy.[3] In fact, CNM people embody a broad range of identities—politically, ethnically, geographically, racially, sexually, financially, gender-wise, age-wise, and more. For example, in *Polyamory in the 21st Century*, Deborah Anapol included a cross-cultural analysis of polyamory around the world—with emphases on China, India, Europe, Australia, and New Zealand,[4] demonstrating how CNM varies across cultures. In terms of United States CNM populations, Balzarini and colleagues' research has challenged prior findings and assumptions that CNM groups are demographically homogenous,[5] and documented the vast diversity of social identities present in people who identify as polyamorous.[6] These findings were congruent with Rubin and colleagues' study from a few years earlier.[7] Along the same lines, Kathy Labriola, a CNM author who provides low-cost counseling for CNM people in California, expressed that she encounters many more CNM people of color and/or of lower socio-economic status in her practice than are accounted for in most academic research. While she noted that her client base may not be representative of the CNM community as a whole, she has a distinct perspective on the types of CNM people who typically are not represented in academic studies or media appearances—partly because folks with less social advantage cannot take the risk of being "outed" as CNM and lose the privilege they have (I explained this more thoroughly in Chapter 10). Additionally, they might consider other identity variables as being more central to their identity than CNM. Labriola described these dynamics in an email:

> Almost all my poly clients are working-class people, most of whom are struggling to survive financially in the overpriced Bay Area. I also have a lot of clients out of state that I see by Skype or through phone sessions, and most of them are low-income or working-class people as well. . . . I see a lot of poly

clients who are people of color, POC make up about one-third of my poly clients, they are primarily African-American, Chinese-American, and South Asian and Southeast Asian immigrants from India, Indonesia, Vietnam, and Thailand. A small number are American-born Latinx and a few are Latinx immigrants from Central American nations, Mexico, and Brazil. . . . About 90% of my clients are LGBT, more bisexuals/pansexuals and trans folks than strictly lesbians or strictly gay males. . . . I do think that there are a lot more POC people, working-class folks, and queer people involved in CNM relationships than are being counted in these research studies and in popular media portrayals. I believe that is because these are people who are not as likely to be interviewed or to be accessible to researchers or as likely to respond to a survey. I believe that this is at least partly because they are struggling with survival issues and are more likely to identify as POC or Queer or working-class FIRST, and poly or CNM second or third or fourth, and not see it as such an important part of their identity as white middle-class heterosexuals do. I also think there is a much higher potential "price" for them to be "out" about their CNM relationship orientation, as they are already dealing with racism, homophobia, and economic hardships, and don't need the additional risk of losing their jobs or their children due to coming out as poly.[8]

This discrepancy between CNM representation and participation contributes to a knowledge gap in both academia and the broader culture. Because so many social identities within the CNM community have been under-represented in research and the media, there is a paucity of expertise regarding how these factors impact particular aspects of non-monogamous relating. In particular, how social positionality intersects with the subjective experience of compersion is, as of yet, uncharted territory. While this was not a focal point of my original research,[9] I recognized in writing this book that this was an important missing angle that warranted, at the very least, an initial—though abbreviated—introduction to the topic.

Before diving into the specifics of my findings, I want to emphasize that this chapter does not wholly represent the vast array of experiences that can happen at the juncture of compersion and social positionality. I restrained my inquiry to six prisms of identity—age, ability, gender, sexual orientation, race, and socioeconomic status—for the sake of time and space. As such, many other vectors, such as neurodiversity, immigration status, standards of conventional attractiveness, religion, cultural background, and more did not receive focused attention in this book. I also acknowledge the absence of aromantic, asexual, and agender individuals from my study and hope that future literature will bring more visibility to these groups. While not every person may see themselves represented in this chapter, I hope readers will enjoy broadening their understanding of compersion through the unique stories contained in these pages. I personally have gotten my mind (and my heart) blown open many times while conducting the interviews that brought this chapter to life.

THE RESEARCH PROCESS

To gain a better understanding of compersion from the lens of social positionality, I conducted additional interviews with over half (nine out of 17) of my original participants, four to five years after their initial interviews, focusing on the impact of identity within their CNM relationships and experiences of compersion. Also, to offer a more inclusive range of perspectives on the intersection of racial identity with compersion, I conducted additional interviews with five new BIPOC participants. Finally, I conducted personal interviews, over Zoom or email, with esteemed colleagues (book authors, prominent social media creators, and community leaders) in the field of CNM: Kathy Labriola, William Winters, Kevin Patterson, Evita "Lavitaloca" Sawyers, Millie Boella, and Sarah Stroh.

To complement the interview data, I also reviewed relevant published materials. While no previous literature addresses the intersection of various identities with compersion *specifically*, some authors have explored the intersection of CNM with the variables of age;[10] race;[11] socioeconomic status;[12] disability;[13] sexual orientation and gender;[14] neurodiversity;[15] and a combination of intersectional factors.[16] To summarize, this chapter relies on three main sources of information:

1. Qualitative data from my original study;[17]
2. Existing literature relevant to CNM and social positionality;
3. Additional rounds of journalistic interviews, conducted in 2022 and 2023, with:
   (a) over half my original participants (nine out of 17 agreed to have a follow-up interview with me, including two who had changed their gender identities);

(b) five new participants, recruited to bring in more racially and ethnically diverse viewpoints and perspectives: Jamila, a half-Black, half-White heteroflexible woman; Tyrone, a 38-year-old Black bisexual man; Sue, a 79-year-old half-Korean, half-Japanese heterosexual woman; Trent, a 43-year-old heteroflexible Black man; and George, a 53-year-old heterosexual Black man (these are pseudonyms);

(c) Kathy Labriola, author of *Polyamorous Elders*,[18] a foremost expert on the intersection of aging and CNM (Zoom);

(d) Kevin Patterson, author of *Love Is Not Colorblind* (Zoom);[19]

(e) William Winters, founder of the *Bonobo Network*, a polyamorous community in the San Francisco Bay Area (Zoom);

(f) Evita "Lavitaloca" Sawyers, author of *A Polyamory Devotional*[20] (Zoom);

(g) Millie Boella, creator of the popular social media account *Decolonizing Love* (email); and

(h) Sarah Stroh, a popular social media creator and relationship coach specializing in CNM (email).

Before diving into the six vectors of identity I studied systematically—age, ability, gender, sexual orientation, race, and socioeconomic status—I highlight the most novel and counterintuitive themes that emerged across these categories. These include the surprising impact of compounded discrimination on compersion, and compersion as a strategy of resistance.

IS COMPERSION A PRIVILEGED EMOTION? THE SURPRISING IMPACT OF COMPOUNDED DISCRIMINATION

Mononormativity is a system of power and oppression that contributes to structural discrimination against people in CNM relationships and is institutionally enforced via compulsory monogamy.[21] As members of a relational minority group, CNM practitioners are systematically stigmatized due to their relational practices. They frequently encounter CNM-related discrimination, harassment, and violence, and these are often without recourse because of the lack of legal protection from discrimination based on relationship behavior.[22]

While this system is harmful to everyone who is currently involved in a CNM relationship, individuals with more privilege tend to experience more societal freedom around their relational status since they can typically afford to take more social risks. This has been documented in many publications as well as in the original data herein.[23]

In addition, members of marginalized communities may internalize the impact of systemic oppression and discrimination in the form of negative inner narratives regarding self-worth and desirability, which may negatively impact one's sense of inner security (see Chapters 7 and 8), and consequently, inhibit compersion in CNM situations. Negative comparison can be particularly painful when one's metamour embodies certain social privileges that one does not carry. Millie Boella, creator of the popular social media account *Decolonizing Love*, encapsulated this by saying that "marginalized folks more than others might struggle with compersion when their metas resemble privileges they don't have." This dynamic shows up not only for folks who already practice non-monogamy, but also for those who would never consider it—this calculation stemming specifically from the anticipation of comparative triggers from social hierarchies, desirability politics, and compounded discrimination.

While it would be tempting to thus hypothesize that social disadvantage correlates with compersion *negatively*—I discovered that this is not necessarily the case. I found that two main factors of resiliency (see Chapter 10)—connecting with a supportive community, as well as critically questioning normative beliefs and systems—were often highly emphasized by members of marginalized groups, and that in turn, these resiliency factors would create fertile conditions for compersion. Of course, my data is based on people who self-selected as having experienced compersion, and therefore, it is not an accurate representation of everyone practicing CNM. Nevertheless, these meaningful and somewhat surprising findings bring nuance and insight to our understanding of compersion for folks of different backgrounds.

Why were the resiliency factors of community belonging and willingness to question social conventions particularly salient for folks with less privilege? When it came to community bonds, this made sense from both a needs-based as well as cultural perspective. Many vectors of privilege (whiteness, wealth, heteronormativity, physical and mental ability, etc.) typically correlate with a more individualistic way of life: folks with greater privilege often have the resources to function more independently (see relevant studies in the section on socioeconomic status); they are also generally culturally raised in siloed nuclear family models where there is an emphasis on privacy and independence—rather than interdependence and mutual aid. Conversely, community bonds tend to be more important, and even vital, in minoritized populations. In terms of the willingness to question established conventions and embrace CNM values, folks who already lived outside of privileged normativities were sometimes more likely to question other normative assumptions, as they were part of the same interconnected system of oppression. Having an "outsider status" in one area could make them more likely to also reject and dismantle internalized mononormativity—which in turn promotes compersion. These two factors of resilience—community belonging and a critical view of mononormativity—worked together.[24]

For example, being part of the LGBTQ+ community had predisposed several of my participants to come out as non-monogamous, because they had a preexisting willingness to defy social conventions and typically spent time in sex-positive environments where folks were more likely to embrace a fluid view of gender, sexuality, and relationships—and therefore, were more likely to understand and support non-monogamy. Older CNM folks could be socially disadvantaged in many areas due to ageism; however, CNM folks in upper age ranges often had more to gain, and less to lose, from being openly non-monogamous. If they were retired or empty nesters, they were no longer worried about losing jobs or child custody based on their relationship choices. They would also benefit greatly from an interconnected community of metamours taking care of each other's needs—which promoted compersion. Furthermore, people with lower socioeconomic means often found more reasons to be compersive when they were able to create supportive polycules to share expenses and family responsibilities with metamours, rather than trying to make ends meet in a traditional siloed nuclear family model. A similar paradox arose among Black, Indigenous, Latin, or Asian folks who grew up in tight-knit, traditionally religious communities: while they typically faced heightened discrimination when coming out as non-monogamous, they were often predisposed to thriving in interconnected CNM communities where self-determination and solidarity are basic values. While it might seem that economically affluent, cisgendered, able-bodied White people would have an easier time being compersive due to the abundance of resources yielded to them—they may have been raised with strong values of individualism that present a psychological obstacle to deep empathy and real sharing.

In sum, what I encountered in my study was a lot of surprising data that defied my prior hypotheses about CNM and privilege. One of the main themes was the significance of compersion as a *strategy of resistance* for members of marginalized communities—a concept that I believe can inspire folks of all backgrounds, and of all relationship styles, to practice love as a positively defiant stance against systems of both inner and outer oppression. I particularly thank Evita "Lavitaloca" Sawyers, author of *A Polyamory Devotional*,[25] for her thought partnership on this particular topic. Her coining of the phrase "compersion as resistance" helped me integrate much of the data in this chapter, and further understand the connection between compersion, identity development, and the process of coming out as CNM.

COMPERSION AS RESISTANCE

Beyond compersion not being a "privileged emotion," my research showed that compersion can be a form of resistance to interconnected systems of social power that label some folks as valuable, and others as disposable, based on arbitrary demographic characteristics.

Being sidelined due to race, ethnicity, socioeconomic status, age, gender, sexual orientation, disability, or other identity can impede compersion, especially toward people perceived as having unearned social advantages. Additionally, the adoption of CNM may seem more risky, as it implies losing yet more social power by not conforming to the dominant systems in one more sphere.[26] However, some folks in my study reported that their experiences of marginalization brought about an increased sense of defiance, agency, and self-determination that made them *more* inclined to reject mononormativity—as it is part of the same system of oppression that historically pigeonholed them into second-class citizenship status.[27] Furthermore, rejecting mononormativity—not only by opting out of monogamy as a relationship structure and behavior, but also at the *thought and emotional levels*—combats the idea that they should feel trapped in a sense of scarcity. Thus, cultivating a compersive orientation to intimate relationships became an intrinsic part of a healing and liberation process from internalized oppression.

In other words, while systems of racism, ageism, heternormativity, ableism, classism, or other -isms had sent messages such as, "You are not enough. You are less than. You are disposable and replaceable. You can't afford to share, to give, to support others because you don't have enough for yourself," some folks would rebuke these narratives as a strategy of resistance, and replace them with messages such as, "There is enough love for everyone. I *have* plenty, and I *am* plenty. I am valuable and irreplaceable. I have enough to share."

While this phenomenon emerged through many bits and pieces in my participants' accounts, it congealed during my conversation with Evita "Lavitaloca" Sawyers—thus I cite her at length:

> For some marginalized folks, rejecting normative concepts such as monogamy is a form of resistance. Monogamy has roots in capitalism and colonialism. So for many non-monogamous folks, their participation in non-monogamy is a form of resisting ideas about love and relationships that were imposed upon us by these systems. And not only do they reject the notions of how we "should" be in relationships as dictated by standard societal ideals, but they reject the notions of how we should FEEL about relationships as dictated by standard societal ideals, to include the experience of compersion. It is a form of resistance for them to assert that even though everything around them says that they are supposed to feel jealous, threatened, or negative about their partners seeking fulfillment in romantic and sexual relationships with others, that they are instead going to choose to feel joy, peace, and encouragement about their partners' other relationships because to feel the reverse is to be in agreement with the dominant culture's ideas about relationships. More than just reject the more problematic notions of monogamy in behavior and practice, they reject them in thought and feeling and their compersion is part of that rejection.[28]

Sawyers's perspective demonstrates a sense of personal agency that can be empowering for many people. In addition to articulating a path that supports marginalized folks on their CNM journeys, I believe this angle has profound implications for anyone who struggles with self-worth, independently from their walk of life or identity.

Healing Inner Oppression through Resistance

In my coaching practice, I see people of all different backgrounds struggling with the pain of inadequacy, fears of abandonment, or feeling less than—and these pain points often get particularly triggered by non-monogamy. Whether a person's fear and wounds stem from dysfunctional family dynamics, verbal or physical abuse, bullying, discrimination, abandonment, rejection, or anything else—these dynamics tend to be internalized into a lack of self-love, causing intricate layers of emotional pain, self-perpetuating narratives, and destructive relational patterns that keep love elusive and scarce.

In these cases, compersion can be a form of resistance against not only external forms of oppression but also *inner oppression*—especially given the fact that there is a revolving door between the two. Of course, some people have been dealt a much more privileged hand than others—which is why considering power dynamics and social positionality is crucial in the study of any socioemotional phenomenon.

That said, the concept of compersion as resistance can carry a redemptive quality for anyone who experiences an internalized sense of scarcity and deprivation and wishes to create a more secure, abundant, and loving relational life. In other words, resisting both inner and outer systems of oppression pertains to everyone. In CNM contexts, this can be supported by aligning oneself with compersive attitudes and behaviors. As I spelled out in Chapter 4, "Two Kinds of Compersion," attitudes and behaviors are more fundamentally important to relationship quality—and also easier to invoke—than embodied compersion. This emphasizes the potential for agentic thinking and actions. Aligning oneself with a *love ethics*, as bell hooks spelled out,[29] can be done even when difficult emotions are present. To this point, Sawyers affirmed that even though she does not believe that the *emotion* of compersion is necessary to create harmonious CNM relationships, she considers her *behavioral orientation* toward compersion to be core to her "polyamorous integrity." She summarized this in one sentence: "I hold an ethic of compersion even when I don't always experience the FEELING of compersion."

In the following pages, I offer vignettes and observations from my interviews on how different identities may intersect with compersion. I organized the rest of this chapter under six themes: (1) age/stage of life, (2) disability, (3) gender, (4) sexual orientation, (5) race, and (6) socioeconomic status.

COMPERSION AND AGE/STAGE OF LIFE

People's predisposition to experiencing compersion can definitely evolve over time—according to changes in needs, desires, and relational dynamics at different stages of their lives. Along with these changes, their "compersion map"—what fosters or hinders compersion for them specifically—develops. As it goes for all the positionality variables I highlight in this chapter, age is only one factor at play in each of those situations, and it needs to be contextualized within an ecosystem of other factors that impact compersion.

While there is a paucity of literature on this topic,[30] my research has yielded fascinating trends. I organized this section using the life stages most reflected in my data: mid-30s, 40s, 50s, and 60s, 65 and over, and finally, post-death compersion.

Mid-30s, Parenthood, and Compersion

Since I had the pleasure of interviewing over half of my original participants (nine out of 17) four to five years after the initial interviews in 2018, some fascinating information came up around the evolution of compersion over time and with changing life priorities. For example, Bethanne, a nonprofit activist who was 29 years old at the time of the first interview, was 34 at the time of the second one and explained that the characteristics of her compersion experiences had changed along with her life stage. She mentioned that she had become less committed to polyamory in recent times because she was now prioritizing finding a stable anchor partner with whom she could build a family. Although she still preferred open relating and avowedly felt skeptical of entering a monogamous partnership as a way to find more relational stability, she no longer considered polyamory a must. Connected to her unfulfilled desire for anchor partnership, she had been experiencing somewhat less compersion toward her current lovers. However, she also remarked that aging—which correlated with her deepening spiritual practice and psychological maturity—had allowed her to augment her capacity to hold many emotions, as well as uncertainty. This allowed her to experience new depths of both jealousy *and* compersion (see Chapter 1 for more detail on Bethanne's experience with this). When I asked how she perceived that her age intersected with compersion, she reflected:

> I feel like it really relates to life phase. I could imagine many iterations of this cycle where I'm really wanting a specific thing, but I feel very skeptical of this, that seemingly monogamy is going to serve, like building a family in an efficient timeline. [*laughs*] And that makes me put the blinders up, and makes me more focused in a particular way. And that being contrasted with my 20s or even my 40s, when there's just, like, probably more stability or more expansion, either or, that enables exploration, or actually, more capacity for uncertainty. Because a lot of poly requires a lot of capacity for uncertainty.

Bethanne's nuanced response shows the fluidity of compersion in regard to other factors—such as what needs and desires she prioritized, and what needs and wants were currently unfulfilled.

Jamila, a 36-year-old participant, was in a similar situation. She identified with and preferred polyamory as a relationship structure but was unsure as to whether she would be able to build a family while practicing polyamory without an anchor partner. She explained,

> I've been grappling with labeling myself as polyamorous because I'm also at the age where I've been thinking more about family planning. And I keep thinking about, how am I going to do this, am I going to co-parent, am I going to, you know, do something traditional and then go back to my polyamorous roots, like, what's the plan? I don't really have one yet.

As a counterpoint to the perceived difficulties of combining motherhood and CNM, Sarah Stroh, a non-monogamy coach and expert, shared her thoughts with me on being pregnant while non-monogamous:

> A lot of people have asked me if now that I'm pregnant, I'm feeling a natural urge to be more monogamous. And honestly, I find this question bizarre. Humans did not evolve in monogamous nuclear family structures. We're meant to raise children in tribes, not just with one other adult. Now that I'm pregnant, I'm more invested in maintaining my loverships, my friendships and my partnerships than I ever have been.[31]

For Jamila and Bethanne, the fear was not so much that they could not raise a child within a polyamorous family structure, but rather that they may not be able to find a partner who would be both a wonderful co-parent and CNM partner within their biological timeline for getting pregnant. Sarah already had stable CNM relationships before getting pregnant and did not feel the need to become monogamous as she was expecting a child. Thus, her experiences of compersion were not particularly affected by her stage of life.

Similarly, Natasha, a physician who was 34 at the time of the first interview and 38 at the time of the second, had remained in the same hierarchical CNM partnership and had since given birth to a child. She recounted that her experiences of jealousy and compersion had not changed very much. She was thankful that having moved to the Southwest of the United States had provided her with substantial opportunities to connect with CNM community, including a "niche group" of CNM mothers in their late 30s nicknamed "hot mamas gone wild."

These various accounts highlighted the intersection of age, relationship status, and gender in these women's experiences of compersion and CNM. Contexts of community and partnership had a lot to do with each person's ability to create secure non-mononormative family structures. This changed depending on folks' specific life situation, geographical location, and more—so again, there is no one-size-fits-all in regard to parenting and polyamory. Elisabeth Sheff's book, *The Polyamorists Next Door*,[32] dives deeper into this theme and provides additional stories of CNM families.

Mid-30s CNM Scarcity

Jo added a unique perspective on compersion in mid-30s. They started practicing polyamory in their early 20s, were 29 at the time of the first interview in 2018, and 34 at the time of the second interview—while also in the process of transitioning and affirming their gender. (I elaborate more on Jo's experience of compersion as a trans man in the section of gender.) On the one hand, they commented on the fact that their substantial polyamorous tenure had yielded valuable practice, experience, and knowledge on how to make CNM work well—which naturally makes compersion more likely to arise. On the other hand, being now in their mid-30s posed specific challenges that weren't present in their 20s:

> When you're younger, you kind of feel entitled to the next person showing up immediately. Like, you can just jump. Everyone's disposable. The next person is gonna just come because there's so many people, you're young and hot . . . that's not really the experience as you get older and people are coupled up, and you want something more solid.

The phenomenon that Jo described here could potentially have both negative and positive impacts on compersion, depending on other factors at play. For example, someone might grow insecure as they experience a scarcity of options for new partners, which would result in an enhanced sense of threat to their potential or existing relationships, and therefore hinder compersion. On the other hand, "more solid" and "less disposable" relationships tend to be a more prosperous ground for compersion to bloom—as depth of intimacy, trust, and security with one's partner(s) and metamour(s) relationships have been shown to foster compersion.

In sum, mid-30s were often a turning point in people's lives in regard to their relationship intentions and structures—and changing tides could affect their proclivities to experience compersion, depending on context. Next, I turn to the 40s, 50s, and 60s decades.

Compersion in 40s, 50s, and 60s

Folks in their 40s, 50s, and 60s were often in a favorable stage of life to initiate CNM. Often, they had been monogamously married and had either divorced or become empty-nesters. This was the case for James and Diane, a heterosexual couple in their fifties who I interviewed nearly at five-year interval (spring 2018 and then fall 2022). They had initially become non-monogamous after 30 years of monogamy and had come to a point where they each consistently experienced compersion for one another.

However, they noted that a gender component had altered their CNM experiences over time. The older they got, the easier it seemed for James to connect with new female partners—and the harder it got for Diane to find suitable new male partners. James hypothesized that the dynamics of "supply and demand" with men and women in their age cohort, and in their particular geographical location, had shifted considerably: "Lots of women are chasing very few guys. If you're a guy, you've got lots of opportunities. I think it's life expectancy, mental health, and things like that. A greater proportion of the population is female as you get older." In this particular situation, James (who had three other partners besides Diane at the time of the last interview) would likely have a greater inclination to feel compersive toward Diane (who didn't have other partners at that time) as a result of his newfound privileged position. This was a surprising role reversal from 2018, when Diane had been expressing more compersion for James than he did for her, as a result of her initiating CNM through a discovered affair and initially having an abundance of satisfying dating opportunities. In 2022, she reported that while she still sincerely experienced compersion toward James and his other partners, the scarcity of her dating prospects created a sense of bittersweetness:

> I have a lot of compersion for James, but I do a lot of comparison. I see what James has, and then I see what I have, and I yearn for what he has, and I can't find that. I'm trying to cultivate better relationships, but I can't find that.

Diane also noted that living in a conservative-leaning area of the United States negatively impacted her CNM dating options, which highlighted the intersection of age, gender, and geography.

Sylvia, a Dakota participant in her 50s, had a similar experience. Living in a more rural and politically conservative area, she lamented that being surrounded by highly heteronormative and mononormative communities had kept her from experiencing a thriving CNM life. She framed this both as a geographical and a generational plight: she expressed "aunty compersion" toward younger CNM folks for belonging to a generation for whom alternative sexualities were more widely accepted—and with more years ahead to either move to politically progressive locations or have access to a larger dating pool of like-minded, sex-positive folks, even in politically conservative areas.

For both Sylvia and Diane, the intersection of age, gender, and geography made CNM, and therefore compersion, more difficult. This was different for other members of this age cohort who lived in more progressive locations. Things were also different for James because he had more dating prospects—which may relate to the "Freedom from Full-Time Husbands Compersion" section (under "Gender and Compersion"), where I describe that many divorced or widowed heterosexual women in their 60s and beyond thrive in CNM relationships where they are free from the pressures of being a wife, and are very grateful to date men who are already in established partnerships.

Sixty-Five and Over: A Golden Age for CNM?

It seems that CNM individuals aged 65 and up may have the most optimistic forecast for compersion. First, they often have the most experience dealing with the ups and downs of CNM, and have had ample time to work out challenges, insecurities, and fears. When people find themselves polyamorous in their 70s and 80s, they typically have well-established, secure, and supportive polycules of CNM-experienced folks with whom they share rich histories and little drama. In other words, CNM harmony often comes hand-in-hand with people owning the skill set for creating contexts that invite compersion, such as choosing new partners who are compatible with the existing polycule, effective communication skills, self-confidence, having unlearned mononormative beliefs, and more—and older CNM folks typically have mastered these skill sets over time.

Second, they are the segment of people who typically have the most to gain, and the least to lose, from engaging in CNM. They often benefit in very practical ways from sharing resources and support among a community of lovers, ex-lovers, and like-minded people who feel like "family" rather than "just friends," by belonging to the same polycules or extended CNM communities. As people age and their needs related to caregiving increase, more people's care and attention can make life feel more secure, enjoyable, and connected—which also fosters compersion. As CNM expert and author of *Polyamous Elders*,[33] Kathy Labriola shared in a personal interview,

> Older polys are much more likely to experience a lot of compersion, because they are seeing a lot of the benefits of polyamory that are not as apparent at a younger age. Particularly when it comes to assisting and caregiving, having more people and more metamours is a huge boon . . . having a tightly knit polycule of metamours who are willing to pitch in can become more critical and beneficial than for folks at younger ages.[34]

As I discussed in Chapter 7, the perception of benefits from a partner's other relationship(s) is one of the main factors contributing to the occurrence of compersion. Labriola emphasized that "compersion often grows in those situations where everyone benefits, where benefits outweigh whatever fears and insecurities the jealousy is being sparked by."[35] Indeed, older CNM folks had a lot to gain, and they were also more likely to have worked through lots of personal and relational insecurities that might have plagued them in earlier stages of life. For example, they may have felt more threatened by the presence of other lovers when they were parenting young children—but after their children had grown, the possibility of losing one's partner may have become less threatening. Additionally, the longevity of certain metamour relationships that had lasted decades diminished any sense of threat:

> Many older CNM folks have been in relationships and polycules that have lasted decades—these relationships have stood the test of time and shown themselves to prevail over the fear that they might have dissolved. This is true of nesting partnerships and marriages, as well as of metamour/other relationships. In itself, this can attenuate insecurities and jealousies that were more likely to be present in earlier relational stages.
> Older polys are generally beyond that feeling of being really jealous of the [metamour]. They may have had a lot of struggles around it for years, but the relationship has lasted long enough that it's become clear that this

relationship is not a threat. And that person is here to stay. "I haven't been able to, you know, scare them off or I haven't been able to sabotage that relationship successfully. So I might as well accept it and let's move on." . . . The longevity of both relationships creates security.[36]

In other words, older polyamorous folks had often traveled the spectrum from jealousy, to resignation, to acceptance, to good-faith compersion toward their metamour relationships. Additionally, the tenure of these relationships had increased the amount of empathy that folks could feel toward metamours. People who may have appeared intimidating or invincible at first, may have started to show some vulnerability as they went through personal challenges:

The long-term aspect of these other relationships also increases empathy and caring because they've seen that metamour go through a death of parents or the death of their spouse, and go through that grieving process; it enhances their ability to really empathize. "Well, this is another human being that's going through, you know, pain and loss and wow, I can relate to that, and it kind of taps into that sort of human caring that naturally will come up in a situation like that."[37]

This wonderful ability to humanize and empathize was perhaps never so present as after a metamour has passed away.

Post-Death Compersion

For older CNM folks, the death of lovers, ex-lovers, and metamours was a normal part of life. Changes to polycules over time often had more to do with people developing disabilities or dying, rather than breakups and new partners being added. If death is the great equalizer, it has the power to subdue even the fiercest rivalries. Fred, a 75-year-old retiree (79 at the time of the second interview), recounted attending one of his metamours' wake, and witnessing several women commenting on their common deceased lover's outstanding sexual skills:

I was at that wake, and people started saying how he was such a capable person, and all the crap that people normally say . . . and then someone, one woman said, "he could *really* give head, he gave *great* head," and then my friend, the widow, sort of smiled, and she greatly acknowledged that. And one by one, other people who had been lovers of his acknowledged his sexuality. [*laughs*] I guess that speaks to the issue of compersion. There were a number of his lovers, there was his primary partner, and everybody was just really happy to hear those things as well as all the other good things about him.

In the same vein, metamours who had lost the same partner at the same time often found a level of closeness and empathy that would have been difficult to find elsewhere. While this may fall a bit outside of what would traditionally be considered compersion, it is worth mentioning:

I saw a couple of situations where the husband died and the wife and the girlfriend became closer after that. They were grieving the loss of their partner. They were grieving the loss of the same man, and one woman said to me, "Well, what other woman could possibly understand this? She knows exactly what I'm going through, exactly, because she's lost the same person at the same time." And they've been together through caring for him while he was sick and dying. So, the empathy there is kind of off the charts. Because you're both kind of in the same boat. And there's nothing left to be jealous of.[38]

Indeed, major life transitions—such as birth and death—carry an uncanny power to foster empathy by bringing the spotlight onto a sense of common humanity.

The next step for this area of research would be to further investigate the intersection of age with other vectors of identity such as race, cultural background, couple privilege, sexual orientation, and more. I hope that future research, particularly longitudinal studies, will embrace these opportunities. Next, I turn to the impacts of disability on compersion.

COMPERSION AND DISABILITY

When a person's mind or body falls outside ableist norms that a society privileges, this person may receive the message that their mind or body is a problem that needs "fixing." Yet, many disabilities are chronic and cannot be "fixed." Further, many disabled folks do not want a "cure."[39] Thus, disability justice is not about "curing" disabilities, but about transforming the barriers—attitudinal and material—that society puts in front of disabled people.[40]

The group of people who identify as disabled is vast and diverse. Disability is a large umbrella that includes visible and/or invisible, as well as cognitive and/or physical impairments that limit one's ability to engage with certain activities. Some disabilities are present at birth, others develop later in life. As such, this community is more prevalent than many would imagine. In their seminal book chapter on CNM and disability, Alex Iantaffi stated that "disabled people constitute 26 percent of the adult population in the United States and around 15 percent of the global population . . . [and are] one of the largest minoritized groups and yet one of the most overlooked, especially when discussing sex, sexuality, and relationships."[41] At the intersection of disability and nonomonogamy, disabled CNM people have to juggle the stigma and projections of both CNM and disability at the same time.

However, as with other identities, there is a variety of ways in which people may experience CNM and compersion, based on other factors and vectors of privilege—in particular, whether one has access to loving partner(s) and an inclusive community. Thankfully, communities that bridge sex positivity, diversity, and pride often orient themselves toward values of mutual aid and interdependence. These values can mitigate the isolation and limitations that disabled people often experience, and promote deep interpersonal bonds as well as compersion.

Thus, how individuals with disabilities and their partners experience compersion are very diverse and often paradoxical. I explore some dimensions of this paradox next.

A Combination of Compersion and Envy

CNM and disability may put into juxtaposition compersion and envy. In many cases, someone with a disability may envy their partners and metamours for being able to do things that they themselves cannot do, while also feeling happy and grateful for them. There is a coexistence of pleasure and pain in those situations, reminiscent of the *comperstruggle* concept I discussed in Chapter 6. To illustrate, Jo, who had become disabled between her first (2018) and second (2022) interview, reported:

> It can be hard to feel happy for people who are able to do things that you can't . . . I have health issues and physical mobility issues, and it's hard to feel happy for Sam when he successfully organizes a bunch of group hikes or enjoys himself at dodgeball. It sounds really fun and I wish I could do it, but I am also happy for him. But it's just a little frustrating that I can't also

do it. So, I guess it's like, I'm happy for him that he's doing it, but I wish I could do it too.

Similarly, Kathy Labriola had interviewed folks for whom disability brought about new reasons to be compersive within CNM contexts, while also invoking some jealousy and envy. She recounted,

> I've talked to a number of people that have either, you know, arthritis or some other kind of lupus or fibromyalgia or some other kind of chronic pain syndromes, and a lot of those folks said, "I am too sick to have sex anymore. I'm in too much pain. Sex or just even affection can be very physically painful. And I'm so grateful that my partner has another partner for sex and affection, because you know, they need, want, and deserve that. I can't provide it anymore. I'm sad that I'm missing out myself on that, but the pain makes it not any fun. So I'm not gonna do it. And so thank goodness, they're not having to do without that and just be angry and resentful that they have to take care of me and I can't even provide any kind of sexual relationship for them."
>
> So sometimes these are people that have been intensely jealous of their metamour, and now that's changed. *Some are experiencing a combination of jealousy and compersion.* It's oftentimes more like envy, in that, "oh, I'm envying my partner and their partner because they can have, you know, a wonderful sex life, they can have all this wonderful cuddling, and I can't, or I'm tired, and I'm in pain." . . . So there's pain and there's pleasure there, and there's the sadness that you can't have that with them, but that you're feeling compersion because while someone else is able to have that with someone else, and so they're not missing out on anything.[42]

In some cases, a disabled person would even conclude that their metamour had saved their relationship, as they supposed that without that person, their own relationship would have ended because of their inability to meet their partner's needs:

> A few people have said it's an even more complex combination, because they're thinking, "Well, if my partner didn't have that with someone else, if we weren't poly, they probably would have divorced me by now." Because their needs would not be met in this relationship. And so just from a sort of selfish point of view, I'm glad we're poly—if we were in a monogamous relationship, how miserable would that have been for them? They would probably end up deciding to end the relationship.

For some of Kathy Labriola's participants, the occurrence of a disability had even turned intense jealousy of a metamour into extreme gratitude for their presence. This came as a "shocking revelation" for some people:

> There's at least a number of people that said, "Well, you know, I used to be insanely jealous, because I thought oh, you know, my partner's gonna leave me for this other person. Now, I think, well, if they didn't have this other person, they'd probably leave." For some people, that's a pretty shocking revelation. They've been spending years being jealous, worrying, oh, they're gonna leave me for this other person. They're gonna love them more, or whatever; well, now, having that relationship makes it possible for them to stay in the relationship with me.[43]

Just like with aging, the presence of a disability could lend itself to the creation of ecosystems of care that promoted mutual support and aid, and consequently, fostered compersion.

Ecosystems of Care

Stories of compersion emerging in circumstances that involve a disabled partner often involve gratitude for being part of a polycule where people are available and willing to support one another. The emphasis on the need for caring community often leads people with disability to create interconnected cultures where mutual aid is normalized. On this topic, Bethanne commented:

> Often, disability communities need to be connected and have forms of mutual support inherently, or kind of more practically, and that leads to a lot more sharing and overlapping and mutually supporting relationships. So in all those ways, I think there's just like a cultural support system to enable the practice [of compersion].

To illustrate how the occurence of a disability could lead to compersion in a CNM setting, Kathy Labriola recounted the story of a woman's husband who was injured in a car wreck and became disabled—and how this tragic situation, mitigated by the resiliency factor of community belonging, led to this woman's compersiveness:

> She was the only caregiver for him and luckily, he also had a girlfriend and they were in an openly poly situation. And the girlfriend, you know, really

stepped up and was coming over and providing respite care, so that the wife could rest and go out and see her friends and see the grandchildren and all of that. Even though she had had a lot of jealousy before this happened, she became very grateful and compersive toward that girlfriend.[44]

This is another example of a counterintuitive, and bittersweet, turn of events—where a loss of independence creates unforeseen avenues toward gratitude and positive empathy.

Pandemic and Disabilities

The COVID-19 pandemic has highlighted how non-monogamous relationships could become more difficult for folks with chronic immunity concerns. Access to in-person parties and mingling opportunities became dangerous for many people, widening the existing accessibility gap. However, partners of those folks sometimes got creative in terms of creating safe ways to share intimacy, which is a wonderful form of compersion. Tyrone, a 38-year-old facilitator, gave the example of planning virtual play parties and orgies for his lovers who were homebound:

> Having space for people who can't meet people because they are homebound, or have a level of fear of leaving because of the pandemic, there can be a disconnect if you're dating someone who is outside and meeting people. I've had that in a relationship where my partner was jealous because I had a life that's active and more vibrant than theirs. If my partner was at home, I would have a zoom orgy. Yeah, it's like, you don't have to go outside, we can still connect and be intimate. And that's inviting non touch but you are still being very intimate in groups and we're communicating that we're witnessing each other and each other's pleasure. I've done that with 6 to 25 people. I've had a virtual play party once, for my friends and my lovers. So it's just being creative with how you can be in connection with each other when your partner or you doesn't have or isn't able to be in spaces that require play or connection.

In this story, Tyrone described how he mitigated his partner's envy and jealousy by creating a positive and inclusive experience for them. This is a good example of how a disabled person's partner can support them in experiencing more pleasure, connection, and belonging.

In sum, while disability presents many accessibility challenges for CNM folks, it also brings opportunities for mutual care—which may generate novel avenues for compersion between partners and metamours. Next, I turn to the intersection of gender and compersion.

COMPERSION AND GENDER

My final study sample comprised 11 women, eight men, one trans man, and two nonbinary-identified persons. Two of the men and two of the women specified some flexibility in their gender identity through the following descriptors: "Male ish," "Male—though not too heavily," "Female gender-queer," and "Female (very loose attachment to my gender identity)." One participant, Jo, was in the process of transitioning from female to male at the time of their second (2022) interview, and now used "he/they" pronouns; I changed their pseudonym from Alice (in my initial 2021 dissertation[45]) to Jo in this book to accommodate their different gender identities across the two interviews, and to reflect the fact that they changed their name in real life. I also used the "they" pronoun to refer to them in this book for the sake of consistency (rather than "she" for quotes from the first interview and "he/they" for quotes from the second interview). Additionally, Bethanne, who identified as cis-woman in 2018, identified as gender nonbinary at the time of the second interview (2023) and used "she/them" pronouns. I did not change her pseudonym (as she did not change her name in real life) and elected to use the pronoun "she" to refer to her in this book, for consistency between quotes from each interview. Unfortunately, I was not able to interview agender individuals for this study.

As I mentioned earlier, CNM folks are more likely to identify somewhere on the LGBTQ+ spectrum than the general population. When folks begin to question, or see themselves not fitting into one system of sexual or gender-based normativity—such as heteronormativity, mononormativity, or gender normativity—they are typically more likely to question and become aware of what other "boxes" and social conventions do not match their authentic self. For example, being bisexual or pansexual often goes hand-in-hand with relationship fluidity because being attracted to more than one gender highlights an openness to more than one possibility in a relationship.

While I did not find that folks of certain genders were more predisposed than others to experience compersion, some of my participants' accounts carved a path for understanding how an individual's gender identity and societal gender norms can influence experiences of compersion.

CHAPTER 11

Cis-Dude Compersion

Societal expectations about how individuals should behave in relationships based on gender can certainly influence how people experience compersion. In most heteronormative contexts, men are socialized to express territorial jealousy and mate-guarding behaviors concerning their female partners. Many men would consider "sharing" one's partner with other men, let alone expressing compersion, as a threat to their sense of masculinity and associated social status. Besides, healthy CNM typically requires extensive communication and the ability to express one's needs and feelings openly, which many cis men are socialized not to do. Gender norms can also affect the level of support men offer one another, even within CNM contexts. Thus, straight cis men may face more challenges or stigma in expressing compersion openly—depending on their particular life history, education, subculture, and other contexts.

Of my eight male interviewees, only three identified as straight. Michael, a White 67-year-old bisexual participant, commented on the fact that most men in the United States had an aversion to intimacy with one another, and he imagined this would block compersion. To this point, he exclaimed, "I don't know how straight people do it!" Kevin Patterson, a polyamorous Black man, acknowledged that mononormative culture predisposes cis men to see one another as rivals:

> There's a lot of *Law of the Jungle*, at least with cis men. . . . We're very much socialized to see other men as enemies and rivals, especially in the dating pool, you know? . . . It doesn't just wash off easily because you've declared that you want to do polyamory.[46]

Thankfully, Patterson provided a wonderful template of how cis male metamours can create compersive environments with one another. To counterbalance cultural programing around territoriality and competition, he went the extra mile to make his metamours feel comfortable and defuse any tension:

> Whenever I meet male metamours, I try to lay the hospitality down really thick. Just to break the ice, in terms of, if I know I'm gonna meet another guy, I don't know what kind of guy he's gonna be. Is he gonna be a guy that's like, "Yay, we're meeting our person's person!" or is this gonna be someone who's gonna feel territorial about the whole situation? So I lay it on real

thick like, "Let's hang out, let's watch a game, here's a drink, let's talk about whatever, you know, video games or sports or what have you, just to get out of that tense moment of, you know, which one of us wants to be, like, the top dog here in this situation?" I just walk in really confidently, and I have enough confidence in my polyamory, I have enough confidence in myself and my ability to relate with my partners that I don't mind taking a back seat, just to defuse some possible tension.[47]

Even though relating to another cis man had its potential challenges, Patterson noted that on the bright side, he could relate more closely to them because of their shared gender identity. He recounted giving advice to one of his male metamours a few years back, and this being a bonding moment because of their shared experience with their common female partner:

I had a moment some years ago where my wife was dating a guy. She goes out to some event and a few minutes later, he walks in the front door. And I'm like, "What are you doing here, she's already left," and as it turned out, they were supposed to go to the event together and this was the latest in a series of miscommunications between the two of them. So I find myself giving this guy a bunch of advice that I wish someone had been able to give me in regard to my wife. I'm sitting here telling him everything I know, everything that I've had to learn over the course of being with her for 15, maybe 18 years. So I'm sitting here giving him all the advice that I had on the situation. I was helping keep their relationship together. I feel like that conversation would have gone very differently had my wife's partner not been another cis dude. I feel like the relationship dynamics would have changed, not just between me and this metamour, but between my wife and the metamour. It would have changed my ability to offer up any sort of reasonable advice there.[48]

Indeed, sharing a similar identity—in this case, being a "cis dude"—would bring a two-sided potential effect: on the one hand, it made competitiveness more likely, and on the other, it could promote closeness and collaboration if metamours shared a compersive attitude. Additionally, there are likely differences among cis men of different racial backgrounds and sexual orientations as it pertains to this theme; elaborating on this would require a larger data set, but would certainly be of interest to future studies.

Transgender and Polyamorous

Jo, a software engineer in their mid-30s (29 at the time of the first interview and 34 at the time of the second) was in the process of transitioning from woman to man at the time of their second interview. When I asked them how their gender transition had affected their experiences of CNM and compersion, they mentioned that even though their two male partners were very supportive, dating new people had become somewhat more difficult. Being a trans man in the middle of transitioning, hormonally and surgically, had brought up some fear of rejection. They also brought up that their age, their unwillingness to have children or co-parent, as well their disability status all contributed to the challenge of finding new partners. Here, I cite Jo at length to fully convey the constellation of factors that impacted their intimate relationships:

> There's fear about, like, who wants to sign up for dating me when I'm changing so rapidly? I'm on hormones, and I'm getting top surgery in February, and like, who wants to sign up for that? [*laughs*] . . . Your pool is definitely more limited. It was already limited. Because the whole relationship anarchy thing and stuff and not being available for another primary partner, you know, and also not wanting to have kids. I'm currently not being able to have kids because I had a hysterectomy. And it's not like I was going to have kids. But that's definitely a limiting factor that I've seen is not wanting kids at this age. People who are looking for a more steady partner are often looking for kids or co-parenting their kids, neither of which I'm willing to do. And that's not really because of being trans, but it limits the pool even more. I've got people who are willing to date me right now who are straight men, but that's gonna change. I already have some masculine symptoms. I'm a lot more hairy now, which they may not like, and I'm gonna get top surgery in February. And my voice is a lot deeper. I need to shave my face, otherwise, it's patchy. And like, if I don't shave it one day, are they gonna be grossed out by that? And you know, and it's just more difficult, gay men won't date me either. I kind of have to date bisexual people, so it limits the pool even more. But I find that a lot of trans people prefer dating other trans people. And so it opens up that pool a little bit more.

Jo's account, as a transgender person practicing CNM, portrayed many elements that impact compersion—gender, age, family choices, and the perceived loss of power that comes from having fewer dating options. Their account provides a rich window into how gender intersects with other factors. The following is another example of such an intersection.

"Freedom from Full-Time Husbands" Compersion

Many heterosexual women who had spent the bulk of their lives in monogamous marriages were more likely to become non-monogamous in higher age brackets, relative to their male counterparts or lesbian counterparts. According to Kathy Labriola, widowed or divorced women over 65 often no longer wanted a "full-time husband at home," because they would see it as restricting their hard-earned freedom. In these cases, openly dating a married man could be the best of both worlds: they would reap the benefits from an intimate romantic connection without having to devote themselves to a shared domestic life and caretaking. Often, women in these situations would experience compersion toward their CNM partner's wife. This vignette shows not only the impact of gender on compersion, but the intersection of gender with age and sexual orientation:

> Elder women who are widowed or divorced don't need some of the things they felt they needed in monogamy, like a husband to live with them and help provide financial support for the family or a husband who is going to be a father to their children. As they're aging, a lot of them think a husband would be a big pain in the rear because they're so demanding and keep me from doing the things I want to do in life. Finally, my kids are grown and gone. Finally, I'm retired. I can do whatever the hell I want. I don't want a husband at home that's going to limit me, I'm actually happy that the guy has a wife, so I can do whatever I want.
>
> So for them, the benefits of a poly relationship far outweigh any negatives, because a lot of the things that would have been negative in the past are no longer in existence or no longer operational in their lives. So as a result they either feel neutral toward the metamour, the wife of their partner, or they do feel actual compersion.[49]

Labriola's account relates to how deriving benefits from a partner's other relationships lays a fertile soil for compersion (see Chapter 3). Considering the traditional gender roles that most women over 65 grew up with, there was gratitude in discovering that they could have an intimate relationship with a man without having to become a caretaker. This is a fascinating illustration of how age, gender, and sexual orientation may intersect within a social context where many heterosexual women only get a taste of personal freedom and autonomy after getting divorced or widowed.

"Girlie Girl" and Nonbinary Compersion

While CNM communities were typically known to celebrate a wide spectrum of gender expressions, some intersections of gender and sexual orientation were met with particular warmth and ease. For example, Jamila explained how her gender and erotic expression as a "girlie-girl female" and "straight girl with bisexual tendencies" allowed her to "just kind of slip in" and feel immediately welcomed at the CNM events she frequented. Neither her gender nor her sexual orientation presented any obstacle to community belonging—an element that facilitated compersion according to my study (see Chapters 7 and 10). She noted that this was not the case for her gay and lesbian friends, who felt that they did not as easily find belonging in CNM groups. Jamila recounted:

> As a girlie girl female, that bubbly kinda traditional girl personality is very welcomed and accepted, I don't have any challenges, compared to my lesbian or gay friends . . . they told me it's very heterosexual and it's not as fun for them, it's just not providing that outlet. I just kind of slip in . . . I yield my gender to be the cute bubbly door girl, it's kind of a character . . . I might wear fairy wings . . . I don't know if I do that to make other people comfortable, or if that's just how I feel comfortable in those spaces, because I've gone to festivals for so long . . . to perform that identity feels natural and comforting. Costumes and such.

While Jamila did not directly connect the dots between her gender expression and her experiences of compersion, it is notable that she connected it with her developing ease and comfort within the CNM community.

As a counterpoint, Bethanne, who had changed her gender identity from cis woman to nonbinary between her first and second interview, described how becoming more connected with the queer community allowed her to experience a quality of "queer love" that lent itself more fully to compersion. She had noticed how "more embodied capacity for complexity," "more ease and fluidity of trying on and experimenting and being with different or new structures," as well as "just a lot of love and care and mutual aid and support" in the queer community were vectors for increased compersion. I quote Bethanne at length in the "Sexual Orientation and Compersion" subsection. It is interesting to note that the queering of gender and sexual orientation often come hand-in-hand, as her account demonstrates. Thus, her experience stood in contrast to Jamila's—exemplifying the paradox that weaves through this entire chapter: both privileged and less privileged identities can present assets to experiencing compersion.

SEXUAL ORIENTATION AND COMPERSION

Only five participants in my sample identified as heterosexual. The vast majority (n = 17; 77%) identified as somewhere on the LGBTQ+ spectrum: eight participants identified as queer or pansexual, six as bisexual, and three as heteroflexible. One of the bisexual-identified individuals also added "poly" as part of their sexual orientation—which reflected the perception of polyamory being a categorical orientation, rather than a fluid choice, for this person.

Overall, a LGBTQ+ identity seemed to positively correlate with compersion. As conveyed in Chapter 7, participants who identified with non-heteronormative sexual identities (bisexuality, pansexuality, queerness, or heteroflexibility) said they were predisposed to bend traditional rules in the relationship arena, because they had already embraced an outsider status in other parts of their lives. This matches other research findings about polyamorous individuals being more likely to identify their sexuality in fluid and nontraditional ways.[50] Having already "come out" as LGBTQ+ had often made it easier to come out as non-monogamous, and they typically belonged to more sex-positive and inclusive communities that made compersion more likely to arise.

Bethanne, who had "embraced more of [her] queerness" as well as changed her gender identity from cis woman to gender nonbinary between her first and second interview, described the connection between queerness and compersion delightfully:

> As I've embraced more of my queerness, I've been more integrated into the queer community and there's just, yeah, there's queer love, and queer community is just straight up better at that. [*laughs*] I don't know how to put more concreteness behind that. I just feel like there's a lot more embodied lived capacity for complexity, and there's less taking assumptions and stereotypes at their face value. Obviously, there's a lot less normativity. And so

within that, there's just a lot more ease and fluidity of trying on and experimenting and being with different or new structures. And there's just a lot
of love and care and mutual aid and support, and with that, I think comes
a lot of compersion.

In Bethanne's account, both her gender non-normativity and increased
embrace of her queerness as a sexual orientation had played a role in her
experience, pointing to the intersection of gender, sexual orientation, and
compersion.

Indeed, as I described in Chapter 7, dismantling heteronormativity is
a potent precursor to unlearning mononormativity, which in turn facilitates compersion. Further, being attracted to more than one gender naturally leads folks to question sexual exclusivity. For many participants, a fluid
sexual orientation would also lead to positive experiences of group sex that
would foster compersion. The feelings of integration stoked by group sex
among people who all share an erotic connection would create a positive
relational feedback loop, a feature of compersion I mentioned in Chapter 2.
To illustrate, Tyrone described how group sex felt particularly satisfying to
him as a bisexual man:

> I've had threesomes for seven years. . . . I was just like, "This is my buddy.
> And this is his girlfriend. They love each other. They like me, so we can have
> sex. It wasn't like a big deal." We'd get to have sex and then hang out.

In sum, queerness—and/or sexual orientations that defy heteronormativity—often went hand-in-hand with a mindset of inclusivity and celebration
regarding other axes of "otherness"—such as gender expression, race, disability status, age, and socioeconomic diversity. Thus, as I described in Chapter
10, coming out as LGBTQ+ could invite pride and enthusiasm to come out
as non-monogamous—which facilitated compersion.

RACE AND COMPERSION

How does one's racial identity intersect with compersion? As with the other
themes in this chapter, the answer is nuanced and multifaceted. Individual
experiences of compersion are highly variable depending on a person's
specific life contexts—including their current relational ecosystems and

communities, families of origin, cultural background, geographical location, socioeconomic status, nationality, age, gender, sexual orientation, disability status, religion/spirituality, trauma history, education, individual self-concept, and much more. Just as with the other sections in this chapter, isolating and analyzing the role of race in the "compersion equation" is thus an intricate proposition. Nevertheless, my qualitative interviews led to significant findings around racial representation, identity, and compersion.

Racial Obstacles to Compersion

Racism—in both its systemic and personal manifestations—directly threatens foundations of safety and inclusion which are necessary for compersion to arise in CNM relationships. In particular, the lack of diverse representation in CNM communities, which I explore in more detail later in this section as well as in Chapter 8, can foster stereotyping, exoticizing, fetishizing, colorism, and the possibility of unchecked bigotry in relationships with partners, metamours, and other community members.

Kevin Patterson spoke of his racialized experiences as a polyamorous Black man in *Love Is Not Color Blind: Race and Representation in Polyamorous and Other Alternative Communities*.[51] In a personal interview, he recounted examples of such experiences within CNM communities he belongs to, and how race may impact compersion in his relationships:

> I've always got to be on the lookout for how people are treating me, like, the safety of a situation in regard to race. I've definitely run into people where I got the impression that they wanted to be with me, but they didn't want to be *seen* with me. I've definitely been in situations where somebody didn't know me very well, but felt that me being Black was what I brought to a space, and so they approached me like hey, Black people are here, when really, I'm Kevin, you know? Granted I am super Black, but that's not the way I want to be approached if I'm made to feel welcomed in a space, you know. I want to be addressed for who I am rather than what I am.[52]

Besides these experiences, Patterson explained a concern that racism could impact his metamour's compersion, should they carry unresolved bigotry:

> What I imagine is if one of my metamours had some unresolved bigotry that they were going through, that's going to impact the way that they see my relationship with their shared partner and how much compersion they can or can't feel in that situation.[53]

Along these lines, Millie Boella, creator of the popular social media account *Decolonizing Love*, had witnessed BIPOC friends have trauma responses toward White metamours—which would of course block their capacity to experience compersion:

> I've had BIPOC friends who have told me about being given less respect and affection than their white[54] metas, which, in turn, has now led to a trauma response where they don't have compersion when their partners begin dating white people. In fact, some people I know refuse to date anyone in established relationships with a white partner because of how white supremacy makes people treat their partners with preferential treatment.[55]

This was reminiscent of the ways couple privilege often creates preferential treatment toward established long-term partners that are considered part of the "primary couple"—a privilege that may be compounded by the legal and institutional privileges afforded to married couples. Indeed, some CNM folks often hesitate or refuse to partner with married folks, as they rightly fear that they would always remain "secondary"—and therefore may never feel completely safe, honored, and cherished as equals.[56] It is interesting to note the parallels between these two different systems of power and privilege.

Similarly, colorism and desirability politics were a prominent obstacle to people's compersion, when relationship dynamics "rubbed against" some factors of privilege such as how skin pigmentation gets associated with class, status, and beauty. Evita "Lavitaloca" Sawyers provided the personal example of her compersiveness being challenged when her partner would date a lighter-skinned woman—as well as the intersection of age in metamour relationships:

> My identities impact my experience of compersion when something my partner is doing with someone else activates any internalized programming I have as a result of my identities or triggers any feelings of scarcity I may carry around from my life experience with my identities. . . . For example, if a partner dates someone lighter skinned than me, feeling compersion may be more challenging because of internalized colorism that asserts that "lighter skin" is more appealing. Consequently, I may feel more threatened by their lighter skinned partner, believing that my partner is more physically attracted to them than they are to me as a darker skinned woman. Another example could be that as a woman in my forties, my partners dating younger women/femmes can sometimes activate insecurity in me because as women,

we are socialized to view aging as a loss of value and desirability. Fortunately, since I have been at this for some time now, even when I notice that I'm experiencing some barriers to compersion due to situations like these, I am practiced in choosing to align my thoughts and behavior, even when my emotions may not be on board, with my polyamorous integrity which is to be a supportive and encouraging partner to my partners as they pursue relationships and connections that bring them fulfillment.[57]

As a contrast, Millie Boella recounted how she had associated a lack of compersion with both lighter-skinned and darker-skinned metamours—as well as metamours who were either younger or older than herself. While she noted that jealousy and compersion were more of a reflection of the security of the relationship than these triggers in and of themselves, this quote portrays the complexity and uniqueness of each situation as it pertains to the intersection between identity, inner security, relational security, and compersion:

> He was Black, and when he dated someone whiter and younger, I assumed it was reflective of his previous preference for whiteness. But when the next person he was with was dark-skinned, I felt that my Blackness wasn't sufficient as someone Brown/Light-skinned and mixed race. When he eventually cheated on me with someone older, I attributed it to my not being mature enough for his tastes. But he was just triggering insecurities, and the mind creates narratives to make sense of a relationship that was never full of love, and where I was always starving for affection. So, I think compersion/jealousy can be a reflection of the health of your relationship.[58]

These quotes demonstrate how thin the veil is between personal and political spheres—and how one cannot consider intimate relationships in isolation from their many contexts. Because compersion requires positive empathy—for which feeling seen, welcomed, cared for, and included are prerequisites—racial prejudice and trauma can create barriers to feeling "on the same team" with certain metamours based on racial dynamics.

Additionally, it is generally riskier for folks who belong to marginalized racial groups to come out as non-monogamous than for those with racial privilege. Being publicly labeled as sexually outside the norm, or deviant—whether CNM, kinky, or both—can lead to losses of social advantages that some folks cannot afford to part with. Therefore, it can be dangerous for people who fear financial, legal, or familial punitive repercussions, to openly connect with CNM communities. As Eli Sheff and Corie Hammers explained in *The Privilege of Perversities: Race, Class, and Education among Polyamorists and Kinksters*,

> Being accused of being a pervert can have detrimental consequences, and although everyone involved in "perverted" sex risks social censure, people unprotected by social advantages are more vulnerable to the discriminatory impacts of this sexual stigma than are those shielded by racial and/or class privileges.[59]

As I explained in Chapter 10, obstacles to coming out as non-monogamous can make it difficult to release internalized mononormativity, and therefore, compersion may be more difficult to access. On the other hand, when one can come out to a trusted and supportive community, breaking social barriers can become easier thereafter—and compersion can become an embodiment of a celebratory spirit of resistance and radical love.

Racial Discrimination as a Catalyst to Dismantling Mononormativity

Discrimination works in complex social ways. Along with incalculable hardship, belonging to a marginalized group has the potential to breed solidarity, tight-knit friendships, loyalty, community belonging, empathy, and a spirit of resistance toward other hegemonic normativities. If the dominant culture has already been proven to be harmful and oppressive through racial oppression and discrimination, why trust its further mandates—such as mononormativity?

As I described at the beginning of this chapter, compersion can then become a resistance strategy for members of marginalized groups—especially those that espouse collectivist ways of being. Thus, in cases where conformity or submission to the cultural hegemony is not possible or desirable, breaking other social norms can become easier—and this may catalyze compersion among members of trusted communities.

For example, Fred and Sue, an interracial couple in their late 70s (both 75 at the time of the first interview, and 79 at the time of the second), had faced intense racial discrimination from a young age. Sue was a half-Korean, half-Japanese refugee who had been born in Shanghai during the Japanese occupation of 1943. Her family had "escaped death numerous times before she was six years old." Her husband, Fred, on the other hand, was "one of only two Jewish guys in [his] high school." They had both grown up as social out-siders because of their racial, ethnic, and religious backgrounds. Becoming an interracial couple in their 20s had reinforced that status. However, Fred recounted that having faced so much hardship in their communities had predisposed them to—rather than preventing them from—violating other social norms, including monogamy:

> I think the reason that people are maybe more predisposed to violating the social norms is if they grow up being outcasts in the first place. Both Sue and I were sort of outsiders in the context of our growing up, so we felt that outsiderness, that otherness, and so it was like, "They want us to be monogamous, get married, have the white picket fence, 2.1 point one children or whatever the hell it is, and we looked at that and thought, why the hell should we do what they say? I mean, they nastied us the whole time. Why should we bother? You know, pigeonholing us into that set of norms." And so, the more people told us we shouldn't do it, the more pissed off we got. I don't know if that's . . . I've read that when that happens to people, they develop low self-esteem, but we just got angry about it. I mean, not yelling and screaming at you, but more like, "You're telling us to do that, so fuck you!"

What gave Sue and Fred the resilience to become openly non-monogamous despite every other vector of discrimination they were facing? The answer seems to lie in both community belonging and agentic thinking. Sue explained that while her parents faced a lot of persecution throughout their lives both in Asia and in the United States, they had "managed to land on their feet, always through their friendships, and it was generally through art. They were outliers to begin with. I mean, they're very independent-minded people to be artists." She also mentioned that her parents were atheists, while the rest of her family was very religious. Thus, the propensity for agentic thinking and community building were deep-rooted values in her family of origin, even though she was the first person in her known lineage to practice CNM.

Thus, being on the receiving end of race-based discrimination sometimes went hand-in-hand with the process of rejecting compulsory monogamy. For people like Sue and Fred, consciously rejecting compulsory monogamy and adopting a mindset of nonconformist love fundamentally supported the emergence of compersion.

CHAPTER 11

Radical Love, Collective Liberation, and Compersion

The connection between radical love in intimate relationships and collective liberation has been drawn by several prominent Black and Indigenous authors. For example, Ruby B. Johnson described the potential of polyamory in fostering personal sovereignty and collective liberation in her editor's note to a *Special Issue of the Journal of Black Sexuality and Relationships on Polyamory and Other Relational Constellations*:

> Polyamory is about building relationships and connections. . . . In my experience, I have found kinship (i.e. intentional family) and solidarity (i.e. "We are in this together.") are inherent attributes of Black polyamorous communities. . . . Polyamory opens individuals up to create the partnerships that work [for] them. It's not about the exclusion of monogamy but inclusion of other relationship options such as polyamory. The liberation is shifting the governance of the relationship to the individual versus imposed cultural expectations.[60]

Because racially marginalized cultures often embody more collectivist than individualist traditions, and have long histories of precolonial non-monogamous sexualities and family structures, folks in these groups may have a different relationship with CNM than White folks. On the one hand, they may feel ill at ease and underrepresented in mostly White polyamorous communities (as I described in Chapter 8 and in the next section), yet on the other, non-monogamy may resonate particularly deeply as they connect the dots between colonialism, racism, and compulsory monogamy—and trace CNM to their ancestral roots.

When CNM becomes an act of political reclamation and radical solidarity, it is viewed as more than a "lifestyle"—but as a cornerstone of a social paradigm based on justice and equity. As Yakas and Lopez explained,

> Systems of oppression are, by their nature, disabling—and this includes compulsory monogamy. And like other systems of oppression, it's not disabling by mere historical accident. Indigenous scholar Kim Tallbear's work in critical polyamory asserts that compulsory heterosexual monogamy was strategically used in colonial efforts to subjugate and eradicate Indigenous ways of being. In the Americas, many pre-colonial cultures embraced sexual and gender fluidity; this was also true in Aotearoa/New Zealand. And among the many cultural genocide tools in their arsenals, colonialists forced heteronormativity, mononormativity, and a gender binary upon Indigenous cultures.

> Building on the work of queer theorists, Kim Tallbear therefore refers to compulsory monogamy as "settler sexuality," which she defines as "both heteronormative and homonormative forms of 'love,' 'sex,' and 'marriage' that are produced along with private property holding" in settler nations. . . . Kim Tallbear's work reveals how mononormativity is born at the intersections of colonization, white supremacy, and cisheteropatriarchy.[61]

In this passage, Yakas and Lopez highlighted the work of Kim Tallbear in linking different systems of oppression to compulsory monogamy—which is particularly personal to Indigenous communities, but finds echo in countless cultural lineages around the globe, especially the Global South. What becomes clear is that freedom from one vector of oppression is interconnected with freedom from the others—and that relationship choices, as well as compersion, can be used as political acts of defiance, collective reclamation, and liberation.

This is reminiscent of Black feminist scholar bell hooks's advocacy for a society based on care and justice, rather than domination—and how this starts with practicing a "love ethic" in one's personal life. In *All About Love: New Visions*, she showed that attempts to control or dominate others are simply incompatible with love:

> When we choose to love we choose to move against fear, against alienation and separation. The choice to love is a choice to connect—to find ourselves in the other. . . . Domination cannot exist in any social situation where a love ethic prevails.[62]

A love ethic fosters collective liberation, thereby resisting systems of domination. Compersion, which rests on a commitment to honor one's and other people's personal sovereignty, may thus be particularly resonant, both philosophically and emotionally, for people who know firsthand about the harms of hegemonic oppression.

Representation and Inclusivity in CNM Communities

For most BIPOC participants, embracing a paradigm of nonconformist radical love was typically conditional on one's ability to access an inclusive CNM community. When these were out of reach, whether because they did not exist in one's geographical area or because of fear of repercussions and loss of privilege, these folks encountered more challenges than their White counterparts in building thriving relational ecosystems that felt like home. Nearly all of my participants, from all racial and ethnic backgrounds, had noticed a lack of racial diversity within CNM communities, especially in more conservative and/or less diverse geographical areas. Because community belonging is key to validating and *affirming* one's non-monogamous identity and fostering compersion (see Chapter 10, "The Role of Coming Out and Pride in Compersion"), folks who did not have access to inclusive communities would face greater obstacles on their CNM journeys.

For example, Sylvia, a 59-year-old Dakota participant who identified as solo polyamorous, encountered challenges finding local like-minded partners who could relate to her cultural background and philosophy. The sheer scarcity of potential lovers in her geographical area rendered compersion difficult. Conversely, Lisa, a 41-year-old White participant living in the Pacific Northwest, noted that the "poly-themed meetups, munches, play parties, all those sorts of things" she attended were "disproportionately White." When asked how she thought her racial background intersected with compersion and CNM, she responded: "I absolutely think my racial background plays a role because this community felt accessible to me. . . . There is something about how we are constructing these communities that is definitely bent toward White culture." She also remarked that she had "pretty much universally heard" from her BIPOC partners and friends that they "didn't feel invited, and kind of fought their way into CNM spaces." As someone who periodically organized local play parties, she was working to find ways to foster inclusivity to tip the scale toward more adequate representation.

The "Black Guy in Front of the Room"

On that note, it seemed that not being White was one effective way to create inclusive CNM communities as an organizer. William Winters, founder of the Bonobo Network, a CNM community in the San Francisco Bay Area, discussed how his being Black helped other racially marginalized folks feel more inclined to join events such as picnics, workshops, and play parties. He explained that "being the Black guy in front of the room" is "helpful in bringing folks together. Folks of color who might otherwise be pretty hesitant to go into majority or even plurality White spaces, they see me as the person who's leading the thing, and they're like, 'Okay, I'll give this a chance.'"[63] Winters also reflected on how his positionality gives his institutional power to affect the culture of diversity, inclusion, and acceptance within the CNM spaces he leads:

> It also means that I actually have institutional power with respect to how the community comes together and how policies are made, and what our stances are around the work of inclusion, like building inclusive communities. That means I can influence the White folks who join our communities, you know, like everyone who joins has to fill a tremendously long application, everyone has to answer questions like, "What does Black Lives Matter mean to you?" "Are you a feminist, why or why not?" "What, if anything, does the phrase systemic oppression mean to you?" and "True or false, transgender men are men, and transwomen are women, and why." I think that there are lots of potential correct answers, and there are just like a handful of incorrect answers.[64]

The idea that BIPOC leadership greatly impacts the level of diversity in CNM event attendance was confirmed by Natasha, a 38-year-old White participant living in the US Southwest. She noted that although the local CNM scene was mostly White, "The couple of play parties I've gone to that are run by a person of color were very diverse."

While there is undeniably much progress to be made in terms of improving racial diversity in CNM spaces, there is also cause for optimism. Jamila, a 36-year-old half-Black, half-White member of the San Francisco Bay Area polyamory community, reported witnessing increased levels of inclusion in recent years:

> When I went to parties before, there were no other Black and Brown people there. That only became more of a thing later, with effort put behind some of these parties. . . . And then money. All those parties and events cost us $60 or $70 to attend. I think that has something to do with the lack of diversity that happens in those spaces. But I think that also is changing. I mean, I've noticed that change over the last few parties I've gone to.

Here, Jamila noted the intersection between race and socioeconomic status. Another impactful factor in this conversation was geographical location.

Geography and Representation

While many participants had recently witnessed an evolution in the racial diversity of their local CNM groups, this was not the case in every

CHAPTER 11

geographical area. This may be due to general demographics, politics, religion, and other social factors. For example, James, a White participant living in New Mexico, reported that CNM communities in his area were "pretty darn White":

> Most of the diversity is in the LBGTQ spectrum and not so much racially. I attribute that mostly to some of the minority populations tend to be much more religious, traditionally religious. New Mexico is a very strong Catholic state, and then its Hispanic populations, you know, even more strongly Catholic. I think that that has a reflection on the demographics. . . . I can't remember ever running into somebody from Islamic background [in a CNM community].

Indeed, the CNM "scene" differed greatly from location to location. Some cities were known to be home to more racially inclusive CNM communities, which led some BIPOC folks to visit and even move to those areas. Tyrone, a 38-year-old bisexual Black man, had found it difficult to find Black CNM partners—particularly male—in most cities, except for Atlanta, Oakland, and New York City. He then geared his travels to these locations:

> I run in a lot of spaces that are predominantly White, because I'm super hippie dippie, very sex positive and kink oriented. Depending on what city you live in, it's just not diverse at all. But I'm a part of a lot of groups that are POC oriented such as *poly and play*. . . . I haven't found a lot of Black men, actually at all, that have the education and tools around non-monogamy that I would desire. . . . It's literally why I moved to Atlanta, because of the desire to be around more POCs that have the tools, and I've connected to people in Atlanta for that reason. It's a predominantly Black city. And there are gradients of every type of Black person, and there's non-monogamy and tantric, sex-positive kinky groups that are all specifically Black. . . . I have to know what cities to go to that have a predominant level of kinky, polyamory, or non-monogamy, in cities like Atlanta, Oakland, or New York.

In sum, what I found in my interviews about the intersection of race and compersion was heavily mitigated by the availability of inclusive CNM communities—which in turn was dependent on contexts such as geography, religion, spirituality, culture of origin, education, and socioeconomic status. I turn to this latter factor next.

SOCIOECONOMIC STATUS AND COMPERSION

While there are financial barriers to access in some CNM communities, the impact of socioeconomic status on compersion itself is mixed. As I stated in previous chapters, being financially independent and having access to resources can help folks feel more secure in their relationships, and therefore feel less threatened and more generous in regard to their partners' other relationships. Because jealousy is to a large degree an evolved threat response connected to survival (see Chapter 1), being dependent on a partner for one's sustenance could make it more difficult to wholeheartedly share that partner with other lovers.

However, there are circumstances where metamours are adding to a polycule's financial security and well-being, rather than threatening to take away from it. These circumstances are fertile for compersion, by way of stoking feelings of gratitude and being on the same team. This phenomenon was similar to the connections between age, disability, and compersion explored earlier: when a metamour was seen as a positive contribution to the relational ecosystem, compersion would flourish. For example, Kathy Labriola reported that CNM relationships where many people contribute to the economic stability of a household can reduce financial stress and give everyone more time and freedom: "Having financial difficulties sometimes really enhances compersion because someone if someone is dependent financially on the partner and metamours, they're often very grateful that their metamours are there and that those relationships exist and that they're being given support."[65]

Additionally, psychological research indicated that socioeconomic privilege and empathy are negatively correlated and that less wealthy individuals often display more empathy, generosity, and prosocial behaviors. Stellar and colleagues conducted comparative studies of "lower-class" versus "upper-class" (constructs associated with financial wealth, educational attainment, and occupational prestige) individuals concerning compassion. They found that individuals with lower socioeconomic statuses reported elevated dispositional compassion, relative to their counterparts in higher socioeconomic brackets.[66] Similarly, Piff and colleagues found that "despite experiencing life stressors on a more chronic basis," folks in lower socioeconomic categories "appear to be more engaged with the needs of others."[67] Across different empirical studies, they showed that folks with less socioeconomic privilege proved to be more generous, charitable, trusting, and helpful, compared with their more privileged counterparts. They hypothesized that this finding may have to do with wealth and abundance bringing a sense of freedom and independence from others, which allows people to be more self-focused. In other words, having to rely less on others reduces the need to care about their feelings. Conversely, acts of generosity and benevolence strengthen social bonds—and these bonds may be more meaningful for folks with less economic means:

> We speculate that, relative to upper class individuals, lower class individuals construe themselves more in terms of their relationships to others, and this self–other overlap may account for their heightened sensitivity to other people's welfare. Another potential area of inquiry is class-based differences in approaches to communal and exchange relationships. For instance, whereas upper class individuals' prosociality may hinge on expectations of reciprocity and exchange, communal orientations among lower class individuals may predispose them toward prosocial behavior even when they do not expect others to be immediately prosocial in return.[68]

Applied to compersion and non-monogamy, the quote could suggest that less wealthy people may be more predisposed to thriving and experiencing compersion in CNM relationships—which is a more communal way to approach intimacy, compared to the monogamous nuclear family model.

Of course, many other contextual factors need to be taken into consideration. For example, compounded challenges like disability or living in rural or conservative areas where CNM is particularly stigmatized could make it particularly difficult for lower socioeconomic status folks to thrive in CNM relationships. The lack of access to CNM resources and communities could present challenges for those with less disposable income to benefit from the sense of belonging that often comes with the ability to attend events and access CNM-informed care. Alex Iantaffi described how challenging economic circumstances often intersect with disability and other factors:

> Financial access can be a barrier in many ways. Someone might not be able to attend CNM conventions, events, or resources due to cost, for example. This would reduce networking possibilities within CNM communities, as well as access to information. . . . Many therapists who are CNM-affirming might be more likely to work in private practice and not accept health insurance. They might offer sliding-scale fees and pro-bono spots, but there is still a limited number of those to go around. A sliding-scale spot might still be too expensive if someone is living on disability benefits, for example. Another

way in which financial access can be an issue is in dating and relationships. While love might be limitless, financial resources are not, and being in multiple romantic and/or sexual relationships can be costly, depending on people's expectations around dates, vacations, gifts, and so on.[69]

Another relevant consideration is that people with less economic security may have more to lose by coming out as non-monogamous. The loss of a job based on CNM discrimination could have a greater negative impact on someone who lives paycheck to paycheck or lacks privilege in other areas as well. Additionally, maintaining multiple intimate relationships can be time-consuming in a way that excludes folks who have to work multiple jobs to make ends meet, or are under financial stress. As James hypothesized, "If you're spending all your time eking out an existence, and you struggle economically, I think you have less time for cultivating new relationships. It's pretty time consuming."

In sum, the intersection between socioeconomic privilege and compersion is a complex, multifaceted, and at times counterintuitive one. Like with all other identity factors, it is impossible to divorce its impact from other elements—such as whether someone feels included, supported, safe, and loved in their relationship ecosystems and larger communities.

CONCLUSION: THE DOUBLE-EDGED SWORD OF OTHERNESS

My goal with this chapter has been to shine a light on how social positionality may impact compersion. I hope readers found the unique stories in these pages as thought-provoking as I did while gathering them.

Overall, I found the relationship between identity and compersion to be non-linear, paradoxical, and often counterintuitive. While individuals who experience discrimination based on age, disability, gender, sexual orientation, socioeconomic status, race, or ethnicity face unique obstacles when it comes to CNM and compersion, there are two main mitigating factors that may come into play to enhance positive empathy:

(1) *Agentic thinking*. Many folks with marginalized identities feel particularly predisposed to bending social rules, which facilitates the process of dismantling internalized mononormativity. Because dominant systems of power have betrayed them, they are often more psychologically

ready to embrace an "outsider status" in other parts of their lives—i.e., embracing a non-monogamous ideology and set of values—which in turn, promotes compersion.

(2) *Community belonging.* Additionally, members of marginalized communities are often more likely to belong to tight-knit, supportive communities built on values of mutual aid, diversity, inclusion, and sex-positivity. Embodying a "chosen family" mindset can be a catalyst for overcoming individualism and promoting inclusive love and resource sharing—which allows compersion to flourish.

These two factors of resilience were often highly prevalent for folks who had been discriminated against—which had the potential to mitigate the obstacles to compersion that could arise from social disadvantages.

While each person is infinitely more complex than the matrix of their particular identities, the prism of social positionality offers unique and important insight into the dynamics of our relational and personal experiences. Perhaps, through expanding dialogue into these under-explored topics, we might not only gain more knowledge and understanding of ourselves and our differences but also begin to approach bell hooks's *love ethic* where "the choice to love is a choice to connect—to find ourselves in the other."[70]

NOTES

1. Evita "Lavitaloca" Sawyers, personal communication, October 2, 2023. Reprinted with permission.
2. Harper, 2024.
3. Rubin et al., 2014; Balzarini et al., 2019
4. Anapol, 2010.
5. For example, Jenks, 2014; Noël, 2006; Wheeler, 2011; Sheff, 2005; Sheff & Hammers, 2015.
6. Balzarini et al., 2019.
7. Rubin et al., 2014.
8. Kathy Labriola, personal communication, February 6, 2020.
9. Thouin-Savard, 2021.
10. Labriola, 2022.
11. Johnson, 2019; Patterson, 2018.
12. Sheff & Smith, 2022.

13. Iantaffi, 2022; Yakas & Lopez, 2023.
14. Schippers, 2016.
15. Gonzalez, 2023; Yakas & Lopez, 2023.
16. For example, Alexander, 2022.
17. Thouin-Savard, 2021.
18. Labriola, 2022.
19. Patterson, 2018.
20. Sawyers, 2023.
21. For example, Rothschild, 2018.
22. Moors & Ramos, 2022.
23. For example, Vaughan & Burnes, 2022.
24. Also see chapter 9 for a description of how these factors interact with one another.
25. Sawyers, 2023.
26. Sheff & Hammers, 2015.
27. For example, Tallbear, 2014.
28. Evita Sawyers, personal communication, October 2, 2023.
29. hooks, 2001.
30. Exceptions include Fleckenstein & Cox II, 2017; Labriola, 2022.
31. Sarah Stroh, personal communication, September 5, 2023.
32. Sheff, 2014.
33. Labriola, 2022.
34. Kathy Labriola, personal communication, October 10, 2022.
35. Kathy Labriola, personal communication, October 10, 2022.
36. Kathy Labriola, personal communication, October 10, 2022.
37. Kathy Labriola, personal communication, October 10, 2022.
38. Kathy Labriola, personal communication, October 10, 2022.
39. Hahn & Belt, 2004.
40. https://disabilityphilanthropy.org/resource/what-is-disability/
41. Iantaffi, 2022, p. 157.
42. Kathy Labriola, personal communication, October 10, 2022.
43. Kathy Labriola, personal communication, October 10, 2022.
44. Kathy Labriola, personal communication, October 10, 2022.
45. Thouin-Savard, 2021.
46. Kevin Patterson, personal communication, September 14, 2023.
47. Kevin Patterson, personal communication, September 14, 2023.
48. Kevin Patterson, personal communication, September 14, 2023.
49. Kathy Labriola, personal communication, October 10, 2022.
50. Manley et al., 2015.
51. Patterson, 2018.
52. Kevin Patterson, personal communication, September 14, 2023.
53. Kevin Patterson, personal communication, September 14, 2023.

54. In the rest of the book, I capitalized "White" and all other racial qualifiers in accordance with the *Publication Manual of the American Psychological Association*, 7th edition; in this quote, however, I reproduced Millie Boella's original non-capitalization of "white" from her written communication.

55. Millie Boella, personal communication (email), October 4, 2023.

56. I elaborate on the impact of couple privilege and compersion in Chapter 8, under "Obstacles to Ideological Commitment to CNM Values"; see also Balzarini et al., 2017.

57. Evita Sawyers, personal communication, October 2, 2023.

58. Millie Boella, personal communication (email), October 4, 2023.

59. Sheff & Hammers, 2011, p. 198.

60. Johnson, 2019, pp. viii, xi.

61. Yakas & Lopez, 2023, p. 338.

62. hooks, 2001, pp. 93, 98.

63. William Winters, personal communication, June 5, 2023.

64. William Winters, personal communication, June 5, 2023.

65. Kathy Labriola, personal communication, October 10, 2022.

66. Stellar et al., 2012, p. 1.

67. Piff et al., 2010, p. 771.

68. Piff et al., 2010, p. 781.

69. Iantaffi, 2022, p. 164.

70. hooks, 2001, p. 93.

PART VI

CONCLUDING THOUGHTS

CHAPTER 12

CAN COMPERSION BE LEARNED?

In Western cultures we are taught to act as if we are sharing, but we are never taught to actually share.
—Kenya K. Stevens, love coach and author of *UPLVL Communication*[1]

Embracing a non-monogamous relationship structure means that jealousy can hardly be avoided. Therefore, learning to remain "on the same team" as partners and metamours, especially when difficult emotions arise, can be one of the most determinant factors in folks' ability to sustain harmonious relationships over time. As prior research has shown that compersion positively correlates with relationship satisfaction in CNM partnerships,[2] understanding how compersion emerges, and how it may be fostered, should help create more fulfilling relational ecosystems.

Simply put, learning to cultivate compersion is about gaining greater access to love—even in places where love does not flow habitually. While doing this can be confronting and take effort, it should not be framed as a rejection of one's truth. Rather, it can be recognized as an intentional expansion of one's psycho-emotional range to include more opportunities for empathy and gratitude.

Before diving in, I wish to reiterate a caveat I offered in the introduction, under the section "Should Compersion Always Be a Goal?" There, I warned readers against weaponizing the "ideal of compersion" as an instrument of blame rather than inspiration. In particular, attempting to convince oneself or one's partner to "be more compersive" in circumstances where disrespectful, abusive, nonconsensual, or unethical dynamics are at play may be counterproductive, at best—or a form of gaslighting, at worst. In those settings, a lack of compersion may be showing up as a perfectly healthy reaction to an unhealthy situation.

Besides, any perceived lack of compersion is always best met with curiosity and compassion, rather than shame or judgment. There may be many steps a person needs to take—such as naming, understanding, and bringing healing to challenging emotions and patterns—before they can access any form of compersion. I explore this more thoroughly in Chapter 1, "Developing a Non-Mononormative Relationship to Jealousy as a Foundation for Compersion," and in Chapter 6 under the section, "Comperstruggle."

That said, I imagine most people who picked up this book (just like those knocking on the door of my coaching practice) want to understand how compersion *can* be cultivated. I use the present chapter to summarize the most practical wisdom I encountered in my research, as well as to offer a collection of recommendations that can assist CNM folks and their therapists/ counselors in understanding the path ahead when one sets out to foster more empathic love in their relationships.

I sectioned this chapter into seven approaches to learning compersion: (1) learning by creating a "fertile terrain"; (2) learning by example; (3) learning by unlearning; (4) learning by shifting paradigms; (5) learning through practice; (6) learning by cultivating empathy; and finally, (7) learning by doing.

LEARNING BY CREATING A "FERTILE TERRAIN"

One of the most important messages of this book is that there are contexts that promote compersion, and other contexts that hinder it. Understanding what may block compersion is the first step in inviting more of it. On my website, www.whatiscompersion.com, I offer a downloadable worksheet where folks can identify their "compersion strengths and bottlenecks." CNM people and their therapists/counselors can use this self-assessment tool, based on my Compersion Roadmap (see Chapters 7 and 8), as a guide to evaluate how to invite more compersion into their lives.

Once folks become aware of their compersion bottlenecks, they can elect to spend more time and energy understanding and resolving obstacles in these particular areas. Once major blocks have been identified and attended to, creating a fertile terrain for compersion means cultivating more elements that promote it within the different layers of one's relational ecosystem. These elements include inner and outer security, kindness, care, compassion, transparency, communication, trust, consent, positive connection with metamours, community support, and much more. Being a "compersion gardener" is to look for and invest in opportunities to cultivate elements that propagate positive empathy and gratitude—and to weed out the obstacles as much as possible.

LEARNING BY EXAMPLE

Many participants in my study recounted learning compersion by example. Being surrounded by a supportive CNM community, as I emphasized in Chapters 7 and 10, allowed folks to be exposed to compersion in others— therefore, it could become normalized and more easily enacted. Stepping into CNM subcultures where one can witness other people expressing compersion in their intimate relationships has the power to create new paradigms around meaning-making, emotions, thoughts, attitudes, and behaviors— models that defy mononormativity.

William Winters, founder of the Bonobo Network—a CNM community in the San Francisco Bay Area—recounted having learned compersion through observing others in communities of practice. He explained that witnessing compersion in others helped him realize that CNM "could be just fine" for him:

> I would say that a lot of the socio-emotional learning that I have done has come from being actively involved in community. . . . I just observed how relaxed people were with one another, and how easy it was for people to be looking at their partners flirt with other people, and maybe even have physical cuddles or make out, or whatever, and it was all *just fine*—and I didn't know that it could be just fine. And when I learned that it could be just fine, *I let myself let it be fine!* [*laughs*] And I would say that compersion soon followed.[3]

Without seeing other people modeling compersion, it can be difficult to imagine it or even believe in its possibility. Because humans are social creatures, we learn behaviors through observing and imitating others. This is why having role models and a supportive CNM community can be so impactful in "learning" compersion—and "unlearning" mononormativity.

LEARNING BY UNLEARNING

Several participants in my study felt that compersion was not something that needed to be learned or created, but rather something that would be uncovered through the process of *removing what was in the way of it*—such as fear, lack of trust, or internalized mononormativity. Thus, they described that compersion was not a result of learning as much as *unlearning*: unlearning the cultural frameworks that caused them to interpret their partners' romantic and sexual feelings for others as a betrayal and rejection.

Lisa, a 41-year-old faculty counselor, eloquently explained this process—emphasizing that compersion can happen when "cultural expectations [are] removed":

> I think that the core of [compersion] is being able to get in touch with a level of intimate empathy that has some of the cultural expectations removed. I think it is possible for anyone to experience compersion, but many of us are held back from it because of prejudices and social expectations. So it's pretty natural, when it happens. It doesn't feel like, you know, I'm trying to train myself to have compersion. It's just very natural. But the part that you have to train is to recognize and let go of some of these stereotypical expectations.

For Lisa, compersion was a natural state that was hidden by mononormative conditioning. Similarly, James, a 54-year-old scientist engineer, spoke of his experience of developing compersion as a process of removing blocks to it, rather than learning something new:

> I think it was a matter of removing the elements of fear that contributed to shielding it, or the other emotions that were being generated. So I don't know if I learned it. I think I allowed it to express itself and be felt without competing for other feelings, or being washed away by other feelings. . . . Because the sense of somebody being intimate with your primary partner is, you know, we were always taught for that to be a very threatening thing. That's almost an archetypal sort of concern that one would have, and so you have decades of learning. . . . Seeing stories and novels where that's an incredibly jarring event. I think part of it is just having an expression of it as a different sort of entity.

James, who had entered CNM after discovering that his wife had an affair and then deciding to become openly non-monogamous, had needed to shift paradigms in order to experience compersion. Indeed, unlearning mononormativity is nothing short of a paradigm shift.

LEARNING BY SHIFTING PARADIGMS

Many participants remarked that non-monogamy required a shift in paradigmatic thinking—a theme Jessica Fern and David Cooley emphasized in their latest book, *Polywise*.[4] Unlearning a lifetime of monogamous conditioning, as I described earlier, was a multilayered process. Shifting into a new paradigm where compersion was available could seem like a leap into a world where a different philosophy, mindset, and skillset was at play. Kevin Patterson, author of *Love's Not Color Blind*,[5] described this shift in philosophy from a monogamous to a non monogamous paradigm:

> Just based on the way socialization is, a lot of us are trying to *win*, and not trying to *partner*. And I think just having compersion as a concept that people can identify with, and hopefully do identify with . . . just the same way I needed to hone my communication skills for my polyamory, those communication skills transfer to every other aspect of my life. Compersion can be the same way, where I know there are times where I'm rooting for someone to win, even though I don't have anything to gain, and part of that stems from me figuring out compersion with my polyamory.[6]

According to Patterson, truly caring about someone else's well-being without anything to gain was a concept that clashed with mainstream culture. Indeed, expressing love and support beyond the socially acceptable borders of what society deems normal or acceptable was nothing short of revolutionary. Patterson emphasized how this was particularly true for cisgender men in America:

> The way cisgender men are socialized in America, it's not always easy to find people who give a genuine fuck about your well-being, you know, outside of family, or people you've known for forever. So for me to roll up on someone who society tells me is an enemy or a rival, or something like that, and for me to congratulate them on their success is, you know, that's more of a future than I want.[7]

"Giving a genuine fuck," as Patterson stated, was a quality that could be cultivated through intentional practice akin to those of ancestral spiritual traditions.

LEARNING THROUGH PRACTICE

For some participants, cultivating compersion was an intentional practice. As I described in the introduction, muditā is one of the four brahmavihārās, or qualities of the enlightened person—and Buddhist practitioners have elaborate practices around cultivating that quality, along with the other three: mettā (loving-kindness), karunā (compassion), and upekshā (equanimity). According to Buddhist tradition, these qualities are interconnected and build upon each other.

Bethanne, an experienced meditator, said that she used mettā (loving-kindness) practice to invite more compersion into her experience of CNM:

> It's kind of like practicing mettā. You know, the Buddhist practice, it's quite literally, just like, "I wish my partner well and I am joyful that they are experiencing joy." . . . It's exactly like mettā, "I wish my partner joy. I wish them happiness." Or whoever, partner in the broadest sense of the word.

Jorge Ferrer has written at length about the relationship between compersion in CNM and muditā—including ways to put it into practice.[8] In *Love and Freedom: Transcending Monogamy and Polyamory*, he described how the practice of muditā (or sympathetic joy[9]) could be applied to intimate relationship contexts to "transform jealousy and thus support greater relational freedom."[10] He explained,

> In the context of open relationships or jealousy-triggering social situations in both poly and mono relationships, for example, one may begin the practice of sympathetic joy with oneself ("May I be joyful"), then proceed with one's partner ("May my partner experience joy with this person"), before extending the practice to the person interacting with one's partner ("May she experience happiness with my partner"), and ending with a more integrative statement such as, "May this relationship bring joy and growth to me, my partner, and this third person."[11]

Ferrer then suggested that the practice could be undertaken "with one's partner(s), as well as in small groups of intimately related or unrelated people struggling with jealous feelings."[12] Doing this may help lessen the sense of shame and isolation that often compounds with the pain of jealousy, by helping normalize these emotions and open the heart through the power of human love and connection. It would be wonderful for future research to investigate the impact of mettā or muditā practice on compersion in CNM. If this style of practice seems a bit formal or esoteric for some, another way to practice compersion may simply be through cultivating empathy.

LEARNING BY CULTIVATING EMPATHY

There is an increasing amount of literature documenting the benefits of empathy, as well as evidence showing how mindfulness practice can catalyze empathy.[13] Although empathy is not a panacea, and can certainly have downsides—for example, some people may have difficulty achieving emotional regulation because of an exaggeratedly porous sense of self—cultivating more empathic understanding and connection can, in the context of intimate relationships, foster compersion.

Along these lines, James spoke of inviting empathy "in a place that feels a bit unusual" as a meaningful vector for compersion:

> To me, compersion is largely grounded in empathy. So a lot of it is, I think, learning to be okay to be vulnerable a little bit, and then also to embrace and understand your empathy. And then express that in a place that feels a bit unusual.

Similarly, William Winters spoke of compersion as a muscle that could be developed:

> I think that practice can be like building a muscle. Developing greater sensitivity to your partner's joy. Actually, being curious about your partner's joy is also very helpful. To the extent that they are actually experiencing joy, learning about it, asking, "what is good for you about this relationship?" You know, like, "What do you like about this person? What's fun? What's supporting your happiness or growth, or whatever it is, that's attracting you to this person?" Being able to align with them on that, and see that through their eyes can be helpful potentially.[14]

Winters also described his shifting from being "stuck in [his] own experience" to cultivating a state of empathy. He described his ability to look at the world through his partner's eyes as a vector for compersion:

One of the biggest roadblocks for compersion for me was certainly being really stuck in my own experience. The more I was stuck in my own experience of anxiety or whatever, the less it was easy to empathize with my partner. I imagine that if you can get outside of yourself for a few moments by trying really hard to get into your partner's head, like trying really hard to focus on somebody else's experience, maybe, just maybe, it'll make the compersion thing a little easier for you.[15]

Cultivating positive empathy as a way to invite more compersion in one's relationships was directly aligned with the first component of compersion (see Chapter 2). Nurturing gratitude was the other side of the coin for Winters: "I really started looking for reasons to experience that as opposed to looking for reasons not to." He concluded with encouraging words: "I do think that once you find your way to it, whatever way that is, it can potentially become something that's easier to access."

LEARNING BY DOING

Last, compersion could be learned by "doing"—in other words, behaving in compersive ways. As an analogy, folks who are learning to play baseball primarily learn by playing; and those wanting to learn compassion typically do so by adopting compassionate behaviors, as a way to make compassion a more integral part of their lives. Cultivating compersion is similar: choosing compersive actions despite not necessarily *feeling* compersive can be a powerful stance.

For example, CNM folks might show support toward their partner's other relationships by sharing positive and encouraging words, helping them get ready for a date, being kind to their metamours, or, at the very least, not getting in the way or attempting to sabotage these relationships.

In Chapter 5, "Spectrum of Compersion," I noted that cultivating a compersive attitude often was a building block to emotional or embodied compersion; this attitude could include supportive actions and behaviors toward a partner's other relationships. On that note, Evita "Lavitaloca" Sawyers, author of *A Polyamory Devotional*,[16] regarded compersive actions and attitudes as a way to actualize her "polyamorous integrity." Even though she did not view compersive feelings as necessary for harmonious CNM, she practiced an "ethic of compersion":

I am who I want to be, overall, to my partners, and so we can feel those feelings and there's that space where we can navigate through those emotions. Maybe I'll talk to my partner about it. Maybe I'll talk to a friend. Maybe I'll go eat a pint of ice cream and cry, or whatever. But I'm able to kind of go, okay, well, what is our polyamorous integrity? I'm gonna lead with my integrity, and what I want to show up as overall.[17]

Indeed, compersion encompasses not only emotions—but also attitudes, thoughts, and actions. Acting compersively toward partners and metamours is something one can *do*—and since actions are easier to invoke than feelings, compersive behaviors are a great place to begin cultivating a compersive life.

CONCLUSION

The vast majority of my research participants believed that given a healthy and supportive relational context, anyone could develop compersion. This process encompassed fostering a favorable context for its emergence, unlearning mononormative beliefs, and cultivating practices that led to positive empathy and gratitude.

I did not include materials on working with jealousy and envy in this chapter, as I covered the topic at length in Chapter 1. However, I want to reemphasize that inviting compersion, in a vast majority of cases, involves reckoning with challenging emotional dynamics such as jealousy, envy, fear, and competitiveness. Rather than suppressing these emotions, I recommend developing a non-mononormative relationships with them to allow compersion to bloom. As I explained in Chapter 6, jealousy and compersion are not mutually exclusive; in fact, people generally need to be willing to experience a wide breadth of emotions to reveal the fullness of an open heart against the odds. This path is nonlinear and highly personal; it requires patience, curiosity, self-compassion, and the will to transform.

NOTES

1. Kenya K. Stevens, personal communication, August 26, 2023. Reprinted with permission.
2. Aumer et al., 2014.

3. William Winters, personal communication, June 5, 2023.

4. Fern & Cooley, 2023.

5. Patterson, 2018.

6. Kevin Patterson, personal communication, September 14, 2023.

7. Kevin Patterson, personal communication, September 14, 2023.

8. Ferrer, 2007, 2019, 2021.

9. Coren, 2023.

10. Ferrer, 2021, p. 62.

11. Ferrer, 2021, p. 62.

12. Ferrer, 2021, p. 62.

13. For example, Berry et al., 2018; Cheang et al., 2019.

14. William Winters, personal communication, June 5, 2023.

15. William Winters, personal communication, June 5, 2023.

16. Sawyers, 2023.

17. Evita Sawyers, personal communication, October 2, 2023.

PARTING WORDS

Compersion, Personal Transformation, and Social Change

Compersion exists on the outer reaches of what mononormative culture defines as love, yet in its essence, our ability to have empathy and cultivate care between self and other is at the core of what makes us human. In most social situations, wholeheartedly celebrating our loved one's joys and successes is a marker of good character and emotional maturity; however, in intimate partnerships, it can seem inconceivable to support our partners' pleasure when it derives from intimacy with another person. The taboo and painful nature of sexual jealousy confronts our most deeply rooted and ingrained fears. While non-monogamy is certainly not for everyone, understanding the compassionate quality of compersion can benefit all people—particularly those who wish to transcend the limitations of a zero-sum paradigm of love or wish to build relationships beyond couple-centric models of family and intimacy.[1]

The existence of compersion in CNM relationships disrupts the assumption that jealousy is the only valid or possible response to intimacy beyond monogamy; its documentation thereby contributes to dismantling the binds of mononormativity. As a society, undoing mononormativity would invite all people to make relational choices out of personal agency, authenticity, and relational freedom[2]—rather than from default assumptions or social pressures. Systems of sexual and relational normativity—such as heteronormativity, mononormativity, and couple-centrism—not only perpetuate stigma and discrimination toward individuals who do not adhere to the norms, they also impose limits on every person's imagination and freedom over the course of their lives. Thus, we all become freer when these normativities melt away.

Beyond the personal and individual benefits that embracing compersion can bring to relationships, imagining a world where positive empathy is increasingly common gives me hope for positive social change. This is because creating a hospitable *environment* for compersion—individually, relationally, and socially—requires a deep commitment to integrity, autonomy, openness, honesty, care, consent, freedom, safety, solidarity, equity, and kindness. Being compersive requires both empathy and gratitude, and it highlights the deeply interconnected nature of human relationships. Creating a relational life that embodies the necessary conditions for compersion represents a remarkable feat *in and of itself*—because these are conditions of healthy relating. As such, cultivating a fertile environment for compersion to grow and evolve is more important than focusing on it as an end goal.

Of course, learning to love beyond an entrenched paradigm of competition is not easy. As bell hooks described, it requires bravery and the willingness to "face our fears":

> To live our lives based on the principles of a love ethic (showing care, respect, knowledge, integrity, and the will to cooperate), we have to be courageous. Learning how to face our fears is one way we embrace love. Our fear may not go away, but it will not stand in the way.[3]

Under this lens, compersion may be framed as a lifelong guiding principle—one that challenges us to become more generous and supportive to ourselves and to one another in a variety of contexts. To this aim, expanding the traditional definition of compersion and including the many ways it may be experienced—through thoughts, attitudes, behaviors, emotions, and in different relationships—can help democratize its impact and benefits. As I have shown in this book and through this research, compersion is not only a *feeling*. It is also an *orientation to relationships*—a way people can choose to treat one another, based on principles of deep caring and collaboration.

At the collective level, compersion may develop another level of significance in current times of social and ecological crisis. There is an unmistakable relationship between mononormativity—a system that glamorizes possessive love through language, media, and pervasive messaging in everyday life[4]—and the overarching patriarchal, extractive, and territorial dynamics governing the world's political and economic powers.[5] While these structures have served human beings' evolutionary agenda from the perspective of expansion and conquest,[6] they have now brought our species face-to-face with an unsustainable, constrained, and grim future. If we are to change course, we need to shift away from the domineering philosophy that underlies our "grow-or-die" economic model,[7] and toward a commitment to collaboration, equity, and sustainability throughout society.

Suggesting that compersion could have something to do with our evolutionary trajectory may seem like a reach. However, microcosms of personal experience often hold relevance within the arc of human progress. In this case, the existence of compersion reveals the possibility for a relational paradigm built on radical cooperation and trust rather than domination and fear. As Boone speculated,

> If jealousy has been "programmed" into the human psyche due to past adaptational challenges and evolutionary needs, then does the much more recent advent and intentional cultivation of an opposite emotion—compersion—represent a mere outlier of an anomalous counter-evolutionary current? Or rather, does it show evidence for an emerging change in trajectory for human social and relational evolution? I would argue for the latter, because as we look at the specific cultural and environmental differences between the times of our ancestors and our own time, it is clear that the adaptational challenges for survival and reproduction that we face now are very different from those of millions of years ago.[8]

Thus, understanding compersion might be a key to unlocking the transformational potentials of our times. If personal relationships are the seed crystals of larger social change, the reality of compersion demonstrates that a more beautiful world is within reach.

NOTES

1. *Couple-centric bias* is the widespread mononormative bias that all people have or should desire a "couple" relationship; Ansara, 2023.
2. See Jorge Ferrer's *Love and Freedom: Transcending Monogamy and Polyamory*, 2021, for an exploration of the concept of *relational freedom*.
3. hooks, 2001, p. 101.
4. See Kean, 2015, for a list of examples of mononormativity in everyday life.
5. Emens, 2004; Rothschild, 2018; Kean, 2015.
6. Harari, 2014.
7. For example, Sandler, 1994; Smith, 2010.
8. Boone, 2019, p. 10.

REFERENCES

Alexander, A. A. (2022). Intersectionality in CNM relationships. In M. D. Vaughan & T. R. Burnes (Eds.), *The handbook of consensual non-monogamy: Affirming mental health practice* (pp. 138–150). Rowman & Littlefield.

Anapol, D. M. (1997). *Polyamory: The new love without limits.* IntiNet Resource Center.

Anapol, D. T. (2010). *Polyamory in the 21st century: Love and intimacy with multiple partners.* Rowman & Littlefield.

Angelou, M. (1994). *I wouldn't take nothing for my journey now.* Bantam.

Ansara, Y. G. (2023). Getting real about monogamism: Disrupting mononormative bias in sex therapy and relationship counselling. In *Relationally queer* (pp. 5–23). Routledge. https://doi.org/10.4324/9781003260561-2

Aron, A., & Aron, E. N. (1986). *Love and the expansion of self: Understanding attraction and satisfaction.* Harper & Row.

Ashton, M. C., Paunonen, S. V., Helmes, E., & Jackson, D. N. (1998). Kin altruism, reciprocal altruism, and the Big Five personality factors. *Evolution and Human Behavior, 19*(4), 243–255. https://doi.org/10.1016/S1090-5138(98)00009-9

Aumer, K., Bellew, W., Ito, B., Hatfield, E., & Heck, R. (2014). The happy green eyed monogamist: Role of jealousy and compersion in monogamous and nontraditional relationships. *Electronic Journal of Human Sexuality, 17.* Retrieved from http://www.ejhs.org/volume17/happy.html

Ballard, J. (2020, January 31). One-third of Americans say their ideal relationship is non-monogamous. *YouGov.* Retrieved from https://today.yougov.com/society/articles/27639-millennials-monogamy-poly-poll-survey-data

Balzarini, R. N., Campbell, L., Kohut, T., Holmes, B. M., Lehmiller, J. J., Harman, J. J., & Atkins, N. (2017). Perceptions of primary and secondary relationships in polyamory. *PloS one, 12*(5), e0177841. https://doi.org/10.1371/journal.pone.0177841

Balzarini, R. N., Dharma, C., Kohut, T., Campbell, L., Lehmiller, J. J., Harman, J. J., & Holmes, B. M. (2019). Comparing relationship quality across different types of romantic partners in polyamorous and monogamous relationships. *Archives of Sexual Behavior, 48*(6), 1749–1767. https://doi.org/10.1007/s10508-019-1416-7

Bancroft, J. (1999). Central inhibition of sexual response in the male: A theoretical perspective. *Neuroscience & Biobehavioral Reviews, 23*(6), 763–784. https://doi.org/10.1016/S0149-7634(99)00019-6

REFERENCES

Bancroft, J., Graham, C. A., Janssen, E., & Sanders, S. A. (2009). The dual control model: Current status and future directions. *Journal of Sex Research, 46*(2–3), 121–142. https://doi.org/10.1080/00224490902747222

Bancroft, J., & Janssen, E. (2000). The dual control model of male sexual response: A theoretical approach to centrally mediated erectile dysfunction. *Neuroscience & Biobehavioral Reviews, 24*(5), 571–579. https://doi.org/10.1016/S0149-7634(00)00024-5

Barker, M. (2005). This is my partner, and this is my ... partner's partner: Constructing a polyamorous identity in a monogamous world. *Journal of Constructivist Psychology, 18*(1), 75–88. https://doi.org/10.1080/10720530590523107

Barker, M.-J., & Langridge, D. (2010). Whatever happened to non-monogamies? Critical reflections on recent research and theory. *Sexualities, 13*(6), 748–772. https://doi.org/10.1177/1363460710384645

Barratt, B. B. (2010). *The emergence of somatic psychology and bodymind therapy.* Palgrave Macmillan. https://doi.org/10.1057/9780230277199_14

Barrett-Lennard, G. T. (1981). The empathy cycle: Refinement of a nuclear concept. *Journal of Counseling Psychology, 28*(2), 91–100. https://doi.org/10.1037/0022-0167.28.2.91

Basson, R. (2000). The female sexual response: A different model. *Journal of Sex & Marital Therapy, 26*(1), 51–65. https://doi.org/10.1080/009262300278641

Batson, C. D. (2009). These things called empathy: Eight related but distinct phenomena. In J. Decety & W. Ickes (Eds.), *The social neuroscience of empathy* (pp. 3–13). MIT Press. https://doi.org/10.7551/mitpress/9780262012973.003.0002

Batson, C. D., Batson, J. G., Slingsby, J. K., Harrell, K. L., Peekna, H. M., & Todd, R. M. (1991). Empathic joy and the empathy-altruism hypothesis. *Journal of Personality and Social Psychology, 61*(3), 413–426. https://doi.org/10.1037/0022-3514.61.3.413

Bauer, R. (2014). *Queer BDSM intimacies: Critical consent and pushing boundaries.* Routledge. https://doi.org/10.1057/9781137435026

Ben-Ze'ev, A. (2022). I am glad that my partner is happy with her lover. In A. Pismenny & B. Brogaard (Eds.), *The moral psychology of love* (pp. 127–150). Rowman & Littlefield.

Berry, D. R., Cairo, A. H., Goodman, R. J., Quaglia, J. T., Green, J. D., & Brown, K. W. (2018). Mindfulness increases prosocial responses toward ostracized strangers through empathic concern. *Journal of Experimental Psychology: General, 147*(1), 93. https://doi.org/10.1037/xge0000392

Betzig, L. (1989). Causes of conjugal dissolution: A cross-cultural study. *Current Anthropology, 30*(5), 654–676. https://doi.org/10.1086/203798

Bhugra, D. (1993). Cross-cultural aspects of jealousy. *International Review of Psychiatry, 5*(2–3), 271–280. https://doi.org/10.3109/09540269309028317

REFERENCES

Block, S. M. (2015). Erotica: cuckold. In *The international encyclopedia of human sexuality* (pp. 339–340). Wiley. https://doi.org/10.1002/9781118896877.wbiehs135

Bockting, W. O. (2014). Transgender identity development. In D. L. Tolman, L. M. Diamond, J. A. Bauermeister, W. H. George, J. G. Pfaus, & L. M. Ward (Eds.), *APA handbook of sexuality and psychology, Vol. 1: Person-based approaches* (pp. 739–758). American Psychological Association. https://doi.org/10.1037/14193-024

Boone, D. (2019). *Non-jealousy in polyamorous relationships: Countering evolution, or driving it forward?* Unpublished manuscript. California State University, Chico. Retrieved from https://www.academia.edu/19579836/Non-jealousy_in_Polyamorous_Relationships_Countering_Evolution_or_Driving_it_Forward

Bordo, S. (1987). *The flight to objectivity: Essays on Cartesianism and culture*. Suny Press.

Bradford, N. J., & Syed, M. (2019). Transnormativity and transgender identity development: A master narrative approach. *Sex Roles, 81*(5–6), 306–325. https://doi.org/10.1007/s11199-018-0992-7

Brake, E. (2011). *Minimizing marriage: Marriage, morality, and the law*. Oxford University Press.

Brown, T. (2002). A proposed model of bisexual identity development that elaborates on experiential differences of women and men. *Journal of Bisexuality, 2*(4), 67–91. https://doi.org/10.1300/J159v02n04_05

Bryson, J. B. (1991). Modes of response to jealousy-evoking situations. In P. Salovey (Ed.), *The psychology of jealousy and envy* (pp. 178–210). Guilford Press.

Buss, D. (1994). *The evolution of desire: Strategies of human mating*. Basic Books.

———. (2000). *The dangerous passion: Why jealousy is as necessary as love or sex*. Free Press.

Buunk, B. P. (1982). Anticipated sexual jealousy: Its relationship to self-esteem, dependency, and reciprocity. *Personality and Social Psychology Bulletin, 8*(2), 310–316. https://doi.org/10.1177/0146167282082019

Buunk, B. P., & Dijkstra, P. (2004). Men, women, and infidelity: Sex differences in extradyadic sex and jealousy. In J. Duncombe, K. Harrison, G. Allen, & D. Marsden (Eds.), *The state of affairs: Explorations in infidelity and commitment* (pp. 103–120). Lawrence Erlbaum. https://doi.org/10.4324/9781410610652-6

Carmi, Z., & Sadeh-Saadon, L. (2021). *A few is the new two: Real stories of non-monogamous relationships*. Self-published.

Cass, V. C. (1979). Homosexual identity formation: A theoretical model. *Journal of Homosexuality, 4*(3), 219–235. https://doi.org/10.1300/J082v04n03_01

———. (1984a). Homosexual identity. *Journal of Homosexuality, 9*(2), 105–126. https://doi.org/10.1300/J082v09n02_07

———. (1984b). Homosexual identity formation: Testing a theoretical model. *Journal of Sex Research, 20*(2), 143–167. https://doi.org/10.1080/00224498409551214

Chalmers, H. (2019). Is monogamy morally permissible? *The Journal of Value Inquiry, 53*(2), 225–241. https://doi.org/10.1007/s10790-018-9663-8

———. (2022). Monogamy unredeemed. *Philosophia, 50*(3), 1009–1034. https://doi.org/10.1007/s11406-021-00445-0

Chapman, G. (2009). *The five love languages: How to express heartfelt commitment to your mate.* Moody.

Cheang, R., Gillions, A., & Sparkes, E. (2019). Do mindfulness-based interventions increase empathy and compassion in children and adolescents? A systematic review. *Journal of Child and Family Studies, 28,* 1765–1779. https://doi.org/10.1007/s10826-019-01413-9

Clanton, G. (1996). A sociology of jealousy. *International Journal of Sociology and Social Policy, 16*(9/10), 171–189. https://doi.org/10.1108/eb013274

Clardy, J. L. (2019). Monogamies, non-monogamies, and the moral impermissibility of intimacy confining constraints. *Journal of Black Sexuality and Relationships, 6*(2), 17–36. https://doi.org/10.1353/bsr.2019.0019

Clardy, J. L. (2023). *Why it's okay to not be monogamous.* Routledge.

Coleman, E. (1982). Developmental stages of the coming out process. *Journal of Homosexuality, 7*(2–3), 31–43. https://doi.org/10.1300/J082v07n02_06

Cole, S. W., Kameney, M. E., Taylor, S. E., & Visscher, B. R. (1996). Elevated physical health risk among gay men who conceal their homosexual identity. *Health Psychology, 15*(4), 243–251. https://doi.org/10.1037/0278-6133.15.4.243

Collins, P. H., & Bilge, S. (2020). *Intersectionality* (2nd ed.). Polity Press.

Conley, T. D., Matsick, J. L., Moors, A. C., & Ziegler, A. (2017). Investigation of consensually nonmonogamous relationships: Theories, methods, and new directions. *Perspectives on Psychological Science, 12*(2), 205–232. https://doi.org/10.1177/1745691616667925

Conley, T. D., & Moors, A. C. (2014). More oxygen please!: How polyamorous relationship strategies might oxygenate marriage. *Psychological Inquiry, 25*(1), 56–63. https://doi.org/10.1080/1047840X.2014.876908

Conley, T. D., Moors, A. C., Matsick, J. L., & Ziegler, A. (2013). The fewer the merrier?: Assessing stigma surrounding consensually non-monogamous romantic relationships. *Analyses of Social Issues and Public Policy, 13*(1), 1–30. https://doi.org/10.1111/j.1530-2415.2012.01286.x

Conley, T. D., Ziegler, A., Moors, A. C., Matsick, J. L., & Valentine, B. (2013). A critical examination of popular assumptions about the benefits and outcomes of monogamous relationships. *Personality and Social Psychology Review, 17*(2), 124–141. https://doi.org/10.1177/1088868312467087

Coren, D. (2023). Sympathetic joy. *Erkenntnis,* 1–11. https://doi.org/10.1007/s10670-023-00677-4

Crenshaw, K. (1990). Mapping the margins: Intersectionality, identity politics, and violence against women of color. *Stanford Law Review, 43,* 1241.

REFERENCES

Cruz, J. (2016). A utilitarian defense of non-monogamy. *Polymath: An Interdisciplinary Arts and Sciences Journal, 6*(2), 46–52.

Daly, M., Wilson, M., & Weghorst, S. J. (1982). Male sexual jealousy. *Ethology and Sociobiology, 3*, 11–27. https://doi.org/10.1016/0162-3095(82)90 027-9

D'Augelli, A. R. (1994). Identity development and sexual orientation: Toward a model of lesbian, gay, and bisexual development. In E. J. Trickett, R. J. Watts, & D. Birman (Eds.), *Human diversity: Perspectives on people in context* (pp. 312–333). Jossey-Bass/Wiley.

de Sousa, R. (2017). Love, jealousy, and compersion. In C. Grau & A. Smuts (Eds.), *The Oxford handbook of philosophy of love* (pp. 1–23). Oxford University Press. https://doi.org/10.1093/oxfordhb/9780199395729.001 0001

de Waal, F. B. (2008). Putting the altruism back into altruism: The evolution of empathy. *Annual Review of Psychology, 59,* 279–300. https://doi.org/10.1146/annurev.psych.59.103006.093625

Deri, J. (2015). *Love's refraction: Jealousy and compersion in queer women's polyamorous relationships.* University of Toronto Press. https://doi.org/10.3138/9781442624566

Deri, S., & Zitek, E. M. (2017). Did you reject me for someone else? rejections that are comparative feel worse. *Personality and Social Psychology Bulletin, 43*(12), 1675–1685. https://doi.org/10.1177/0146167217726988

Donaghue, C. (2015). *Sex outside the lines: Authentic sexuality in a sexually dysfunctional culture.* Benbella Books.

Drescher, J. (2004, October 1). The closet: Psychological issues of being in and coming out. *Psychiatric Times, 21*(12). Retrieved from https://www.psychiatric-times.com/view/closet-psychological-issues-being-and-coming-out

Dryden, J. (2015). This is the family I chose: Broadening domestic partnership law to include polyamory. *Hamline Journal of Public Law and Policy, 36*(1), 162–188.

Duma, U. (2009). *Jealousy and compersion in close relationships: Coping styles by relationship types* (Doctoral thesis). Available from GRIN Verlag.

Easton, D., & Hardy, J. W. (2009). *The ethical slut: A practical guide to polyamory, open relationships and other adventures.* Celestial Arts.

Eisenberg, N. (2002). Empathy-related emotional responses, altruism, and their socialization. In R. J. Davidson & A. Harrington (Eds.), *Visions of compassion: Western scientists and Tibetan Buddhists examine human nature* (pp. 131–164). Oxford University Press. https://doi.org/10.1093/acprof:oso/9780195130430.003.0007

———. (2010). Empathy-related responding: Links with self-regulation, moral judgment, and moral behavior. In M. Mikulincer & P. R. Shaver (Eds.), *Prosocial motives, emotions, and behavior: The better angels of our nature* (pp. 129–148). American Psychological Association. https://doi.org/10.1037/12061-007

REFERENCES

Emens, E. (2004). Monogamy's law: Compulsory monogamy and polyamorous existence. *New York University Review of Law and Social Change, 29*(2), 277–376.

Emmons, R. A., & Shelton, C. M. (2002). Gratitude and the science of positive psychology. In C. R. Snyder & S. J. Lopez (Eds.), *Handbook of positive psychology* (pp. 459–471). Oxford University Press.

Erel, U., Haritaworn, J., Rodríguez, E. G., & Klesse, C. (2010). On the depoliticisation of intersectionality talk: Conceptualising multiple oppressions in critical sexuality studies. In Y. Taylor, S. Hines, & M. Casey (Eds.), *Theorizing Intersectionality and Sexuality: Genders and Sexualities in the Social Sciences* (pp. 56–73). Palgrave Macmillan. https://doi.org/10.1057/9780230304093_4

Falco, K. L. (1991). *Psychotherapy with lesbian clients: Theory into practice.* Brunner/Mazel.

Fern, J. (2020). *Polysecure: Attachment, trauma and consensual nonmonogamy.* Thorntree.

Fern, J., & Cooley, D. (2023). *Polywise: A deeper dive into navigating open relationships.* Thornapple.

Ferrer, J. N. (2007). Monogamy, polyamory, and beyond. *Tikkun: Culture, Spirituality, Politics, 22*(1), 37–43, 60–62.

———. (2018). Mononormativity, polypride, and the "mono-poly wars." *Sexuality & Culture, 22*(3), 817–836. https://doi.org/10.1007/s12119-017-9494-y

———. (2019). From romantic jealousy to sympathetic joy: Monogamy, polyamory, and beyond. *International Journal of Transpersonal Studies, 38*(1), 185–202. https://doi.org/10.24972/ijts.2019.38.1.185

———. (2021). *Love and freedom: Transcending monogamy and polyamory.* Rowman & Littlefield.

Fisher, H. E. (2016). *Anatomy of love: A natural history of mating, marriage, and why we stray.* W.W. Norton.

Fleckenstein, J. R., & Cox II, D. W. (2017). The association of an open relationship orientation with health and happiness in a sample of older US adults. *Sexuality & Ageing,* 106–128. https://www.tandfonline.com/doi/abs/10.1080/14681994.2014.976997

Flicker, S. M., Thouin, M., & Vaughan, M. D. (2022). Factors that facilitate and hinder the experience of compersion among individuals in consensually non-monogamous relationships. *Archives of Sexual Behavior, 51,* 3035–3048. https://doi.org/10.1007/s10508-022-02333-4

Flicker, S. M., Vaughan, M. D., & Meyers, L. S. (2021). Feeling good about your partners' relationships: Compersion in consensually non-monogamous relationships. *Archives of Sexual Behavior, 50*(4), 1569–1585. https://doi.org/10.1007/s10508-021-01985-y

REFERENCES

Flicker, S., & Sancier-Barbosa, F. (2024). Your happiness is my happiness: Predicting positive feelings for a partner's consensual extra-dyadic intimate relations. *Archives of Sexual Behavior.* https://doi.org/10.1007/s10508-023-02766-5

Fox, J., Picciotto, G., Cashwell, C. S., Worthington Jr., E. L., Basso, M. J., Brow Corrigan, S., Toussaint, L., & Zeligman, M. (2020). Religious commitment, spirituality, and attitudes toward God as related to psychological and medical help-seeking: The role of spiritual bypass. *Spirituality in Clinical Practice, 7*(3), 178–196. https://psycnet.apa.org/doi/10.1037/scp0000216

Fredrickson, B. L. (2001). The role of positive emotions in positive psychology. *American Psychologist, 56*(3), 218–226. https://doi.org/10.1037/0003-066X.56.3.218

Fredrickson, B. L., & Branigan, C. (2001). Positive emotions. In T. J. Mayne & G. A. Bonnano (Eds.), *Emotion: Current issues and future directions* (pp. 123–151). Guilford Press.

Freud, S. (1923). The ego and the id. In *The standard edition of the complete psychological works of Sigmund Freud, volume XIX (1923–1925)*, 1–66. Hogarth Press.

Friedman, H. L. (2013). Transpersonal self-expansiveness as a scientific construct. In H. L. Friedman & G. Hartelius (Eds.), *The Wiley-Blackwell handbook of transpersonal psychology* (pp. 203–222). Wiley. https://doi.org/10.1002/9781118591277.ch11

Gable, S., Gonzaga, G., & Strachman, A. (2006). Will you be there for me when things go right? Supportive responses to positive event disclosures. *Journal of Personality and Social Psychology, 91*(5), 904–917. https://doi.org/10.1037/0022-3514.91.5.904

Gable, S. L., Gosnell, C. L., Maisel, N. C., & Strachman, A. (2012). Safely testing the alarm: Close others' responses to personal positive events. *Journal of Personality and Social Psychology, 103*(6), 963–981. https://doi.org/10.1037/a0029488

Gable, S. L., Reis, H. T., Impett, E., & Asher, E. R. (2004). What do you do when things go right? The intrapersonal and interpersonal benefits of sharing positive events. *Journal of Personality and Social Psychology, 87*(2), 228–245. https://doi.org/10.1037/0022-3514.87.2.228

Garcia-Romeu, A., Himelstein, S. P., & Kaminker, J. (2015). Self-transcendent experience: A grounded theory study. *Qualitative Research, 15*(5), 633–654. https://doi.org/10.1177/1468794114550679

Glaser, B. G., & Strauss, A. L. (1999). *The discovery of grounded theory: Strategies for qualitative research.* Aldine de Gruyter. (Original work published in 1967.)

Goetz, A. T., Shackelford, T. K., Romero, G. A., Kaighobadi, F., & Miner, E. J. (2008). Punishment, proprietariness, and paternity: Men's violence against women from an evolutionary perspective. *Aggression and Violent Behavior, 13*(6), 481–489. https://doi.org/10.1016/j.avb.2008.07.004

REFERENCES

Greenberg, S. E. (2019). Divine kink: A consideration of the evidence for BDSM as spiritual ritual. *International Journal of Transpersonal Studies, 38*(1), 220–235. https://doi.org/10.24972/ijts.2019.38.1.220

Giuliani, C. R. (2023, July 25). Love, liberty, and the pursuit of polyamory: A look under the covers of nonmonogamy and its burgeoning civil rights battle. *Vanity Fair.* Retrieved from https://www.vanityfair.com/style/2023/07/love-liberty-and-the-pursuit-of-polyamory

Gonzalez, A. (2023). *Nonmonogamy and neurodiversity: A more than two essentials guide.* Thornapple Press.

Goodman, W. (2022). *Toxic positivity: Keeping it real in a world obsessed with being happy.* Penguin.

Guerrero, L., Trost, M., & Yoshimura, S. (2005). Romantic jealousy: Emotions and communicative responses. *Personal Relationships, 12*(2), 233–252. https://doi.org/10.1111/j.1350-4126.2005.00113.x

Guittar, N. A. (2013). The meaning of coming out: From self-affirmation to full disclosure. *Qualitative Sociology Review, 9*(3), 169–187.

Gusmano, B. (2018). Coming out through an intersectional perspective: Narratives of bisexuality and polyamory in Italy. *Journal of Bisexuality, 18*(1), 15–34. https://doi.org/10.1080/15299716.2017.1416510

Haag, P. (2011). *Marriage confidential: Love in the post-romantic age.* HarperCollins.

Halpern, E. L. (1999). If love is so wonderful, what's so scary about MORE? *Journal of Lesbian Studies, 3(1/2),* 157–164. https://doi.org/10.1300/J155v03n01_17

Hamilton, J. E. (2020). *Triangular trouble: A phenomenological exploration of jealousy's archetypal nature in polyamorous individuals.* Pacifica Graduate Institute. Dissertation.

———. (2023, October 2). *Comperstruggle: When you want to feel joy but keep getting stuck in jealousy.* [Blog]. Retrieved from https://www.jolihamilton.com/blog/comperstruggle

Hamilton, J. E., Morrison, N. R., & Gioa, A. N. (2024). Jealousy: A comparison of monogamous and consensually non-monogamous women's experience. *Cogent Mental Health, 3*(1), 1–42. https://doi.org/10.1080/28324765.2023.2283006

Hahn, H. D., & Belt, T. L. (2004). Disability identity and attitudes toward cure in a sample of disabled activists. *Journal of Health and Social Behavior, 45*(4), 453–464. https://doi.org/10.1177/002214650404500407

Harari, Y. N. (2014). *Sapiens: A brief history of humankind.* Random House.

Harding, J., & Pribram, E. D. (2004). Losing our cool? Following Williams and Grossberg on emotions. *Cultural Studies, 18*(6), 863–883. https://doi.org/10.1080/0950238042000306909

Hardy, J. W., & Easton, D. (2017). *The ethical slut: A practical guide to polyamory, open relationships and other freedoms in sex and love* (3rd ed.). Ten Speed Press.

REFERENCES

Harper, A. J., & Swanson, R. (2019). Nonsequential task model of bi/pan/poly-sexual identity development. *Journal of Bisexuality, 19*(3), 337–360. https://doi.org/10.1080/15299716.2019.1608614

Harper, T. A. (2024). Polyamory, the ruling class's latest fad. *The Atlantic*. Retrieved from https://www.theatlantic.com/ideas/archive/2024/02/polyamory-ruling-class-fad-monogamy/677312/

Harris, C. R. (2003). A review of sex differences in sexual jealousy, including self-report data, psychophysiological responses, interpersonal violence, and morbid jealousy. *Personality and Social Psychology Review, 7*(2), 102–128. https://doi.org/10.1207/S15327957PSPR0702_102-128

Hart, S., & Carrington, H. (2002). Jealousy in 6 month-old infants. *Infancy, 3*(3), 395–402.

Haupert, M. L., Gesselman, A. N., Moors, A. C., Fisher, H. E., & Garcia, J. R. (2017). Prevalence of experiences with consensual nonmonogamous relationships: Findings from two national samples of single Americans. *Journal of Sex & Marital Therapy, 43*(5), 424–440. https://doi.org/10.1080/0092623X.2016.1178675

Heap, S. H., & Varoufakis, Y. (2004). *Game theory: A critical text*. Psychology Press.

Heckert, J. (2010). Love without borders? Intimacy, identity, and the state of compulsory monogamy. In M. Barker & D. Langdridge (Eds.), *Understanding non-monogamies* (pp. 255–266). Routledge.

Heinlein, R. A. (1961). *Stranger in a strange land*. Ace.

Hoffman, M. L. (1981). Is altruism part of human nature? *Journal of Personality and Social Psychology, 40*(1), 121–137. https://doi.org/10.1037/0022-3514.40.1.121

Holton, J. A., & Walsh, I. (2017). *Classic grounded theory: Applications with qualitative and quantitative data*. Sage. https://doi.org/10.4135/9781071802762

hooks, b. (2001). *All about love: New visions*. HarperCollins.

Hupka, R. B., & Bank, A. L. (1996). Sex differences in jealousy: Evolution or social construction? *Cross-Cultural Research, 30*(1), 24–59. https://doi.org/10.1177/106939719603000102

Hypatia from Space. (2018). *Compersion: Polyamory beyond jealousy*. Self-published.

Iantaffi, A. (2022). Disability and CNM relationships. In M. D. Vaughan & T. R. Burnes (Eds.), *The handbook of consensual non-monogamy: Affirming mental health practice* (pp. 157–176). Rowman & Littlefield.

Janssen, E., & Bancroft, J. (2007). The dual-control model: The role of sexual inhibition and excitation in sexual arousal and behavior. In E. Janssen (Ed.), *The psychophysiology of sex* (pp. 197–222). Indiana University Press.

Jenks, R. J. (2014). An on-line survey comparing swingers and polyamorists. *Electronic Journal of Human Sexuality, 17*, 1–15. Retrieved from http://www.ejhs.org/volume17/swing.html

REFERENCES

Jenkins, C. S. I. (2015). Modal monogamy. *Ergo: An Open Access Journal of Philosophy, 2*(8), 175–194. https://doi.org/10.3998/ergo.12405314.0002.008

Johnson, R. B. (2019). Black and polyamorous. *Journal of Black Sexuality and Relationships, 6*(2), vii–xiv. https://doi.org/10.1353/bsr.2019.0017

Kaplan, H. S. (1979). *Disorders of sexual desire and other new concepts and techniques in sex therapy* (Vol. 2). Simon & Schuster.

Kean, J. (2015). A stunning plurality: Unravelling hetero-and mononormativities through HBO's *Big Love. Sexualities, 18*(5–6), 698–713. https://doi.org/10.1177/1363460714561718

Kleinplatz, P. J. (2006). Learning from extraordinary lovers: Lessons from the edge. *Journal of Homosexuality, 50*(2–3), 325–348. https://doi.org/10.1300/J082v50n02_16

Klesse, C. (2007). *The spectre of promiscuity: Gay male and bisexual non-monogamies and polyamories.* Ashgate.

———. (2016). Marriage, law and polyamory: Rebutting mononormativity with sexual orientation discourse? *Oñati Socio-legal Series, 6*(6), 1348–1376. Available at SSRN: https://ssrn.com/abstract=2891035

Klesse, C., Cardoso, D., Pallotta-Chiarolli, M., Raab, M., Schadler, C., & Schippers, M. (2022). Introduction: Parenting, polyamory and consensual non-monogamy. Critical and queer perspectives. *Sexualities.* Online first publication. https://doi.org/10.1177/13634607221114466

Knight, C. (2004). Review of the book *Cultures of multiple fathers: The theory and practice of partible paternity in Lowland South America* (S. Beckerman & P. Valentine, Eds.). *Journal of the Royal Anthropological Institute, 10*(1), 206–208.

Kolesar, A. E., & Pardo, S. T. (2019). The religious and philosophical characteristics in a consensually nonmonogamous sample. *International Journal of Transpersonal Studies, 38*(1), 99–117. https://doi.org/10.24972/ijts.2019.38.1.99

Kuper, L. E., Wright, L., & Mustanski, B. (2018). Gender identity development among transgender and gender nonconforming emerging adults: An intersectional approach. *International Journal of Transgenderism, 19*(4), 436–455. https://doi.org/10.1080/15532739.2018.1443869

Labriola, K. (2013). *The jealousy workbook: Exercises and insights for managing open relationships.* Greenery Press.

Labriola, K. (2022). *Polyamorous Elders: Aging in Open Relationships.* Rowman & Littlefield.

Lehmiller, J. J. (2018). *Tell me what you want: The science of sexual desire and how it can help you improve your sex life.* Da Capo Press.

———. (2020). Fantasies about consensual nonmonogamy among persons in monogamous romantic relationships. *Archives of Sexual Behavior, 49,* 2799–2812. https://doi.org/10.1007/s10508-020-01788-7

REFERENCES

Lehmiller, J. J., Ley, D., & Savage, D. (2018). The psychology of gay men's cuckolding fantasies. *Archives of Sexual Behavior*, 47, 999–1013. https://doi.org/10.1007/s10508-017-1096-0

Levitt, H. M., & Ippolito, M. R. (2014). Being transgender: The experience of transgender identity development. *Journal of Homosexuality, 61*(12), 1727–1758. https://doi.org/10.1080/00918369.2014.951262

Lewis, L. A. (1984). The coming-out process for lesbians: Integrating a stable identity. *Social Work, 29*(5), 464–469. https://doi.org/10.1093/sw/29.5.464

Manley, M. H., Diamond, L. M., & van Anders, S. M. (2015). Polyamory, monoamory, and sexual fluidity: A longitudinal study of identity and sexual trajectories. *Psychology of Sexual Orientation and Gender Diversity, 2*(2), 168–180. https://doi.org/10.1037/sgd0000098

Masters, W. H., & Johnsons, V. E. (1966). *Human Sexual Response*. Brown.

Mathes, E. W., Adams, H. E., & Davies, R. M. (1985). Jealousy: Loss of relationship rewards, loss of self-esteem, depression, anxiety, and anger. *Journal of Personality and Social Psychology, 48*(6), 1552–1561. https://doi.org/10.1037/0022-3514.48.6.1552

Mazur, R. (1973). *The new intimacy: Open ended marriage and alternative lifestyles*. toExcel Press.

McCarty, R. (2016). The fight-or-flight response: A cornerstone of stress research. In G. Fink (Ed.), *Stress: Concepts, cognition, emotion, and behavior* (pp. 33–37). Academic Press. https://doi.org/10.1016/B978-0-12-800951-2.00004-2

McLean, K. (2007). Hiding in the closet?: Bisexuals, coming out and the disclosure imperative. *Journal of Sociology, 43*(2), 151–166. https://doi.org/10.1177/1440783307076893

Meneses, R. W., & Larkin, M. (2012). Edith Stein and the contemporary psychological study of empathy. *Journal of Phenomenological Psychology, 43*(2), 151–184. https://doi.org/10.1163/15691624-12341234

Meyer, I. H. (2003a). Prejudice as stress: Conceptual and measurement problems. *American Journal of Public Health, 93*(2), 262–265. https://doi.org/10.2105/AJPH.93.2.262

———. (2003b). Prejudice, social stress, and mental health in lesbian, gay, and bisexual populations: Conceptual issues and research evidence. *Psychological Bulletin, 129*(5), 674–697. http://doi.org/10.1037/0033-2909.129.5.674

———. (2015). Resilience in the study of minority stress and health of sexual and gender minorities. *Psychology of Sexual Orientation and Gender Diversity, 2*(3), 209–213. https://doi.org/10.1037/sgd0000132

Moore, P. (2016, October 3). Young Americans are less wedded to monogamy than their elders. *YouGov*. Retrieved from https://today.yougov.com/society/
Lehmiller, J. J., Ley, D., & Savage, D. (2018). The psychology of gay men's cuckolding fantasies. Archives of Sexual Behavior, 47, 999–1013. https://doi

Lehmiller, J. J., Ley, D., & Savage, D. (2018). The psychology of gay men's cuckolding fantasies. Archives of Sexual Behavior, 47, 999–1013. https://doi.org/10.1007/s10508-017-1096-0.org/10.1007/s10508-017-1096-0 articles/16622-young-americans-less-wedded Lehmiller, J. J., Ley, D., & Savage, D. (2018). The psychology of gay men's cuckolding fantasies. Archives of Sexual Behavior, 47, 999–1013. https://doi.org/10.1007/s10508-017-1096-0 -monogamy?redirect_from=%2Ftopics%2Flifestyle%2Farticles Lehmiller, J. J., Ley, D., & Savage, D. (2018). The psychology of gay men's cuckolding fantasies. Archives of Sexual Behavior, 47, 999–1013. https://doi Lehmiller, J. J., Ley, D., & Savage, D. (2018). The psychology of gay men's cuckolding fantasies. Archives of Sexual Behavior, 47, 999–1013. https://doi.org/10.1007/s10508-017-1096-0 .org/10.1007/s10508-017-1096-0-reports%2F2016%2F10%2F03%2Fyoung -americans-less-wedded-monogamy

Moors, A. C. (2017). Has the American public's interest in information related to relationships beyond "the couple" increased over time? *The Journal of Sex Research, 54*(6), 677–684. https://doi.org/10.1080/00224499.2016.1178208

Moors, A. C., & Ramos, A. (2022). Stigma and prejudice endured by people engaged in consensual mon-monogamy. In M. D. Vaughan & T. R. Burnes (Eds.), *The handbook of consensual non-monogamy: Affirming mental health practice* (pp. 50–73). Rowman & Littlefield.

Moors, A. C., & Schechinger, H. (2014). Understanding sexuality: Implications of Rubin for relationship research and clinical practice. *Sexual and Relationship Therapy, 29*(4), 476–482. https://doi.org/10.1080/14681994.2014.941347

Morelli, S. A., Lieberman, M. D., & Zaki, J. (2015). The emerging study of positive empathy. *Social and Personality Psychology Compass, 9*(2), 57–68. https://doi .org/10.1111/spc3.12157

Morin, J. (1995). *The erotic mind: Unlocking the inner sources of sexual passion and fulfillment.* HarperCollins.

Nagoski, E. (2015). *Come as you are: The surprising new science that will transform your sex life.* Simon and Schuster.

Namu, Y. E., & Mathieu, C. (2007). *Leaving Mother Lake: A girlhood at the edge of the world.* Little, Brown and Company.

Noël, M. J. (2006). Progressive polyamory: Considering issues of diversity. *Sexualities, 9,* 602–620. https://doi.org/10.1177/1363460706070003

Osiński, J. (2009). Kin altruism, reciprocal altruism and social discounting. *Personality and Individual Differences, 47*(4), 374–378. https://doi.org/10.1016/j .paid.2009.04.011

Parrot, W. (1991). The emotional experiences of envy and jealousy. In P. Salovey (Ed.), *The psychology of jealousy and envy* (pp. 3–30). Guilford Press.

Patterson, K. A. (2018). *Love's not color blind: Race and representation in polyamorous and other alternative communities.* Thorntree Press.

Peace, S. L. (2012). *Toward a model of polyamorous identity development* (Unpublished doctoral dissertation). John F. Kennedy University.

Perel, E. (2006). *Mating in captivity: Unlocking erotic intelligence*. HarperCollins.

Perry, D., Hendler, T., & Shamay-Tsoory, S. G. (2012). Can we share the joy of others? Empathic neural responses to distress vs joy. *Social Cognitive and Affective Neuroscience, 7*(8), 909–916. https://doi.org/10.1093/scan/nsr073

Pieper, M., & Bauer, R. (2006). *Mono-normativity and polyamory*. Unpublished paper presented at the International Conference on Polyamory and Mono-Normativity, Research Centre for Feminist, Gender, and Queer Studies, University of Hamburg.

Piff, P. K., Kraus, M. W., Côté, S., Cheng, B. H., & Keltner, D. (2010), Having less, giving more: the influence of social class on prosocial behavior. *Journal of Personality and Social Psychology*, 99(5), 771. https://doi.org/10.1037/a0020092

Pines, A. (1998). *Romantic jealousy: Causes, symptoms, cures*. Routledge.

Pittinsky, T. L., & Montoya, R. M. (2016). Empathic joy in positive intergroup relations. *Journal of Social Issues, 72*(3), 511–523. https://doi.org/10.1111/josi.12179

Pittinsky, T. L., Rosenthal, S. A., & Montoya, R. M. (2011). Liking is not the opposite of disliking: The functional separability of positive and negative attitudes toward minority groups. *Cultural Diversity and Ethnic Minority Psychology, 17*, 134–143. https://doi.org/10.1037/a0023806

Porges, S. W. (2009). The polyvagal theory: New insights into adaptive reactions of the autonomic nervous system. *Cleveland Clinic journal of medicine, 76*(Suppl 2), S86.

Rambukkana, N. (2015). *Fraught intimacies: Non/monogamy in the public sphere*. University of British Columbia Press.

Rambukkana, N. P. (2004). Uncomfortable bridges: The bisexual politics of outing polyamory. *Journal of Bisexuality, 4*(3–4), 141–154. https://doi.org/10.1300/J159v04n03_11

Ravenscroft, A. D. (2004). *Polyamory: Roadmaps for the clueless and hopeful*. Fenris Brothers.

Reynolds, A. L., & Hanjorgiris, W. F. (2000). Coming out: Lesbian, gay, and bisexual identity development. In R. M. Perez, K. A. DeBord, & K. J. Bieschke (Eds.), *Handbook of counseling and psychotherapy with lesbian, gay, and bisexual clients* (pp. 35–55). American Psychological Association. https://doi.org/10.1037/10339-002

Rhoten, K., Sheff, E., & D. Lane, J. (2021). US family law along the slippery slope: The limits of a sexual rights strategy for polyamorous parents. *Sexualities*. https://doi.org/10.1177/13634607211061485

Ritchie, A., & Barker, M. (2006). "There aren't words for what we do or how we feel so we have to make them up": Constructing polyamorous languages in a culture of compulsory monogamy. *Sexualities, 9*(5), 584–601. https://doi .org/10.1177/1363460706069987

Robinson, M. (2013). Polyamory and monogamy as strategic identities. *Journal of Bisexuality, 13*(1), 21–38. https://doi.org/10.1080/15299716.2013.755731

Rodríguez Rust, P. C. (2007). The construction and reconstruction of bisexuality: Inventing and reinventing the self. In B. A. Firestein (Ed.), *Becoming visible: Counseling bisexuals across the lifespan* (pp. 3–27). Columbia University Press.

Rothschild, L. (2018). Compulsory monogamy and polyamorous existence. *Graduate Journal of Social Science, 14*(1), 28–56.

Rubin, J. D., Moors, A. C., Matsick, J. L., Ziegler, A., & Conley, T. D. (2014). On the margins: Considering diversity among consensually non-monogamous relationships. *Journal für Psychologie, 22*(1), 19–37.

Ryan, C., & Jethá, C. (2010). *Sex at dawn: The prehistoric origins of modern sexuality.* HarperCollins.

Samuels, E. J. (2003). My body, my closet: Invisible disability and the limits of coming-out discourse. *GLQ: A journal of Lesbian and Gay studies, 9*(1), 233–255. https://doi.org/10.1215/10642684-9-1-2-233

Sandbakken, E. M., Skrautvol, A., & Madsen, O. J. (2022). "It's my definition of a relationship, even though it doesn't fit yours": Living in polyamorous relationships in a mononormative culture. *Psychology & Sexuality, 13*(4), 1054–1067. https://doi.org/10.1080/19419899.2021.1982755

Sandler, B. (1994). Grow or die: Marxist theories of capitalism and the environment. *Rethinking Marxism, 7*(2), 38–57. https://doi.org/10.1080/08935699408658097

Savage, D. (2014). *American savage: Insights, slights, and fights on faith, sex, love, and politics.* Plume.

Sawyers, E. (2023). *A polyamory devotional: 365 daily reflections for the consensually nonmonogamous.* Thornapple.

Schippers, M. (2016). *Beyond monogamy: Polyamory and the future of poly-queer sexualities.* New York University Press. https://doi.org/10.18574/nyu/ 9781479801596.001.0001

Schwartz, R. (2013). *Evolution of the internal family systems model.* Retrieved from https://www.opa.org/assets/docs/Conference/C21/HANDOUTS/Nancy%20 Morgan%20-%20Evolution%20of%20the%20Internal%20Family%20 Systems%20Model.pdf

Shamay-Tsoory, S. G., Aharon-Peretz, J., & Perry, D. (2009). Two systems for empathy: A double dissociation between emotional and cognitive empathy in inferior frontal gyrus versus ventromedial prefrontal lesions. *Brain, 132*(3), 617–627. https://doi.org/10.1093/brain/awn279

Sheff, E. (2005). Polyamorous women, sexual subjectivity, and power. *Journal of Contemporary Ethnography, 34*(3), 251–283. https://doi.org/ 10.1177/0891241604274263

REFERENCES

———. (2014). *The polyamorists next door: Inside multiple-partner relationships and families*. Rowman & Littlefield.

Sheff, E., & Hammers, C. (2011). The privilege of perversities: Race, class and education among polyamorists and kinksters. *Psychology & Sexuality, 2*(3), 198–223. https://doi.org/10.1080/19419899.2010.537674

Sheff, E. (2014). *The polyamorists next door: Inside multiple-partner relationships and families*. Rowman and Littlefield.

Sheff, E., & Smith, H. A. (2022). Social class and polyamory. In M. D. Vaughan & T. R. Burnes (Eds.), *The handbook of consensual non-monogamy: Affirming mental health practice* (pp. 315–326). Rowman & Littlefield.

Singer, T. (2006). The neuronal basis and ontogeny of empathy and mind reading: Review of literature and implications for future research. *Neuroscience & Biobehavioral Reviews, 30*(6), 855–863. https://doi.org/10.1016/j.neubiorev.2006.06.011

Smith, R. (2010). Beyond growth or beyond capitalism. *Real-world economics review, 53*(2), 28–42.

Smith, R. S. (1976). Voyeurism: A review of the literature. *Archives of Sexual Behavior, 5*(6), 585–608. https://doi.org/10.1007/BF01541221

Sophie, J. (1982). Counseling lesbians. *Personnel and Guidance Journal, 60*(6), 341–345. https://doi.org/10.1002/j.2164-4918.1982.tb00682.x

Sovatsky, S. (1985). Eros as mystery: Toward a transpersonal sexology and procreativity. *Journal of Transpersonal Psychology, 17*(1), 1–32.

Starkweather, K. E., & Hames, R. (2012). A survey of non-classical polyandry. *Human Nature, 23*(2), 149–172. https://doi.org/10.1007/s12110-012-9144-x

Stein, E. (2020). Adultery, infidelity, and consensual non-monogamy. *Wake Forest Law Review, 55*, 147–188. https://doi.org/10.2139/ssrn.3425567

Stellar, J. E., Manzo, V. M., Kraus, M. W., & Keltner, D. (2012). Class and compassion: Socioeconomic factors predict responses to suffering. *Emotion, 12*(3), 449–459. https://doi.org/10.1037/a0026508

Stewart, Z. (2001). What's all this NRE stuff, anyway? Reflections 15 years later. *Loving More, 26*.

Table, B., Sandoval, J. A., & Weger, H. (2017). Transitions in polyamorous identity and intercultural communication: An application of identity management theory. *Journal of Bisexuality, 17*(3), 277–299. https://doi.org/10.1080/15299716.2017.1350897

Tallbear, K. (2014). Couple-centricity, polyamory and colonialism. *The Critical Polyamorist, 28*. [Blog]. Retrieved from http://www.criticalpolyamorist.com/homeblog/couple-centricity-polyamory-and-colonialism

Tam, T., Hewstone, M., Kenworthy, J. B., Cairns, E., Marimetti, C., Geddes, L., & Parkinson, B. (2008). Post-conflict reconciliation: Intergroup forgiveness and implicit biases in Northern Ireland. *Journal of Social Issues, 64*, 303–320. https://doi.org/10.1111/j.1540- 4560.2008.00563.x.

Taormino, T. (2008). *Opening up: A guide to creating and sustaining open relationships*. Cleis Press.

Tarnas, R. (1991). *The passion of the Western mind: Understanding the ideas that have shaped our world view*. Harmony.

Taylor, S. E. (1991). Asymmetrical effects of positive and negative events: The mobilization-minimization hypothesis. *Psychological Bulletin, 110*(1), 67–85. https://doi.org/10.1037/0033-2909.110.1.67

Thouin-Savard, M. I. (2021). *Compersion in Consensually Nonmonogamous Relationships: A Grounded Theory Investigation*. California Institute of Integral Studies. Dissertation.

Thouin-Savard, M. I., & Flicker, S. M. (2023). Compersion. In T. K. Shackelford (Ed.), *Encyclopedia of Sexual Psychology and Behavior* (pp. 1–7). Springer International Publishing. https://doi.org/10.1007/978-3-031-08956-5_2472-1

Tibetan Buddhist Encyclopedia. (2020, November 18). Retrieved from http://tibetanbuddhistencyclopedia.com/en/index.php/Mudita

Titchener, E. (1924). *A textbook of psychology*. Macmillan.

Trivers, R. (2006). Reciprocal altruism: 30 years later. In P. M. Kappeler & C. P. van Schaik (Eds.), *Cooperation in primates and humans* (pp. 67–83). Springer. https://doi.org/10.1007/3-540-28277-7_4

Trivers, R. L. (1971). The evolution of reciprocal altruism. *The Quarterly Review of Biology, 46*(1), 35–57. https://doi.org/10.1086/406755

Tweedy, A. E. (2010). Polyamory as a sexual orientation. *University of Cincinnati Law Review, 79*(4), 1461–1515.

Ursin, H., & Eriksen, H. R. (2004). The cognitive activation theory of stress. *Psychoneuroendocrinology, 29*(5), 567–592. https://doi.org/10.1016/S0306-4530(03)00091-X

Vaughan, M. D., & Burnes, T. R. (Eds.). (2022). *The handbook of consensual nonmonogamy: Affirming mental health practice*. Rowman & Littlefield.

Veaux, F., & Rickert, E. (2014). *More than two: A practical guide to ethical polyamory*. Thorntree Press.

Vohs, K. D., & Baumeister, R. F. (Eds.). (2016). *Handbook of self-regulation: Research, theory, and applications*. Guilford Publications.

Waugh, C. E., & Fredrickson, B. L. (2006). Nice to know you: Positive emotions, self–other overlap, and complex understanding in the formation of a new relationship. *The Journal of Positive Psychology, 1*(2), 93–106. https://doi.org/10.1080/17439760500510569

Weeks, J. (2003). *Sexuality* (2nd ed.). Routledge. https://doi.org/10.4324/9780203425879

Weinberg, M. S., & Williams, C. J. (1974). *Male homosexuals: Their problems and adaptations*. Penguin.

Weitzman, G. (2006). Therapy with clients who are bisexual and polyamorous. In R. C. Fox (Ed.), *Psychotherapy with bisexual women and bisexual men* (pp. 137–164). Harrington Park Press/The Haworth Press. https://doi.org/10.1300/J159v06n01_08

———. (2007). Counseling bisexuals in polyamorous relationships. In B. A. Firestein (Ed.), *Becoming visible: Counseling bisexuals across the lifespan* (pp. 312–335). Columbia University Press.

Weitzman, G., Davidson, J., Phillips, R. A., Fleckenstein, J. R., & Morotti-Meeker, C. (2009). What psychology professionals should know about polyamory. *National Coalition on Sexual Freedom, 7*, 1–28.

Westman, M. (2001). Stress and strain crossover. *Human relations, 54*(6), 717–751. https://doi.org/10.1177/0018726701546002

Westman, M., Brough, P., & Kalliath, T. (2009). Expert commentary on work–life balance and crossover of emotions and experiences: Theoretical and practice advancements. *Journal of Organizational Behavior, 30*(5), 587–595. https://doi.org/10.1002/job.616

Wheeler, S. C. (2011). Poly-tically incorrect: Women negotiating identity, status, and power in polyamorous relationships. (Unpublished master's thesis). San Diego State University, San Diego, CA. Retrieved from http://sdsu-dspace.calstate.edu/bitstream/handle/10211.10/1413/ Wheeler_Sarah.pdf?sequence=1

White, G. (1991). Self, relationship, friends, and family: Some applications of system theory to romantic jealousy. In P. Salovey (Ed.), *The psychology of jealousy and envy* (pp. 231–250). Guilford Press.

Willey, A. (2016). *Undoing monogamy: The politics of science and the possibilities of biology.* Duke University Press. https://doi.org/10.1215/9780822374213

———. (2018). Rethinking monogamy's nature: From the truth of non/monogamy to a dyke ethics of "antimonogamy." *Journal of Lesbian Studies, 22*(2), 235–253. https://doi.org/10.1080/10894160.2017.1340006

Willey, A. (2015). Constituting compulsory monogamy: normative femininity at the limits of imagination. *Journal of Gender Studies, 24*(6), 621–633. https://doi.org/10.1080/09589236.2014.889600

Wilson, M., & Daly, M. (1996). Male sexual proprietariness and violence against wives. *Current Directions in Psychological Science, 5*, 2–7. https://doi.org/10.1111/1467-8721.ep10772668

Witherspoon, R. G. (2018). *Exploring polyamorous resilience and strength factors: A structural equation modeling approach* (Unpublished doctoral dissertation). Alliant International University.

REFERENCES

Witherspoon, R. G., & Theodore, P. S. (2021). Exploring minority stress and resilience in a polyamorous sample. *Archives of Sexual Behavior, 50*(4), 1367–1388. https://doi.org/10.1007/s10508-021-01995-w

Wolfe, L. (2003). *Jealousy and transformation in polyamorous relationships* (Unpublished doctoral dissertation). Institute for Advanced Study of Human Sexuality.

————. (2008). On kittens and the very invented culture of polyamory. *Electronic Journal of Human Sexuality, 11*, 30. Retrieved from http://www.ejhs.org/volume11/Wolfe.htm

Wosick-Correa, K. (2010). Agreements, rules and agentic fidelity in polyamorous relationships. *Psychology & Sexuality, 1*(1), 44–61. https://doi.org/10.1080/19419891003634471

Wosick, K. (2012). *Sex, love, and fidelity: A study of contemporary romantic relationships*. Cambria Press.

Yakas, L., & Lopez, N. A. (2023). Compulsory monogamy is disabling. In S. K. Kattari (Ed.), *Exploring sexuality and disability: A guide for human service professionals*. Taylor & Francis.

York, K. (2020). Why monogamy is morally permissible: A defense of some common justifications for monogamy. *The Journal of Value Inquiry, 54*, 539–552. https://doi.org/10.1007/s10790-019-09727-z

Zal, F. (2022). Inspiring Sexual Attitude Reassessment (SAR). *The Journal of Sexual Medicine, 19*(8), S30–S31. https://doi.org/10.1016/j.jsxm.2022.05.111

INDEX

Page numbers in italics refer to figures and tables.

gaslighting, 13, 158, 247
Gaulle, Charles de, 142
Giuliani, Caroline Rose, 167
gratitude, 71, 99, 119, 158, 164, 173, 219, 220, 247, 248; for authenticity in emotional expression, 60, 64, 136; for benefits of other relationship, 135–36, 165, 177, 194, 225; as a core constituent of compersion, 37, 55, 64, 66; for freedom from fear and pride, 60, *100,* 136, 186; nurturing gratitude, 254, 258; for personal growth opportunities, 63–64; of polycule members, 112, 239; positive empathy and, 109, 115, 128; for relief from guilt, 62–63, *100,* 136; for richness in emotional and sexual life, 56–58, 136; for richness in social life, 58–59; solidarity as linked with, 138–39
group sex, 47, 48, *100,* 123, 128, 129, 135, 228
Guerrero, Laura, 21
Gusmano, Beatrice, 134

Hamilton, Joli, 20, 22, 30–31, 32, 93, 94
Hammers, Corie, 231–32
Harding, Jennifer, 25–26
Hardy, Janet, 141
HEARTS relationship model, 117–18
Heinlein, Robert, 140
HIV prevention, 126
Hoffman, Martin L., 51, 65
hooks, bell, 234
Hypatia from Space, 82, 119

Iantaffi, Alex, 217, 240–41
ideological commitment to CNM values, *100,* 103, 187; CNM meaning-making occurring through, 175–77,

191; ethics and politics, 106–7; full-hearted consent, 104–5, 124, 194; jealousy, non-mononormative stance toward, 109–10; obstacles to, 147–52, 178; pragmatic attitude, 105–6; sex positivity and, 108–9; social conventions, willingness to defy, 107–8
inner security, 103, 104, 117, 177, 196, 231; in compersion model, *176;* factors that hinder, *101,* 147, 152–55, 204; factors that promote, *100,* 110–15, 132, 178; personal needs, meeting, 100, 101, 111, 115–16, 152, 155–57
Internal Family Systems (IFS), 96, 97
intersectional emotion, 26

jealousy, 2, 7, 12, 14, 26, 43, 60, 85, *101,* 122, 126, 210, 247; absence of jealousy, 5, 61; alchemizing of jealousy into desire, 46, 48–51; benevolent neutrality, aiming for, 13, 99; coexistence with compersion, 73, 86, 91, 92–93, 96–97, 177, 218, 255; compersion arising from, 15, 125, 136; comperstruggle, as part of, 29, 93–94; deprivation and, 157, 159–60; different types of, 21–23; disability, role in, 218–19; exclusion jealousy, 22, 128; as fading over time, 125; as a fluid experience, 81, 94–96, 115; holding the emotion of, 84, 96, 209; jealousy-compersion continuum, 82–83; malleability of, 32–34, 48; metamours, jealousy toward, 151, 166, 214–15, 216, 220, 231; in mononormative context, 5, 20–21, 25; non-mononormative jealousy, 21, 28–32, *100,* 105, 109, 117; normative expectations of, 1, 5, 20–21, 27, 62, 142, 257, 259; opportunities

ABOUT THE AUTHOR

Marie Thouin, PhD, is the founder of Love InSight, a Mindful Dating and Relationship Coaching practice where she supports people of all backgrounds to create intentional and vibrant love lives. A leading scholar on the topic of compersion in consensually non-monogamous relationships, she has published seminal research studies and the first encyclopedia entry on compersion. She has also been featured in several magazines and podcasts, including *ELLE*, the *Savage Lovecast*, and *Multiamory*, and is the creator of www.whatiscompersion.com, a popular website that features her research, blogs, and a list of resources on compersion. Thouin also serves as editor at the *International Journal of Transpersonal Studies*, a leading peer-reviewed publication in the fields of transpersonal and whole-person psychologies.

www.ingramcontent.com/pod-product-compliance
Lightning Source LLC
Chambersburg PA
CBHW050336270326
41926CB00016B/3476